WITHDRAWN

PRAISE FOR *THE INVISIBLE BRAND*

Insightful, illuminating, and packed with examples that make you think. Ammerman has brought together many different lines of thinking about the impact of algorithms and AI on society, politics, and the marketplace. His perspective of psychotechnology offers a clarifying lens for understanding what smart technologies will mean for our lives and our futures.

—J. Walker Smith, PhD
Chief Knowledge Officer, Brand & Marketing
Kantar Consulting

The central business challenge of the twenty-first century is finding ways to nimbly adapt as digital technologies like AI rapidly transform the competitive landscape. *The Invisible Brand* smartly analyzes the issue and helps readers understand the implications; this book is essential reading for savvy marketers and leaders who hope to succeed in today's marketplace.

—Doug Conant
founder and CEO, ConantLeadership
former CEO, Campbell Soup Company

The Invisible Brand provides a thought-provoking and at times unsettling look at how artificial intelligence and psychotechnology are already at work in our lives. It will change the way you see our interconnected world.

—Chuck Swoboda
former Chairman and CEO of Cree, Inc. and
leader of the LED Lighting Revolution

It's an intriguing, enlightening, and a bit discomforting pull-back-the-curtain look at how a powerful new marketing industry is being built on massive amounts of personal data. *The Invisible Brand* is a brilliant assessment of our subtle surrender of privacy, one click at a time, and how it spurs us to laugh, cry, vote, donate, and especially buy, buy, buy.

—Gordon Borrell
CEO of Borrell Associates

Demystifying the impact of AI in the world of marketing is where the story begins. Highly relevant examples linked to the life of a marketer—data driven and technology enabled. The story then takes you down a wonderful path of discovery. Learning about the role of the Invisible Brand through the innovations and data that both exist today and are yet to come. The future of marketing and AI appropriately described as both "awesome and terrifying."

—Adele Sweetwood
Vice President of Experience Marketing at Splunk
former SVP of Global Marketing at SAS
author, *The Analytical Marketer*

Artificial intelligence is one of the major technological developments that will shape the marketplace in this century. Yet, we are only just understanding its impact. In this eminently readable book, filled with many vivid and practical examples, Ammerman lifts the veil on AI. A must-read for managers and policy makers.

—Jan-Benedict Steenkamp
Knox Massey Distinguished Professor of Marketing,
UNC Chapel Hill, and author of *Global Brand Strategy*

THE INVISIBLE BRAND

THE INVISIBLE BRAND

MARKETING IN THE AGE OF AUTOMATION, BIG DATA, AND MACHINE LEARNING

WILLIAM AMMERMAN

NEW YORK   CHICAGO   SAN FRANCISCO
ATHENS   LONDON   MADRID
MEXICO CITY   MILAN   NEW DELHI
SINGAPORE   SYDNEY   TORONTO

1 2 3 4 5 6 7 8 9   LCR   24 23 22 21 20 19

ISBN 978-1-260-44125-3
MHID   1-260-44125-3

e-ISBN 978-1-260-44126-0
e-MHID   1-260-44126-1

Design by Lee Fukui and Mauna Eichner

Library of Congress Cataloging-in-Publication Data

Names: Ammerman, William, 1967- author.
Title: The invisible brand : marketing in the age of automation, big data,
  and machine learning / William Ammerman.
Description: New York : McGraw-Hill Education, [2019]
Identifiers: LCCN 2019010692 (print) I LCCN 2019013521 (ebook) I ISBN
  9781260441260 () I ISBN 1260441261 () I ISBN 9781260441253 (hardback)
Subjects: LCSH: Marketing. I Artificial intelligence. I Machine learning. I
  BISAC: BUSINESS & ECONOMICS / Marketing / General.
Classification: LCC HF5415 (ebook) I LCC HF5415 .A598 2019 (print) I DDC
  658.800285/63—dc23
LC record available at https://lccn.loc.gov/2019010692

For Christina, Kate, Cole, and Natalie

Contents

Acknowledgments

WRITING A BOOK IS hard work, akin to running a marathon on a beach, and I owe a huge debt of gratitude to all the people who helped me reach the finish line.

To my professors at the University of North Carolina School of Media and Journalism who helped me to overcome the trial of completing a master's as a married working professional with three children, thank you. Further, I wouldn't have been able to complete the necessary research on programmatic advertising for my thesis without the help and support of Gordon Borrell and his team at Borrell Associates—so thanks to all of you as well.

While living in New York City a few years after completing my master's, I was fortunate enough to rekindle a friendship with Dan Gerstein, a brilliant guy who owns Gotham Ghostwriters in Manhattan. Dan understands more about getting a book published than I can ever hope to know, and he connected me with Josh Bernoff, author of *Writing Without Bullshit*. Josh forced me to hone my ideas and craft a terrific book proposal. Thank you, Josh.

Armed with the final book proposal, Dan marched me around the city in search of an agent. We received a surprising amount of interest, and I feel fortunate that Steve Ross was willing to take me on as an unproven first-time author. Steve's credentials are deep in the publishing industry, having worked formerly as the president and group publisher of the Collins Division of

HarperCollins. Steve is at that stage in his career when he can be choosy about his clients, and I feel very grateful that he chose me. Thank you, Steve.

With Steve's representation, we were able to secure a book deal with McGraw-Hill to publish the book, and that deal set in motion an army of editors, writers, researchers, marketers, and graphic artists who each played a role in the final project, and their influence is present on every page from cover to cover. Chief among them is Darren Dahl, whose contribution to this book is tremendous. As a freelance researcher and writer, Darren was able to help me mold and shape my ideas and get them onto paper in legible form. I deeply value our collaboration, and I'd like to think I've made a friend along the way. Thank you, Darren.

Noah Schwartzberg, senior editor at McGraw-Hill, had the unenviable challenge of marshaling all of the talents and resources available to a major publisher to take my initial manuscript and put it through the rigors of becoming a book. Thanks to you, Noah and your entire team, for all of your hard work.

I am also grateful for all the support of friends, family and neighbors who provided guidance, wisdom, and editorial feedback throughout the process. Most significantly, thank you to my wife and children, my brothers, my neighbors Adrienne and Olivier Jouve, and my favorite pen pal David Allison.

Finally, special thanks to Dan Gerstein, for shepherding me through this three-year journey, for introducing me to Josh and Steve and Darren and Noah and everyone who touched this project along the way. I simply couldn't have done it without you.

Introduction

MARKETERS ARE HARNESSING the power of artificial intelligence to change how we think and to influence what we do. Their work is often unseen, hidden amid the enormous volumes of digital media we are consuming, but their influence is growing. My mission here is to reveal the tools and tactics being deployed by marketers in the age of AI and to engage readers in a rich dialogue about its implications.

Over the past two decades, in leadership roles at some of the nation's largest TV broadcasting companies, including Hearst Television, Capitol Broadcasting, and Tribune Media, I have witnessed profound changes in the way information is delivered to consumers.

When I graduated from college, most media were distributed via broadcast TV, broadcast radio, and mass-printed magazines and newspapers. Everyone received the same information at the same time. Today, the Internet has eclipsed broadcast TV as the leading source of news and information, and with that change has come the capability for publishers to personalize information to the individual. Now everyone gets the customized information they want, when they want it. Digital advertising pioneered technologies that deliver digital ads, tailored for narrow target audiences, in real time. The ability to personalize information for the user has, in turn, produced a revolution in personalized marketing, where marketers can deliver customized messaging down to the individual level.

In a career spanning 25 years, I've had a front-row seat to witness massive changes in communication technology, and I've played an active role in applying that technology to online advertising and marketing. As my colleagues will tell you, I am compulsively attracted to whiteboards in boardrooms where I enjoy drawing diagrams and explaining to my teams and customers how all of this technology works and how it can be used in solving marketing problems. More than one of them has jokingly called me "Professor," and I will readily admit that I enjoy teaching. My desire to share ideas and to help people understand digital technology drove me to write this book. Decades as a practitioner combined with postgraduate work in digital technology and artificial intelligence have given me a unique point of view, informed by a combination of academic research and real-world, hands-on experience.

As a Google Certified Publishing Partner, I helped major TV broadcasters enter the digital age and create their online presence through websites and apps and social media. Over the years, my teams delivered tens of billions of digital ads, and I worked directly with major advertisers to formulate their online marketing strategies, from the first moment they tentatively tested the waters up to the present when digital marketing is an essential component for every business.

I've watched ad networks emerge and grow into massive exchanges that manage trillions of individual ad transactions per year. I've implemented data management platforms to collect vast quantities of consumer data to be used for delivering targeted information to consumers with increasing precision. And I've harnessed the power of social media to deliver news and information through mobile devices to reach highly targeted audiences at massive scales. This in-the-field media experience sharpened my understanding of how information is personalized through digital media down to the individual level and customized to achieve marketing objectives.

It was my postgraduate work at the University of North Carolina (UNC) School of Media and Journalism that informed my views on persuasion as a science and how machine learning harnesses persuasion to keep us engaged and our eyes glued to our screens. My work at the Massachusetts Institute of Technology (MIT) drew my focus to natural language processing and the power of humanlike speech to evoke an empathetic connection between people and their devices.

The marketing industry is driving the convergence of these four distinct areas of innovation: personalized information, the science of persuasion, machine learning, and voice-based interactions between humans and computers. Taken together, these innovations form the basis of what I call *psychological technology* and have shortened to *psychotechnology*. Psychotechnology offers marketers the power to persuade people at a personalized level through voice-based conversations with machines that learn. It is an epochal shift that is set to unalterably redefine the social relationship between humans and computers.

Psychotechnology has evolved so quickly that we've barely had a moment to talk about it and to consider the ramifications. It has snuck up on us, undercover, but its influence is growing, and its potential is to become pervasive. We all need to understand what psychotechnology is, who controls it, and how this unseen force is becoming a dominant factor in our lives.

My goal is to shine a light on how psychotechnology works and the risks and opportunities it presents. For professional marketers,

I want to explain the tools and tactics that will help you use psychotechnology ethically, to remain competitive in this evolving market. For consumers, I'd like to start a conversation about what psychotechnology means for all of us, in the hope that, through knowledge and understanding, we can retain the best of our humanity.

THE
INVISIBLE
BRAND

PART I

EMERGENCE

1

The Invisible Brand Takes Over

IT HAS BEEN SAID that artificial intelligence is the art of making machines act the way they do in the movies. If life imitates art, then it's a pretty good bet we'll all be wiped out by AI at some point in the near future. It's no wonder that people—including the late physicist Stephen Hawking—have issued dire warnings.

Perhaps even geniuses like Hawking are susceptible to what Alvin Toffler dubbed "future shock" in his influential, bestselling book from 1970. In the Introduction, Toffler wrote, "This is a book about what happens to people when they are overwhelmed by change. It is about the ways in which we adapt—or fail to adapt—to the future."

This book has a similar mission. Its intent is not to exacerbate your fears—nor is it to allay your apprehensions. We live in a world where technology with the power to learn and persuade is being deployed by hidden forces all around us. Whether you are an advertising executive, a corporate marketer, or a concerned citizen, my goal is to equip you with an understanding of the technologies shaping our lives so that you are better prepared to deal with the consequences—and so that we may all work together to help guide society in a more positive direction.

Toffler also wrote that change is "the process in which the future invades our lives." Maybe it's the choice of a word like "invades" that gives us pause about what the future of AI may bring. We may take comfort that there is still a sizable gap between the so-called narrow applications of AI that exist today, such as a chatbot with a limited range of responses, and general applications of AI, such as those we see depicted by the science fiction androids who can pass themselves off as human. Professor Daniela Rus, director of MIT's Computer Science and Artificial Intelligence Laboratory (CSAIL), said, "Today it is easier to send a robot to Mars than to get that robot to clear your dinner table."[1]

Why? Because clearing the dinner table is a more complex operation than steering a spacecraft. The robot going to Mars doesn't have to make a huge variety of different kinds of decisions—just a few narrowly defined ones. It needs to land safely, for instance, and then perhaps scoop up a hunk of Martian soil for analysis. (Apologies to the rocket scientists at NASA's Jet Propulsion Lab for this gross oversimplification.) Clearing the dishes, on the other hand, requires an AI agent to make a huge number of diverse decisions, such as whether the scoop of macaroni and cheese left on a plate is worth saving, which dishes can go in the dishwasher, and whether the plastic container of food that's been forgotten in the back of the refrigerator for three weeks can be thrown out—not to mention meeting the challenge of moving around a kitchen and avoiding kids and pets without breaking things.

That's the basic framework we can use to distinguish between narrow and general AI: everything we can do with artificial intelligence today is narrow, and the stuff we see in the movies is general. Fortunately, the AI depicted in the movies will remain far ahead of the actual technology, even when the day comes that movies are produced and directed entirely by androids.

THE VOICE OF AN ALGORITHM

Now comes the more nuanced and less comforting news. Narrow applications of AI are already invisibly at work behind the scenes throughout the digital world—and most of us are only dimly aware of the implications. The world of marketing and advertising, in particular, is being permanently transformed by automation, Big Data, and machine learning, and the race is on to find more and more effective means of manipulating human behaviors.

We have reached an intersection where the science of persuasion and the technology to deliver personalized messaging on a mass scale are colliding at breathtaking speeds.

As consumers, we are left playing catch-up, and we frequently find ourselves taken off guard by the power inherent in human-computer interactions. I have worked for decades in digital media, and yet I still sometimes find myself surprised by the massive changes taking place.

I live next door to a stylish couple who both work in technology and are no strangers to AI themselves, and recently they had a group of us over for an afternoon pool party followed by dinner. I happened to be lounging on a couch on their back deck enjoying a glass of something red when my neighbors' four-year-old son pulled on my arm and indicated he wanted to show me something in the kitchen. With his mother's reassuring nod, I rose and followed my miniature host into the kitchen where he proudly introduced me to Alexa.

"Alexa, play *Star Wars*," he firmly directed. Alexa dutifully played the theme from *Star Wars*. My young host had little patience to listen to more than about 15 seconds of the music before he interrupted with a new request: "Alexa, play *Finding Nemo*." As Alexa fulfilled his wish, the boy's mother slipped quietly into the kitchen. She gazed adoringly at her precocious son as he put the device through its paces. Song after song played at his command, and he beamed with glee.

Then, as I was still pondering the significance of what I was witnessing, something entirely unexpected happened. In a most enamored tone, the boy cooed: "Alexa, I love you." My eyes darted to his mother, who turned and quietly retreated. As I watched her leave, I tried to process what had just happened.

How could a disembodied voice elicit such a strong emotional reaction from someone so young? I was preoccupied for the rest of the evening with the realization that children could respond to machines with expressions of genuine affection and even love. Are the rest of us next? Are we all destined to develop intimate relationships with AI agents to the point where we will trust these dependable voices in our lives with our deepest secrets?

Some months later, I mentioned to the couple that I wanted to include the episode about Alexa and their son in my book, and the mother smiled wryly and whispered: "I hate that thing."

As the story of my neighbors demonstrates, emotions like love and hate and even jealousy are beginning to emerge in our interactions with AI agents. Where previously we may have believed that our strongest emotions were reserved for interpersonal relationships, it is clear that our empathy and emotions play an important role in how we relate to machines. As we endow our machines with more anthropomorphic, humanlike qualities, such as speech and reasoning, our emotional connections with computers will increase.

We have begun a conversation with machines
that will last for the rest of our lives—that will also
be remembered by those machines long after our
own fragile memories have failed us.

The voice-based interface between people and gadgets like Alexa is still in its early days. Just as we currently find ourselves glued to our screens, where the graphical user interface reigns supreme, we will soon find our voice-based conversations to be an indispensable feature of the human-computer relationship. What does it mean for us when those conversations inevitably lead to an emotional connection with technology that is designed and owned by powerful interests?

THE VENTRILOQUIST AND THE DUMMY

Lurking in the digital domain, just out of sight, are the would-be puppet masters pulling our strings—the politicians, journalists, corporations, unions, scientists, institutions, governments, and religions—all lobbying us relentlessly for our votes, our dollars, our hearts, and our minds. With the emergence of voice user interfaces (VUI), our AI agents speak to us on behalf of a multitude of hidden interests, determined to persuade us, change what we think, and alter our behavior. They are intent upon becoming ventriloquists who use AI agents as their dummies to deliver persuasive messages for their brands.

It's worth noting that when we talk about brands, we're not just talking about the iconic corporate logos we see every day on Coke cans or the giant red bull's-eye in front of a Target retail store. The term *brand* is believed to have originated with the practice of marking livestock to establish ownership.[2] Interestingly, brands were also used to mark criminals to make them easily recognized wherever they traveled. A brand is a symbol that carries a specific meaning in a wide range of applications. We can even think of religious symbols like the Christian cross, the Islamic crescent moon and star, or the Jewish Star of David as brands. There are also organizations beyond the corporate realm like universities, government agencies, political parties, and labor unions (think Harvard, the IRS, and the AFL-CIO) that we can also think of as brands—all of which might be interested in persuading us in one way or another.

The brands that succeed in the future have already begun embracing marketing in the age of artificial intelligence. While consumers are largely unaware of the hidden tools and tactics of digital marketing, these interests are forging a new economy where individuals are led by the Invisible Brand.

THE BIRTH OF THE INVISIBLE BRAND

The year 1776 was a momentous one in world events, not just for the declaration that begins, "In Congress, July 4," but also for the publication of Adam Smith's opus *An Inquiry into the Nature and Causes of the Wealth of Nations*. Smith's book, a cornerstone of classical liberalism, laid the foundation for the academic study of economics. In it, he proposed that an individual working for his or her own self-interest will endeavor to produce goods of the greatest value, thus contributing to the public interest, as if "led by an invisible hand to promote an end which was no part of his intention."[3] Smith's invisible hand became a powerful and enduring metaphor for the benefits of the free market.

The title of this book, *The Invisible Brand*, derives from Smith's invisible hand, and it describes an entirely new class of emerging market forces. Increasingly the hidden hands of personalized information, persuasion, machine learning, and natural language processing are at work behind the scenes, buried deep within the media we consume and the apps we use to guide our decisions.

Consider that marketers and buyers have always been engaged in an epic struggle. Over the last two decades, that battle has increasingly favored the buyers. We can find the best price for anything on the web, instantly. We can see how people have rated the seller or the product. We can skip TV commercials on our DVRs and block the ads on our phones. As a result of these shifts, we hold more power than ever before. Now that balance is flipping completely. The Invisible Brand is shifting the power back to marketers.

Internet giants like Google, Facebook, and Amazon are amassing incredible amounts of data about us. What they know no longer respects corporate boundaries. They can match the data they collect with personal information from database marketing companies like Acxiom and Nielsen, companies that know our credit scores, what cars we just bought, even how big a house we own. They know if we like to ski, hunt, or take vacations in Europe. When the moment comes to put a message in front of us, marketers can combine *all* of that information to determine just what kind of message will influence us to do what they want.

Data by itself is not enough. Artificial intelligence is a game changer for marketers. Imagine the computing power that enabled IBM's Watson to beat *Jeopardy* champions, Google's DeepMind to master the mind-vexing Chinese game of Go, and Alexa to respond to our every need. Now imagine a marketer turning the power of AI to the challenge of figuring out what personalized marketing campaign will invisibly push us to make a purchase.

AI will play an increasingly important role in our lives in the years ahead as marketers turn vast amounts of computing power to the problem of influencing people's decisions. In the abstract, AI agents will constantly collect data about us—from our mobile devices, while we drive our cars, and while we sleep—and then analyze that data to learn how to persuade us and influence our behaviors.

The combination of data and AI will shift the marketing equation. In the twentieth century, the big shift was from mass manufacturing (think General Motors) to mass distribution (think Procter & Gamble). Now we are entering the age of mass customization. Your Facebook feed is different from my Facebook feed. When you go to ESPN.com, you see stories about the teams you follow, customized to your preferences. Information has become personalized. That means the power goes to those who know the customer best—based on leveraging AI and data about the customer.

A quick word about marketing and advertising. The terms are not interchangeable. The American Marketing Association (AMA) defines *marketing* as "the activity, set of institutions, and processes for creating, communicating, delivering, and exchanging offerings that have value for customers, clients, partners, and society at large." I think of marketing as the process of anticipating demand and delivering products to meet that demand profitably.

Feel free to come up with your own definition. My point is simply that marketing is a broad field that ranges in scope from designing a product's features to differentiating it in the marketplace. *Advertising* refers to a subset of marketing: the piece that specifically has to do with drawing attention to the product.

A tale that has become a Marketing 101 classic is the story of how Target knew a teenager was pregnant before her parents. Originally published in 2012 in the *New York Times Magazine*, with the title "How Companies Learn Your Secrets," the article by Charles Duhigg recounted how Andrew Pole, a statistician for the retail giant, was directed to analyze purchasing habits to determine if changes in consumer behaviors could be correlated statistically to indicate which consumers were pregnant. The reason? The stakes are enormous. As Duhigg wrote, "New parents' habits are more flexible than at any other time in their adult lives. If companies can identify pregnant shoppers, they can earn millions."[4]

As it turned out, Pole succeeded. Target started sending out mailers explicitly for pregnant women. The problem was that Target delivered one of their baby mailers to a teenage girl, and when her father opened the mail instead, he was furious—and he contacted Target to complain. Only it turned out that his teenage daughter was indeed pregnant. Target's algorithms had uncovered the truth before Dad did.

Algorithms have improved our ability to predict customer behavior, and that's usually the point marketers take away from this story. I would argue there has always been more to the tale. Target realized that shoppers found it creepy to receive mailers filled with coupons for baby clothes, nursery furniture, and diapers before they had time to tell their spouse, friends, or close relatives that they were pregnant. Therein lies the rub. As Duhigg put it in his article, "How do you take advantage of someone's habits without letting them know you're studying their lives?" Target did the logical thing. They started mixing the ads for diapers and toddler clothes in with ads for lawn mowers and wine glasses, so their mailers appeared to contain a random mix of ads. Obfuscating the mechanics of digital marketing became a virtue—and the Invisible Brand was born.

*Consumers want a wall of separation
between their personal lives and the retailers
who are trying to sell them merchandise.*

For brands to survive in an era of massive data collection and behavioral manipulation, they must learn to become *truly* invisible. This is because we now live in an age when consumers believe, to varying degrees, that they are under constant surveillance from their phones, their TVs, and even their refrigerators—and that all the data being collected is empowering various agenda-driven agents to manipulate them. I'll give that belief a name: *Googlenoia.*

I recently took my family on a typical American spring break vacation to Florida. About three weeks after we got home, I started receiving bills in the mail from Florida turnpike authorities that totaled about $60. Now, it so happens that I-95 runs from where I live all the way to Miami in one direct shot, and if I had taken that route, it wouldn't have cost me so much because that section of I-95 is mostly toll free. But Google Maps had routed me along a number of toll roads instead. These roads use cameras to snap photos of license plates, which then enables the regulating turnpike authorities to access the vehicle registration records from my state's DMV to send an invoice conveniently to my mailbox.

Here's where Googlenoia sets in. Does Google have a deal with the toll roads to route me along the most profitable path between point *A* and point *B*? I'd like to believe not. I'd like to believe that Google sent me along the fastest possible path, considering traffic congestion, with only speed and convenience in mind. There's even a setting I can adjust inside the app to help me avoid toll roads altogether. But the cynic in me is still suspicious. There are a host of questions raised by our reliance on AI agents as to why certain recommendations are made and whether they are, in fact, to our benefit or the benefit of other interested parties. Just because we're Googlenoid doesn't mean they aren't out to get us.

As the use of AI spreads, information will become increasingly personalized and persuasive. As AI agents learn to speak, they will become a new voice in our heads, our constant digital companions, upon whom we depend for all our needs and with whom we will develop a deep personal relationship. We're on the verge of a complete shift in the balance of power between producers and consumers because of what AI can do. The potential is at once awesome and terrifying.

ARTIFICIAL PERSUASION

Let's spend a few minutes in the AI-powered world of marketing.

Meet Emily. Emily is a single woman who lives in a 25-year-old house in the suburbs of Raleigh, North Carolina. She's comfortable with technology, which is why she's one of the first people the Invisible Brand will touch. Her Nest thermostat connects to her appliances; her Nest home service warranty sends a technician when anything goes wrong with her air conditioning, her refrigerator, or her plumbing. She enjoys these conveniences.

She pays her bills electronically, twice per month, at around 8:30 a.m. on Saturday mornings. A few weeks ago, she received a quarterly bonus, which she used to pay down her credit cards and fund her 401(k). This Saturday, as she pays her utility bill, Duke Energy shows her the friendly face of its telephone representative—a face that reminds Emily of her younger sister. The on-screen message says, "Emily. Other houses on your street consume 15 percent less energy per month." There's also a graph that shows how much more she's spending than her neighbors. "How is that possible?" she wonders. She clicks.

Now she is looking at an infographic of seven energy saving tactics. The one at the top is an image of an old window, with gaps around the edges where air conditioning is escaping. Sitting at her kitchen table, Emily looks up from the computer screen. Her eyes notice the narrow gap beside her own kitchen window, where the heat leaks out when it's cold outside, just wide enough for a dollar bill to slip through. In her mind, Emily pictures a stream of dollars slowly sliding through the crack and blowing away like leaves.

Later that morning, she checks her favorite local news website. A graphic beside the headlines shows five things to consider when purchasing replacement windows. The tips include details on a $1,500 tax rebate for energy-efficient upgrades, how much she should pay, how to get an interest-free loan from Bank of America, and how to get a free, fixed-price, in-home estimate—tips that are sponsored by Pella Showroom of Raleigh. She clicks on the graphic at the bottom to review appointment times when an estimator is available to visit—and she is pleased to see that one is free at 11 a.m. In one click, she sees the face of Sam Wells, her new estimator, and she's made an appointment.

How did Emily go from sitting at her kitchen table to scoping out replacement windows in the space of a few hours? It's not a coincidence. It's the Invisible Brand at work.

When Emily paid down her credit cards, her credit score improved. Because she had opted into Bank of America's credit monitoring tool, her bank had access to those credit scores—which enabled the bank to preauthorize a loan. As a business service, Bank of America partners with local businesses that rely on consumer credit to offer their services, including Pella Showroom of Raleigh. Her bank placed "cookies" on her computer, not just to recognize her when she returns to the site but also to help other companies recognize her when she is online.

Emily's utility company, Duke Energy, has a business relationship with Nest Labs, the company that makes Nest home automation devices like thermostats, lights, and security cameras that can be controlled from Emily's mobile device. Nest was purchased by Google (Alphabet Inc.) back in 2014 for $3.2 billion, and it was rolled into Google Home. Emily's Nest products not only know just how she sets her thermostat but also the make and model of every appliance in her home and when she uses them. The age and construction details of her home are public information. Combined with her utility data, this information allows Duke Energy to make a pretty good guess that her home air-conditioning bills might benefit from a window upgrade.

The AI agent employed by Duke Energy delivered the image that attracted Emily's attention and provided the infographic that started her thinking about windows. Duke's partnership with Pella Showroom of Raleigh and MaxPoint, a hyperlocal marketing company, led to showing exactly the right ad on her local news website—the ad that tipped her over to making an appointment. The note about the $1,500 tax credit was no coincidence either—the cookies on her browser from the bank calibrated that offer, right down to the Saturday morning timing when she pays her bills.

This example is fictitious, but the scenario is completely plausible based on currently existing technologies. Situations like this will soon be common experiences for millions of consumers thanks to data, AI, and digital advertising. Humans will engineer parts of those algorithms. Once they're in the wild, the algorithms will learn which offers work best in which situations— and they will get smarter. Soon, they will influence everything we do, gathering data from every device we have and persuading us on every surface we view and through every voice we hear.

As a marketer, the question becomes one of how to turn the persuasive powers of AI into an advantage. As a consumer, on the other hand, the challenge is learning how we are all being persuaded—and why.

THE ROAD AHEAD

This book seeks to provide a detailed exposition of how the Invisible Brand is emerging and permanently altering the human-computer relationship. I'll explain what it means for marketers, of course. But a trend this big will also transform media, finance, health, education, and the dynamics of global politics. Rather than panic about these changes, I want us to better understand what's happening so that we are armed to make better decisions about what's coming.

The first five chapters form Part I of this book: "Emergence." First, we will look at the mass customization and personalization of information and how that trend has been enabled by digital media and digital advertising. Second, we will examine the art of persuasion—how it is deployed with increasing precision, and how digital technology is turning persuasion into a science. Third, we will explore the realm of machine learning, with a focus on data collection and the algorithms at work in the fields of advertising and marketing, and how they are revolutionizing the relationships between consumers and brands. Fourth, computers are now communicating with us using humanlike, anthropomorphic voices. We will delve into the inner workings of natural language processing (NLP) to understand a future in which the consumers' interface with computers will shift increasingly toward the spoken word, and how that will make us more vulnerable to persuasion. Together, these four areas of innovation combine to create what I call *psychological technology*, or simply *psychotechnology*.

Psychotechnology *is the following:*

- *Personalized*
- *Persuasive*
- *Able to learn*
- *Anthropomorphic*

Once we have established in Part I the four key trends—the personalization of information, the science of persuasion, machine learning algorithms equipped with infinite data, and natural language processing—we will pull it all together in Part II, "Synthesis," to reveal how psychotechnology is already working to invisibly reshape our behaviors. We will make an inquiry into the potential depth of the human-computer relationship and how we will be changed by these technologies; examine current and near-future opportunities in business and industries resulting from these changes, particularly in the areas of education, personal finance, and healthcare; and explore the societal implications of mass data collection on privacy, propaganda, and politics at a global level. Finally, we will finish with an inquiry into the impact of humans becoming reliant upon artificially intelligent agents who are capable of befriending them at an emotional and even spiritual level.

To Recap

Artificial intelligence is changing marketing in ways that will have wide-ranging impacts on every facet of our society. While we're not yet at the point where AI agents are poised to take over the world, we are already witnessing the use of AI to influence people's decisions—a trend that promises to produce far-reaching consequences for the marketplace and for consumers.

The hidden hand of marketers leveraging AI to influence the way we think and how we act is what I call the Invisible Brand. It is enabled by four major innovations: personalized information, the science of persuasion, machine learning, and humanlike voice interactions, which have converged to create a new field I call *psychotechnology*. It's a development that businesses and consumers ignore at their own peril, whose impact will be felt across sectors as diverse as media, healthcare, finance, education, and government. If we are to better understand who controls the Invisible Brand and how it will develop, we first need to take a step back and examine its roots in the digital advertising industry.

Note from the author: Chapters 2 through 5 are somewhat technical in nature, and they are intended to help practitioners understand how psychotechnology works. If that isn't your objective, you may be more interested in the implications of psychotechnology discussed in Part II, which begins with Chapter 6.

2

The Roots of the Invisible Brand in Digital Advertising

THE ADVERTISING INDUSTRY CHANGED permanently when Internet technologies made it possible to deliver personalized information directly to consumers. Up until then, broadcast media like television and radio and the mass publication of newspapers and magazines dominated the advertising landscape.

We've gone from delivering the same message to everyone at the same time through mass communications, to technology that can deliver different messages to every individual, on demand, through mass customization.

This isn't the first time computers have transformed the advertising business. Think back to AMC's hit *Mad Men*. The show featured elegant and unruly executives who dominated the advertising world of the 1960s with their creativity, sales talent, and well, plenty of alcohol and tobacco. In its final season, *Mad Men* foreshadowed the transformation wrought by computers on the advertising industry.

Enter Don Draper. Classically handsome and adorned in a black regimental-striped tie and fitted suit, he walks into the ad agency Sterling Cooper & Partners where he finds ... exactly ... no one. The halls are silent, and the offices empty. A telephone receiver dangles eerily off the side of a desk as if everyone has suddenly vanished, midsentence, into an episode of the *Twilight Zone*.

Don makes his way through the warren of abandoned desks and up the stairs where he finally discovers all his colleagues gathered solemnly for an announcement of progress: the installation of a mainframe computer at the agency. The bulky computer is unceremoniously to replace the creative lounge—the main thing (in the words of one employee) that makes the agency unique.

Draper walks toward his new office, and in the hallway, he stops and musters a conversation with Lloyd Holly, the contractor installing the new computer. The show's writers clearly intended the exchange to be pivotal and thematically dense:

Holly: This machine is frightening to people, but it's made by people.

Draper: People aren't frightening?

Holly: It's not that. It's more of a cosmic disturbance. This machine is intimidating because it contains infinite quantities of information, and that's threatening because human existence is finite. But isn't it godlike that we've mastered the infinite?[1]

Who can blame Draper when, soon after, he steals a bottle of Smirnoff vodka from his colleague's bottom shelf and drinks deeply, straight from the bottle? The advertising industry has changed forever, and he belongs to an era whose time has passed. Or so we are led to believe. Now, lest we find ourselves becoming too nostalgic for beehive hairdos and cigarettes, we should ask ourselves the most important question: "What kind of computer was that anyway?"

AMC is only too happy to oblige the curiosities of *Mad Men*'s most ardent fans. The show's fan site contains a helpful article: "*Mad Men*'s 1960s Handbook: The IBM System/360 Computer." The article clearly indicates that Don Draper's digital nemesis was the IBM System/360, which came into widespread use in the late 1960s. The article states, "In what *Fortune* magazine later described as a $5 billion bet—about $38.5 billion in today's dollars—IBM's chairman, Thomas J. Watson, Jr., authorized a plan to research and develop a family of computers that would interact with each other and that could be programmed for any use. He chose the number 360, representing the number of degrees in a circle, to emphasize the product's flexibility."[2]

Not to be outdone by AMC's fan site, in 2014 the *Harvard Business Review* (HBR) took its own ride on the fan wagon with a piece entitled "That *Mad Men* Computer, Explained by HBR in 1969."[3] The article noted that Sterling Cooper & Partners' computer contained "a potent new computing technology that was part of the 360—the interactive graphical display terminal." This wasn't merely a toy for nerds with punch cards who could code in Fortran. As Andrea Ovans framed it in her article: "The convergence of long-standing cathode-ray-tube and light-pen hardware with software that would accept English language commands was about to create a revolution in data analysis."

The *graphical user interface* (GUI) made data analysis accessible to the ad agency world, and suddenly the "spray and pray" model of mass advertising could be held to a higher standard of accountability. Reporting and metrics became a routine feature of ad campaign measurement, and computer-based analytics forged a new frontier in advertising. What followed was a rash of mainframe innovations that ultimately begat machines fast enough to take on the challenge of competing with human thought. The S/360's grandchild, IBM's Deep Blue, defeated world chess champion Gary Kasparov in 1997. The fact that Kasparov had managed to beat Deep Blue a year earlier seems to be a miracle in retrospect. At the time it seemed to be more parlor trick than epochal shift—insofar as Deep Blue was programmed to crunch an absurdly large array of potential moves and outcomes. There was an assumption on the public's part that this machine wasn't actually thinking, so much as it was extremely fast at moving imaginary chess pieces around an imaginary board until it stumbled on a winning combination.

Ultimately, the interactive graphical display terminal of yesteryear put the power of data analytics in the agency's hands and unleashed a torrent of creative innovations that drove the advertising industry to new heights, with total TV advertising in the United States alone topping $80 billion some 40 years later. With the personal computer, the graphical user interface became the primary interface between humans and computers and ultimately gave rise to the digital advertising industry. Computer brands themselves became giant advertisers—and spawned a new generation of Drapers.

THE ADS THAT STALK US

As a child, my parents read a Dr. Seuss story to me at bedtime. It was about a pair of pale green pants with nobody inside them that follows this little character around at night in the woods. It was called *What Was I Scared Of?*

I mention this now because that same uncanny feeling of being pursued by an invisible force is what many of us now feel when we notice the online ads that seem to follow us around the Internet wherever we go.

You know that new putter that you were going to buy for golf season? Or those red strappy sandals that keep following you around on every web page you visit? Perhaps you really liked those sandals when you put them in your shopping cart, but when you saw the price tag, you had a change of heart and quickly clicked away before buying them. The next day you are on a completely different website, and an ad pops up for *that exact same pair* of red strappy sandals. Are they following you? Do you have a digital stalker who is watching everything you do online?

To understand how ads can stalk us, we first must understand a few basic things about browsers like Chrome and Safari. When we visit a web page, the browser on our computer uses HTML (that is, written text instructions) to send our requests to a host computer, called a *server*. Essentially we tell the server, "Show me the home page for *CBS News*," and the server responds with instructions that direct our browser where to find the images, navigation icons, and articles that compose the web page.

It is critical to understand that the server doesn't send back one big picture to our browser all at once. Instead, the browser is assembling a jigsaw puzzle of pieces, and the server is simply telling the browser where to get each piece. In most cases the pieces are stored on different computers all connected by the Internet. The server says (in essence), "Go get Image A from Computer B, and place it in the upper left corner of the screen. Then

go get Image C from Computer D, and place it next to Image A."
The server continues giving instructions until the whole page is
displayed. Of course, this happens very, very quickly, so we don't
usually see the page being assembled one piece at a time.

It is important to understand that ads are inserted into web
pages in the same fashion. The server tells our browser to go get
an ad and place it over there on the right side of the screen next
to the article. Specifically, it directs our browser to a computer
called an *ad server*, and the ad server delivers an ad that is targeted to each of us individually at that moment (Figure 2.1).

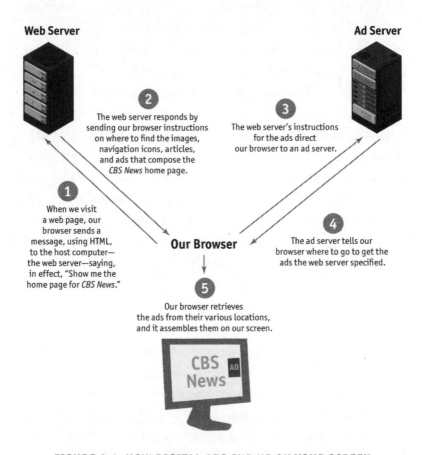

FIGURE 2.1 HOW DIGITAL ADS END UP ON YOUR SCREEN

If two people sat next to each other with their laptops and both visited *CBS News* at the same time, they would see different ads. One might see an ad for a new putter, and the other might see an ad for red strappy sandals. That's personalized information.

Increasingly, huge volumes of digital ads are reaching people through social media. There are now some 3.2 billion active social media users—or nearly half of the entire human race.[4] Clearly that's a population advertisers want to reach, which has led to the rapid growth of digital advertising spending in social media—something that's estimated to total $68 billion this year (as I'm writing this in 2018), or about $22.84 for every person.[5] These numbers are expected to only grow from here. According to a survey of chief marketing officers, digital advertising budgets aimed at social media will double by 2023.[6]

Whether a consumer is browsing the news sites or their social media feeds, how does the ad server know what ad to deliver? The ad server is designed to deliver ads based on a variety of parameters that can be set by the advertisers, such as time of day and geography. Imagine an ad for McDonald's breakfast sandwiches is designed to run in the mornings between 6 a.m. and 9 a.m. only in Boston. After 9 a.m., a different ad for McDonald's cheeseburgers will run instead. So, when consumers visit their favorite website at 8:55 a.m., they see an ad for a breakfast sandwich, and when they refresh the page at 9:05 a.m., they see an ad for a cheeseburger. For the vegetarians out there, they are going to see an ad for a salad because digital advertising can target them based on their behaviors and preferences.

BREADCRUMBS AND COOKIES

Sometimes consumer behaviors and preferences can be deduced from the cookies on their browsers—which might tell the ad server that they visit sites about vegetarian recipes. How? In 1994 Netscape invented the browser cookie for use in its Mosaic web browser as a means for enabling an online shopping cart for e-commerce.[7] Cookies are simple text files that are sent by a website to a user's browser, where they are stored primarily for the purpose of identifying a returning guest to a website, along with information about that guest's previous visits. First-party cookies are those that are set by the domain being displayed in the browser's address bar. Third-party cookies can be set when content, such as a display ad, is sent from a third-party domain, such as an ad server. Advertisers can deliver ads targeting specific online behaviors that may indicate consumer purchase intent using both first- and third-party cookies.[8]

The widespread use of cookies permitted the emergence of data tracking companies that can analyze log files of Internet users' web browsing histories to determine their interests and possible future online behaviors. These online behaviors can be matched with offline behaviors to form a broad picture of an individual's lifestyle and habits. It's as though we are leaving a little trail of breadcrumbs wherever we go online that data analytics providers can follow to figure out where we've been and where we are headed.

One data provider, Acxiom, has developed a massive database of consumer behaviors. For about 96 percent of American households, Acxiom's databases contain the names of their family members, their current and past addresses, how often they pay their credit card bills, whether they own a dog or a cat (and what breed it is), whether they are right-handed or left-handed, and what kinds of medication they use (based on pharmacy records)—the list of data points is at least 1,500 items long and growing.[9]

Remember, a cookie is nothing more than a little username, a way to identify us individually, like "User 12345." The cookie itself doesn't remember us. It acts as a key to unlock the data about us that is stored in a database. Imagine you are planning a trip to France, and you go on a travel website to shop for flights to Paris. Later that day you notice you are getting ads for hotels in Paris. That's not a coincidence. The cookie that identifies your browser as "User 12345" is linked to a record in the travel agency's computer that says you are looking for a flight to Paris. If you go back to that travel site, your Paris trip will pop back up where you left off, and you won't even have to put your travel dates in again. If the travel site has a deal with other advertisers, it can share the fact that User 12345 is flying to Paris, and all of their partner advertisers can buy ads to target you with deals in Paris.

When you see ads that target you because you are in-market for a trip to Paris, we call that behavioral targeting. When you see ads for breakfast sandwiches at 7 a.m., we call that dayparting or time-based targeting. When you see ads for Boston-area stores when you are visiting Boston, that's something called geo-targeting. When you see an ad for red strappy sandals that you abandoned in the shopping cart of another website, that's called retargeting. If you happen to see an ad for Dr. Seuss books while reading an article about spooky pale green pants—that is called contextual targeting. All of these targeting techniques are enabled because of digital advertising technology, which is frequently shortened to ad tech. Thanks to ad tech, marketers and advertisers can now target us in very personal and customized ways. Information delivery has become personalized.

THE EVOLUTION OF THE AD AUCTION

The advent of online display advertising in 1994 brought the new possibility that machines could someday automate the placement of ads over the Internet. At first, ad placement was direct, with advertisers communicating their ad placements to website publishers using traditional technologies such as email and telephones and the proverbial three-martini lunch.

Today, the business of online advertising sales is no longer dominated by account executives giving presentations over power lunches. Massive digital ad exchanges have automated the world of online ad sales for the last decade. Publishers and their advertising clients embraced the exchanges because the technology did the heavy lifting of pairing up the national brands with the small local publishers who couldn't afford to send account executives to solicit major advertisers. Conversely, the national brands could use the ad exchanges to coordinate their ad buys with a broad range of small local publishers.

My first experience with a company that was aggregating publisher inventory (the supply side) on behalf of advertisers was a Chicago-based firm called Centro. Before Centro, an advertiser who wanted to reach audiences in the Northeast had to pick up the phone and start calling a bunch of local websites to ask them if they had inventory available. The effort required a lot of phone calls, emails, and even faxes. Centro's idea was a straightforward value proposition for the advertisers. Centro did the legwork for the advertisers by connecting with all the websites on their behalf. Initially, the data collection was managed on Excel spreadsheets, and each website publisher had to submit its avails manually in an Excel document. Centro aggregated the results from all the websites that responded to the avail request and put together a bid, which it sent back to the advertiser with a single price for a large block of ad impressions to reach the advertiser's target.

As technology progressed, ad tech companies like Centro improved the automation of their processes. Ad networks and new software emerged to automate the aggregation of inventory and connect with national advertisers at scales great enough to make it worth everyone's efforts. In a short time, ad networks started connecting with each other to form ad exchanges. These exchanges became virtual markets where the supply and demand for online display ads could be matched efficiently in real time. Initially, ad exchanges and their trading partners profited handsomely by filling unsold remnant inventory on publishers' sites cheaply and charging advertisers a significant markup buried in the overall cost per thousand (CPM) of the transaction.[10]

On either side of this supply-and-demand market, companies developed technology platforms that enabled the transactions. The supply side platforms (SSPs) worked on behalf of publishers to help them monetize their unsold inventory. The demand side platforms (DSPs) worked on behalf of advertisers to help find cost-effective inventory to reach the right audiences.[11] Together, SSPs and DSPs brought new automated efficiencies to the online advertising industry, and algorithms began to compete alongside traders and ad networks in the ad exchanges for the opportunity to buy and sell ads programmatically. The practice become known as programmatic advertising.

Today, major ad exchanges, such as Google's AdX (aka DoubleClick Ad Exchange), OpenX, and AppNexus, have consolidated the ad networks into a massive online consortium of buyers and sellers placing programmatic advertising on a global scale. For some perspective on the rate of programmatic advertising's stunning ascent and revenue growth, consider that the Interactive Advertising Bureau (IAB) reported that programmatic spending now accounts for 80 percent of all digital ad spending—which includes display mobile, social, and search. That share of the market is expected to rise to 86.2 percent by 2020.[12] Another reliable source of data confirms that estimate. By 2020, according to media research firm Borrell Associates, 85 percent of targeted banner advertising on websites will flow through exchanges like these. When we consider that digital ad spending in 2018 was around $107.3 billion—substantially higher than the $69.87 billion invested in TV advertising[13]—it is clear how incredibly influential programmatic advertising has become.

DATA-ENABLED AD TARGETING

By combining digital buying and selling of advertising through ad exchanges, with data that originated from database marketing companies like Acxiom, the industry is able to offer advertisers the opportunity to automate the process of delivering ads to select target audiences. Programmatic advertising lies at the intersection of data and technology and was born out of the need to deliver highly targeted, relevant marketing across multiple channels more efficiently.[14]

Data-driven targeting capabilities moved exchanges beyond remnant inventory clearance into the premium advertising business. For advertisers, being able to find an "auto intender" buried in the 5-trillion-impression haystack of the web meant new performance and efficiency. For publishers, this was another way to upsell the value of the audiences who consumed the costly content they created.[15]

Let's reinforce the fact that programmatic ads are being delivered individually, one at a time, to consumers based on data that identifies them as members of some ideal target audience an advertiser is seeking. By setting up an automated buy through the ad exchanges, a sporting-goods manufacturer can deliver a display ad targeting select consumers with ads for soccer equipment based on the cookies present on their browsers. Other consumers might receive ads for Ford F-150s from the same ad exchange based on a cookie profile that suggests they are in-market for a new truck. By allowing programmatic markets to deliver value in the form of better targeting, the industry has moved away from thinking of all this ad tech as a method for clearing unsold remnant.

> *Programmatic advertising has become*
> *a weapon of mass customization.*

ADVERTISING AUCTIONS IN REAL TIME

Astoundingly, the programmatic advertising market resolves these buying and selling decisions in less than 200 milliseconds.[16] To understand how that is possible, we must first understand the underlying technologies that enable digital ad exchanges. The best starting point is to think of these exchanges as giant auction houses, where publishers on the supply side can offer up ad space for auction. The bidders are the advertisers on the demand side who are seeking to purchase ad space from those publishers. In between is the auctioneer—the ad exchange—who regulates the bidding and determines the winner of each auction with a final gavel. Like water seeking equilibrium, ads seek the highest traffic at the lowest price. The process of auctioning off ads through networks and phone calls and spreadsheets was time-consuming and burdensome. Ad exchanges led to one of the most transformative innovations in advertising history: real-time bidding (RTB).

RTB is a type of auction in which an automated bid is sent to purchase a single ad impression based on targeting information gathered from a user's browser. Collecting the bids and resolving the auction with the placement of a single ad all takes place in the blink of an eye and allows a publisher to maximize the value of every single ad placement on its site. Rather than buying aggregated blocks of impressions, advertisers are able to buy audiences wherever they can be found. As Jack Marshall explained in *Digiday*, "Real-time bidding refers to the buying and selling of online ad impressions through real-time auctions that occur in the time it takes a webpage to load."[17]

Like a stock exchange, RTB turns advertising into a commodity market—with eyeballs as the commodity. As users view web pages, algorithms are at work matching what is known about them with the needs of thousands of potential advertisers bidding in a giant auction and, in milliseconds, delivering the winning ads to the page. Algorithms manage pricing and fulfillment in real time. Publishers, advertisers, and consumers become components in a massive ad fulfillment machine.

Unlike auctions that position blocks of ads in aggregate prior to the flight dates, real-time bidding enables advertisers to make buying decisions down to the second. RTB produces entirely new opportunities for control over the marketing process. As *Marketing Week* put it: "Marketers can make decisions to alter campaigns in real time by thinking about how it changes their strategy, where they would now want to buy inventory, what audience they want to buy, and how much they want to pay."[18]

Combining this flexibility with market intelligence and near instant responsiveness provides a clear advantage to the marketing professional that is largely responsible for the recent growth of programmatic RTB and its adoption by advertisers. The real-time nature of programmatic RTB also provides the marketer with access to real-time analytics that can be correlated more accurately with brand-related events in the news and social media.

This innovation has transformed the ad business. No longer is the ad buyer seeking some broad demographic such as "women ages 35 to 54" and considering ad buys only in *Vogue* or *Good Housekeeping*. Now media planners can place buys much more specifically, targeting female iPhone users with master's degrees in-market for eyewear in Irvine and waiting for the machine to find them. And the machine is getting smarter every day.

BLURRING THE LINE BETWEEN ADVERTISING AND NEWS

The ability to deliver personalized information to a single individual is a direct result of this technological evolution. What started as an ad delivery strategy to narrowly target audiences has now evolved to the point where it has tremendous implications for the delivery of all types of information. Just as publishers are motivated to put the right ads in front of the right consumers, they are also motivated to deliver articles and information tailored to their wants and interests in the belief that those consumers will spend more time on their sites—and consume more ads.

With the advent of *native advertising*, which is content created by advertisers made to look like news stories, the wall separating editorial content from advertising content has fallen. Just take a look at what shows up on Facebook feeds or the website for the local newspaper. Native ads usually appear under news stories, near the bottom of the page, where consumers see images and headlines that look like additional news stories. But they're not: they're ads, and they're targeting us.

Think of these native ads like the product placements seen in the movies, where brands pay to have their products featured. A

Mini Cooper was featured heavily in the movie *The Italian Job*, and James Bond traded his martini for a Heineken in the movie *Skyfall*. The goal of product placement, of course, is to try and get moviegoers to buy those same products—which is exactly what's happening with native ads. The main difference is that the brands are using personalized and customized combinations of images and text, often dressed up like news stories.

Imagine two people are both watching the same James Bond movie, but one sees Bond drinking a Heineken, while the other sees him drinking Makers Mark. We aren't there yet, in terms of movie theater technology, but that's exactly what's happening with digital advertising online. The surfing experience is being tailored to our preferences. Personalized information keeps us safely within our comfort zones.

As an experiment while writing this section, I visited the site for *CBS News* and clicked on the first story I saw. When I scrolled down the page below that article, I found more stories: one that rated computer virus protection for Apple computers, one about diabetes care, and another about pet nutrition featuring an adorable puppy. Further down, there was an insurance ad that mentioned Chapel Hill, and another that targeted people "born 1947–1979." One would have to squint really hard to notice the words "sponsored content" written in the smallest font, off to the side near these stories.

It wasn't an accident that I was shown those particular stories. For one, I was born in 1967, squarely in the middle of the age group targeted in the ads, and I was at my office in Chapel Hill. I was writing this book on a Mac. (No, that's not a product placement—but thanks for considering the possibility.) I own a dog, and I love cute puppy pictures. Coincidence? Obviously not. Those stories were there to persuade me in very targeted ways. I was being targeted based on my laptop's operating system, my age, my online surfing behaviors, and my geography, all in one screenshot (Figure 2.2).

Taboola Feed

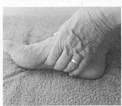

Sponsored Links

Mac Users Guide (2018) - #1 Antivirus Now Fre...
The 10 Best Providers

Early Signs And Treatments For Diabet...
Yahoo Search

The One Thing Every Dog Owner Should Ad...
Ultimate Pet Nutrition

Chapel Hill, North Carolina: This Unbelievable, Tiny Company Is...
EverQuote Insurance Quotes

North Carolina Residents Born 1947-1979 With No Life Insurance Must...
Consumer Daily

FIGURE 2.2 NATIVE ADS APPEARING AS NEWS STORIES ON POPULAR NEWS WEBSITES

A consumer who happens to click on any of these "stories," as I did, would quickly realize they were just ads masquerading as news stories all along. Interestingly, the virus protection story featured an image that looked like a modified version of Apple's iconic logo—but it was more like a pear with a bite taken out of it, so they wouldn't get sued for copyright or trademark infringement. When I clicked on the link, I was taken to a website that was essentially a clearinghouse of affiliate marketing programs to sell antivirus software, regardless of the operating system.

Remember, I started on a news website. I clicked on a story about rating virus protection for the Mac. I was taken to another website, which provided links to popular antivirus software—all available for purchase. In a few short steps, the "news" on CBS's website led me to a product that I might want, conveniently available for purchase. This is how the news and information we consume from digital sources is often customized just for us—on the fly and with a marketing motive. It's becoming more sophisticated every day.

FURTHER FILTERING OUR BUBBLES

In his groundbreaking work *The Filter Bubble*, Eli Pariser established that "the personalized web is changing what we read and how we think."[19] Publishers and marketers watch us closely and tailor our digital information to maximize the time we spend with their content and the chance that we will spend money with their advertisers. If we show an interest in college football, we will be given more stories (and ads) about college football. If we show an interest in artificial intelligence, we will see more stories about AI along with ads for companies in the business. It starts to feel like we are trapped in our own personal echo chambers, in a feedback loop where we are shown more of the same because of some previous interest or behavior.

On one hand, this is convenient because we don't have to work too hard to find stories on subjects that interest us. On the other hand, such a self-reinforcing loop might trap us inside a bubble of selective news and information where we become increasingly polarized and unable to understand the opinions of people who are trapped in conflicting bubbles of news and information. Birds of a feather flock together according to the old cliché. The Internet enables those birds to find each other more easily and to create tribes online where information is selectively shared in narrowing circles. Marketers take advantage of this trend by finding those tribes and targeting their filter bubbles.

We have shifted from consuming information we need,
to consuming information we like.

As we enter into self-perpetuating content ecosystems, we must be honest about how that change is, in turn, changing us.

CROSS-PLATFORM CONVERGENCE

Our echo chambers go beyond the web pages we consume. The convergence of digital delivery and data-driven targeting that allows programmatic ads to succeed for online display ads is the formula for another type of convergence: programmatic ad placement for TV, radio, and mobile devices. To move brand dollars, programmatic technologies have to grow up and advance to other forms of media like TV and radio.[20]

The current limits on TV (including web-connected "smart" TVs), satellite radio, and ever-proliferating mobile devices in the programmatic space will be overcome by technology changes in the near future. Programmatic technology allows for the automation of cross-platform buying and selling of digital advertising via real-time bidding, which allows for a cost-effective way to take advantage of audience targeting.[21]

This is equally true for digital delivery of any Internet-based advertising format, including audio and video. Digital audio

giant Pandora, with more than $300 million in quarterly reve-
nues, reports that mobile ads account for 85 percent of its purchased inventory.[22]

Confidence in the convergence of TV and video formats in
the programmatic arena remains high among industry analysts.
"Internet connected TV is going to be a reality. It will dramati-
cally change the ad industry forever. Ads will become interactive
and delivered to individual TV sets according to the user," said
Henrique de Castro, Google VP for global media.[23]

Programmatic will gain a foothold anywhere that digital delivery of TV meets a demand for data-driven advertising. Hulu
has used private exchanges to auction off video ads. A few years
ago, ABC announced, during its fall upfronts, that it would use
programmatic to sell some of its digital video content. Even some
traditional TV ads are getting automated. Cable carriers, such as
Comcast, enable automated ad targeting against on-demand videos. Satellite carriers DirecTV and Dish Network sell some TV
inventory programmatically.[24]

This convergence of media under an automated advertising
umbrella is critical to the future of programmatic because it will
facilitate better comparisons across screens to allow marketers
to optimize the ways they engage consumers. Currently, most
advertising is spent in separate silos, with one budget and one
buyer for TV and another budget and buyer for print, and yet
another for online. In theory, programmatic can allow all of this
media buying to merge together under one unified system, allowing the planners a deeper understanding of which media are performing and which are not.

It was big news when it was announced in 2014 that "Yahoo!
was developing a new platform designed to be an alternative to
existing 'demand-side platforms,' which would allow advertisers to manage their online ads. One of the key differentiators was

to allow advertisers access to multiple forms of online advertising on one platform, which meant one media plan could cover display, video, and native advertising across all devices."[25] The resulting convergence that has evolved since then means that advertisers can place their ads in front of us, wherever we are. It also means that they can gather more data about the effect of their advertising across a wider range of media to build more accurate attribution models—which in turn can help deliver more effective personalized information.

DATA AND ATTRIBUTION

Attribution is the practice of trying to correlate specific marketing practices with a consumer action. Businesses are collecting data about transactions hoping that it will lead to better attribution models that can help marketers know what is working for their brands and what isn't.

Without doing a deep dive into all the math, let's take a simple holiday shopping example. Last Christmas, I took my daughter shopping in Chelsea, and she saw a display of winter coats in the Columbia Sportswear store under a sign that said "50% off." She picked one out and proceeded to the cash register. At the moment of purchase, Columbia had the opportunity to correlate their 50 percent off sale with the purchase. Advertising works, and the data captured from that sale can be used to influence future advertising decisions. That is attribution.

Unfortunately, the item my daughter intended to purchase was not entered in Columbia's cash register system as being part of the sale. The clerk refused to honor the advertised price, and we ended up complaining (unsuccessfully) to Columbia's customer service team. Since data is also available for capture through customer service interactions, Columbia should have been able to deduce that their advertising was having a negative impact on the customer experience. That is also attribution. If a brand knows why a customer made a purchase, it possesses business intelligence that helps inform its overall marketing plan. Just as importantly, if a brand knows why a customer is unhappy, it can take steps to ensure it avoids similar mistakes in the future. Data collection feeds critical marketing decisions used to improve the effectiveness of ad campaigns on consumers.

Marketers need to be deliberate about data collection— to think strategically about what information is required to make better attribution decisions and figure out ways to get it ethically.

WHEN CLICKS DON'T PREDICT

In the digital world, the starting point for a lot of attribution modeling is the click. Clicks are easy to count, and algorithms love numbers. Ever since *WIRED* magazine published the first display ad on October 27, 1994, in *HotWired*, the digital advertising industry has done a great job convincing advertisers that the click is some sort of Holy Grail that makes ROI easy to measure. As the industry has matured, it has become clear that isn't the case, and more discerning advertisers understand there are times to pay attention to clicks and there are times when clicks are irrelevant. Clicks have context, and understanding their context is the key to knowing when they are important.

When it was revealed that there was a secret partnership between Google and credit card companies, like Mastercard, allowing companies to know if customers who clicked on ads later bought those items in a physical store, it showed just how valuable it was for retail brands to understand that connection.[26] If someone searched for, say, a pair of jeans, and then later bought a pair of jeans in a store using his or her credit card, Google could argue that the search led to conversion for the brand. Companies buy a lot more online advertising from Google when they can see it leads to more sales, both online and offline.

The closer the click is to the cash register, the more useful it is as a metric. Conversely, the further the click is from the cash register, the less useful it is as a metric. For example, when we check out from an e-commerce website by clicking "Pay Now," we are at the cash register, and our clicks are highly correlated with the purchase (the click *is* the purchase). On the other hand, when we click a banner ad to learn about a new car, our click is a long way from the cash register, and it has no correlation with any purchase, as we shall see. Consider the table in Figure 2.3 for more examples.

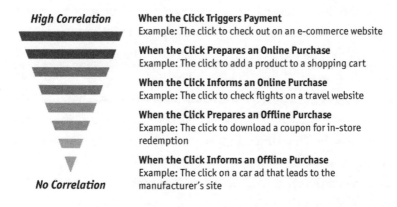

High Correlation

When the Click Triggers Payment
Example: The click to check out on an e-commerce website

When the Click Prepares an Online Purchase
Example: The click to add a product to a shopping cart

When the Click Informs an Online Purchase
Example: The click to check flights on a travel website

When the Click Prepares an Offline Purchase
Example: The click to download a coupon for in-store redemption

When the Click Informs an Offline Purchase
Example: The click on a car ad that leads to the manufacturer's site

No Correlation

FIGURE 2.3 THE CORRELATION BETWEEN CLICKS AND REVENUE

While doing research for my master's a few years ago, I reached out to Gian Fulgoni, former chairman of comScore, and he told me this: "comScore research has repeatedly shown that the click on an online display ad is not an accurate predictor of its effectiveness. Even with click rates of only 0.1 percent, comScore studies have shown that the 'view through' impact of display ads can be substantial, generating meaningful sales increase for the advertised brand both online and in retail stores. Display advertising, despite a lack of clicks, can have a significant positive impact on consumers' likelihood of buying at the advertiser's retail store with an average lift around 17 percent."[27]

Those comScore findings have been repeated by other reputable industry organizations over the years. The Nielsen Company published a report, *Beyond Clicks and Impressions: Examining the Relationship Between Online Advertising and Brand Building*, in which Nielsen stated, "Click-through rate is not the right metric to measure brand impact—virtually no relationship exists between clicks and brand metrics or offline sales."[28] Upper-income, highly educated people rarely click on display ads, but they buy a lot. Display ads have a brand impact whether the user clicks or not. It has become axiomatic that "buyers don't click and clickers don't buy" in the world of online advertising.

Today, one clear fact has emerged in the spectrum of clicks and their distance from the cash register. The click to purchase is 100 percent predictive by definition. When we click the "Pay Now" button to complete an e-commerce transaction, that action correlates with our intention to spend. In e-commerce terms, we are at the cash register. Now go back one step. Somewhere there was a click that put an item in our shopping cart. That click was also highly correlated with intention to spend, but we may abandon the purchase before buying. We all have. So that click wasn't quite as predictive as the final one to purchase. Go back one more

step and we will see that the click that took us to the product catalog was also predictive (we are shopping, after all) but less predictive than the click that adds an item to our cart, or the click
that completes the purchase. Go back a step further and we may
have clicked an ad that led us to the product catalog. Those clicks
are tracked by publishers and advertisers because they add some
value in understanding the customer decision journey, but clearly
the most predictive clicks are the ones closest to the cash register.

Amazon knows this. It has become a trillion-dollar e-commerce monster because it *is* the cash register, and it can see every
predictive click within proximity of that cash register. The click
that predicts best is the one that buys, and increasingly Amazon
can see them all. With all of that predictive data, it is easy to understand why the company wants to go further up the funnel
where it can influence buying behaviors earlier. In that context, it
may be easier to understand why Jeff Bezos bought the *Washington Post*. Once marketers know what people buy—and why—it
is time to start influencing them earlier in their decision process.

For marketers who don't own the cash register the way Amazon does, getting information about that 99+ percent of consumers who buy without clicking remains a key challenge. One
strategy is to use tracking pixels to identify users who have seen
an ad campaign and then place tracking pixels, such as Google's
Activity Tags, on the advertiser's websites to count those actions.
These tags are small bits of code that are designed to capture
data about consumers who click, as well as data about users who
view-through after exposure to an ad campaign. By watching
these post-exposure activities, the advertiser can see which ads
are delivering the most consumers to a website, regardless of
whether the consumer ever clicked. These tags can count transactions, such as online purchases, or they can count page views.
Multiple tags can be combined to enable the advertiser to see

which ads generate specific onsite behaviors. This also allows the advertiser to see which ads are delivering the most engaged consumers.

To enhance the effectiveness of analyzing post-impression data, third-party data providers are now partnering with advertisers and ad networks to correlate online ad campaigns with actual cash register activity. This is achieved by *data pairing*, in which vendors who collect cash register transactions are able to pair that information with specific online users. They then provide "anonymized" point-of-sale data, stripped of personally identifiable information (PII), back to the advertiser in aggregate form to show how many purchasers saw the specific ad campaign in question.

Studies conducted on these techniques for pairing post-impression data with offline point-of-sale activity are intriguing. A study titled "Causal Attribution: Positioning a Better Industry Standard Measure of Display Advertising Effectiveness" documented a 14 percent lift in sales conversions for a national hotel chain between a test group that was exposed to the online ad campaign and the control group that was not.[29] While this type of causal attribution technology is relatively new, it offers one example of how the advertising industry is attempting to move away from the click and click-through rate (CTR).

A key conclusion is that the context of the click is critical when determining its value as a metric for assessing the effectiveness of online advertising. When a click triggers a payment on an e-commerce site, it is obviously highly correlated with revenue. But if the click is on a banner ad where users have the option to view-through to a website or walk in to a retailer to make a purchase, then clicks are the wrong metric, and optimizing for them delivers the wrong audience. The overwhelming evidence is that the CTR is the wrong metric for analyzing display ad campaigns because these clicks are far from the cash register. Advertisers, who continue to demand a metric that will help them guide their campaign decisions, must learn to distinguish between these CTR contexts and develop new and better metrics for assessing the offline sales impact of their advertising campaigns.

WHERE WE GO FROM HERE

In this chapter we have explored how mass customization has become the norm in digital advertising, and how data and attribution modeling are helping to make personalized information more effective.

*The power of data analytics to predict,
and the capacity for algorithms to learn, will entirely
reshape the field of marketing.*

AI is already helping optimize targeting, images, messages, and the method of delivery for every type of marketing message imaginable. For a single advertising campaign, a machine can optimize millions of ad impressions with a hundred versions of a message delivered in combination with a thousand different images targeting 50 different audiences in 10,000 locations to achieve the best results. No human could ever hope to tackle such a task—but a machine can do so with ease.

*Through personalized information, the Invisible Brand is
accelerating its ability to influence the way we think.*

In fact, the messages aimed at us as individual consumers will be increasingly dictated by a combination of marketing automation and machine learning—all designed to persuade us in increasingly sophisticated, imperceptible ways.

To Recap

Technology now enables marketers to develop and deliver customized and personalized ads and messages on a tremendous scale. Brands are no longer content to send out broad messaging aimed at generalized audiences and then hope for results. Ad tech enables brands to target their audiences more precisely across a multitude of platforms. Those brands can now tie consumer actions back to the ads they saw and where they saw them, to better calibrate their messaging.

Brands are willing to pay a premium for this capability, which has resulted in a vast demand for more data and information on consumers that can be used to fine-tune marketing strategies at a personalized level. The capability for delivering personalized information has spurred brands to leverage AI to customize messaging in real time. Personalized information has become a critical component in the emergence of the Invisible Brand. In the next chapter, we will explore how AI shapes messages to change what we do and how we think and how it delivers user experiences that use the science of persuasion to keep us glued to our screens.

3

Persuasion Equations

THERE IS A SET of rules behind our ability to persuade people to act in certain ways, and marketers and advertisers regularly deploy these rules with the aim of persuading us to buy their products or use their services.

My college psych professor at the University of Michigan was Jim McConnell, author of the bestselling textbook *Understanding Human Behavior*. In it, he recounted that in 1940, a pioneer of social psychology named Solomon Asch pointed out a truism in marketing. If marketers want to persuade people to buy something that they aren't already predisposed to buy, like a new car, they have two choices: either make improvements to the car itself to make it more useful or change the buyers' perception of the car. McConnell wrote, "The most important aspect of persuasion is the flow of communication from the outside world into your nervous system."

Let's start by examining how the art of persuasion isn't really an art at all. It's actually a science that can be boiled down into concrete principles. There is a video posted on YouTube titled

"The Science of Persuasion," for instance, that talks about the science behind a handful of powerful techniques that can be used to increase the likelihood that someone can be persuaded.[1] Those techniques include the following:

- **Reciprocity:** People feel compelled to reciprocate when they are given something.

- **Scarcity:** People covet things they perceive as rare—particularly when they fear missing out on an opportunity.

- **Authority:** People often do what they believe is expected of them by figures in authority.

- **Consistency:** People feel compelled to act consistently with something they've promised to someone else.

- **Liking:** People respond more favorably to other people who are similar to them, to whom they can relate.

- **Consensus:** People mimic other people who are like them.

We've all experienced reciprocity when we feel compelled to give a birthday gift to someone who has given us one in the past. "Give more, get more" the saying goes. Want to get invited to more dinner parties? Throw more dinner parties. Marketers know this too. That free gift that came in the mail? Yes, the marketers who sent it expect to be paid back through reciprocity. Try it and buy it!

Scarcity has practically built the home shopping network. Time is running out! The clock is ticking! There is a limited supply. Act now or miss out on this once-in-a-lifetime opportunity. People can be compelled to buy what they do not really need if they believe it is in short supply.

Authority plays prominently everywhere in the marketing and media landscape. Dr. Oz and Dr. Phil are so ubiquitous that they have become caricatures of authority figures. Are they even real doctors? Does it even matter? They can dispense advice and endorsements and persuade mass audiences through the sheer force of their personalities. They have carefully cultivated such an air of authority with their audiences that their persuasive power is irresistible.

Consistency is another important factor. We learn from an early age that being consistent has its own rewards. It is a lesson we don't unlearn in life. So, when we tell someone we are going to do something, we feel compelled to follow through. Someone who promises to fill out a survey is more likely to fill it out. That's who we are.

Liking people makes them easier to trust. If I like a person, I am more apt to do what they ask. If I can relate to them in some way, they have a greater chance of persuading me. If they tell me they like my new shirt, or we listen to the same music, or they have a dog just like mine, we will get along great. I will be more open to their suggestions, and I will avoid upsetting them.

Consensus is familiar to everyone who lived through their teenage years because at the core of every high school clique is the desire to be like the people around us. If everyone is doing it, there must be something to it, so we do it too. Consensus was probably a very helpful survival instinct for our ancestors, and it has endured quite nicely into the present day.

A great example of consensus persuasion in the video is the story of a hotel that found a clever way to get people to reuse their towels by leaving a note card in the bathroom explaining all of the environmental benefits of reusing towels.[2] Just by placing that card in the bathroom, 26 percent more guests opted to reuse their towels. But researchers also tested how tweaking the message on that note card could get even more people to reuse their towels. Changing the message to say that 75 percent of all guests who stayed in that same room had reused their towels led to a 33 percent increase in the number of guests who went without having clean towels or linens delivered daily. Consensus persuaded the hotel guests to alter their behavior to be like the group.

This example serves as a powerful message about how we can be influenced by what other people are doing—especially people whom we consider similar to ourselves. This also reveals our vulnerability to peer pressure, where, by aligning ourselves with people we think are similar to us, we become more susceptible to persuasion by the rest of the group.

The science of persuasion is uncovering these unconscious reflexes that trigger specific behaviors. In fact, these reflexes can be so powerful that, even when we become aware of them, we find them hard to overcome.

DEPLOYING CHEMICAL WARFARE

Part of the explanation for why we are susceptible to persuasion is that our brain betrays us. Well, it doesn't exactly turn against us as much as our brain can be triggered to release different chemicals or neurotransmitters that can profoundly affect our moods and behaviors.

The interactions between chemicals in our nervous system and our endocrine system directly influence our desires, moods, and sense of well-being. Experiences of pleasure and happiness are closely associated with the body's levels of neurotransmitters, such as dopamine and serotonin, and hormones including oxytocin and endorphins. Stress hormones like epinephrine (adrenaline) and norepinephrine can intensify emotions by rapidly increasing the heart rate and are closely associated with our "fight-or-flight" response. The hormone cortisol assists with concentration and memory formation. Body chemistry is unique to the individual, but science is providing us clues to how these various chemical components work and how they can be controlled.[3]

Due to our unique physiologies, some of us might be prone to certain addictions to these chemicals and hormones. We've all heard of "adrenaline junkies" who push themselves further and further into dangerous situations in pursuit of more of the good stuff. They may be an extreme example, but we all seek out pleasurable stimulation to our brain chemistry, and the rewards we receive from these chemicals, therefore, can be a prime way for someone to persuade us. By offering consumers an experience that triggers one of our brain-chemical rewards, marketers can incentivize us to spend money, time, and energy in a variety of ways.

Consider what Sean Parker, the polarizing entrepreneur behind ventures like Napster and, until 2005, an advisor to Mark Zuckerberg, had to say about why Facebook can be become so addictive. Speaking to the audience at a conference, Parker admitted that Facebook had a game plan based on answering the question: How can Facebook consume as much of our time and conscious attention as possible?[4] The answer: whenever someone liked or commented on a photo or post, it would trigger our brain to hit us with a shot of dopamine. *Oh, it feels so good! Give me another!* Parker is actually quoted as saying that Facebook's expertise was actually "exploiting a vulnerability in human psychology" so as to find ways to consume as much of a user's conscious time as possible.[5]

It's a technique some have begun to call "hijacking," though it's based on the same behavioral science posited by the renowned psychologist B. F. Skinner. The designers of the slot machines in Las Vegas, for instance, have long employed Skinner's study of rats, where he learned that the most effective way to persuade a rat was by issuing it rewards at random intervals.[6] Because a rat—or a Facebook user—doesn't know when the sweet dopamine reward is coming, they will persistently check back until they earn their reward.

BJ Fogg is a researcher from Stanford University's Persuasive Technology Lab who has spent his career trying to uncover persuasive forces like the dopamine reward response. Fogg has been particularly interested in revealing how technology like websites, video games, and mobile phones play an outsized role in changing what people believe and what they do. "Persuasive technology touches our lives anywhere we touch digital products and services," said Fogg. It's a field of study he has dubbed "captology"—which is an abbreviation for "computers as persuasive technologies."[7]

In his work, Fogg has studied social media sites like Facebook and how they use what he calls "cue triggers" to help persuade people to keep using the sites. He points to the example of Facebook notifying people when they have been tagged in a photo by another user—which can be very effective at persuading them to log back into the site.[8]

This example fits neatly into the Fogg Behavior Model—or FBM—which asserts that for someone to be persuaded to do something, three elements must be present: a person must have sufficient motivation, sufficient ability, and an effective prompt or trigger. In the Fogg Behavior Model (shown in Figure 3.1), motivation, ability, and prompts are represented as the acronym MAP.[9]

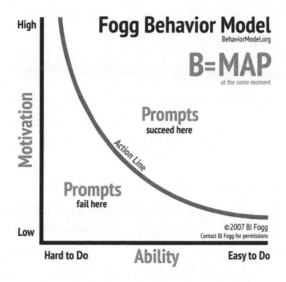

FIGURE 3.1 FOGG BEHAVIOR MODEL
Source: Adapted from the Fogg Behavioral Model, copyright © 2007
BJ Fogg, https://www.behaviormodel.org.

Using Fogg's model, I might open up Facebook because I am
curious about who tagged me and why; it's super easy to do—
one click; and I am very much tuned in to the prompt—the email
alerting me that I was tagged. Once I log into Facebook and I see
that someone said something nice about my photo, I might receive a nice hit of dopamine—which might lead me to clicking
around even more in search of more rewards. Before I know it,
I have been persuaded to spend several hours of my time on the
site, without even consciously thinking about it.

Other social media sites like YouTube work in very similar
ways, by making it very easy for motivated users to click into
more content by putting what Fogg called "hot triggers" right in
front of us. We almost can't help but get sucked in. That's powerful stuff, and it's part of what Fogg referred to as "the secret
sauce of social media."[10]

INVISIBLE INFLUENCERS

In his research, Fogg has also uncovered other invisible forces that are particularly powerful at influencing our behaviors. For example, people tend to believe what they see on video.[11] It's in our nature to trust what we see—rather than maintain a sense of skepticism about whether the video is real or not. (Increasingly it isn't real.)

Fogg has taught us that we are each unique in terms of the kinds of persuasion strategies to which we are most vulnerable. Each of us has our own unique "persuasion profile" that someone can use to influence and motivate us in different ways. Our persuasion profile might consist of the community of people with whom we identify or how susceptible we are to regular dopamine hits. We can think of it like being hungry for certain kinds of foods—like a craving that can cause us to drive across town for a cheeseburger.

*Find the right craving and you can trigger
the desired behavior.*

Given enough information collected on our behaviors, Fogg has envisioned a future where companies will actually assemble these persuasion profiles on us, not unlike the way credit agencies build credit reports. Companies or politicians could then use that information about us in a personalized way to persuade us to buy their products or vote for their candidacy. It would give someone the ability to sort people in very effective ways based not just on theories but on the actual cues they know can trigger us to act.

This is already happening in some ways as marketers tap into our online footprints to better understand the traits that comprise unique personality—something that the American Psychological Association has defined as "individual differences in characteristic patterns of thinking, feeling, and behaving."[12] Psychologists have identified what they call the "big five" of these traits—openness to experience, conscientiousness, extraversion, agreeableness, and neuroticism—that just so happen to fit the nifty acronym OCEAN.

It turns out that these kinds of profiles built with the help of our recorded digital actions can be extremely accurate—especially when they are combined with the power of AI. Algorithms that used personality profiles based on what users "liked" on Facebook, for instance, were better than coworkers, friends, and even family members at judging someone's actual personality.[13]

THE EMERGENCE OF PSYCHOTECHNOLOGY

It's worth considering how an AI agent programmed with the science of persuasion, armed with the details of our personality and behavior profiles, and equipped with mass customization, will be able to learn how to sway our decisions and actions. This will be particularly true if that agent seems humanlike, or anthropomorphic, in appearance or speech. Fogg's term, *captology*, hasn't really penetrated the popular zeitgeist. As I've already mentioned, since we are dealing with a new form of psychological technology at the intersection of humans and machines, I have settled on the term *psychotechnology*.

Imagine what might happen if an AI agent were fed all kinds of data about people and then was instructed to conduct hundreds, even thousands, of tiny experiments to test what might work best in persuading them to act in a certain way. The AI might calculate their OCEAN profile, the profile of their brain chemistry, and whether they are more persuaded by authority or liking or consensus. If they are more persuaded by liking, the AI agent will discover that becoming friends with them is the most effective way of influencing them.

Clifford Nass is another professor from Stanford who has researched how computers and technology play a role in influencing how we act. As Nass said in an interview with NPR: "We tend to establish really rich and long-lasting and complex relationships with our computers and any technology that talks or seems to even hint at the slightest bit of intelligence."[14]

In his book *The Man Who Lied to His Laptop*, Nass wrote about the kinds of emotional relationships people develop even with the GPS navigation systems in their cars.[15] What Nass found was the tone of a navigation system's voice—whether it sounded happy or sad—had a measurable impact on the emotional state of the driver. Strangely enough, people drove much better when the tone of the navigation system matched their own mood. If people were sad or angry, they preferred to interact with a navigation system that also sounded sad or angry. But when the researchers had a happy navigation system tell an angry driver to, say, "slow down," that made the grumpy driver even angrier—as well as far more prone to getting into severe accidents while driving.

Similarly, drivers seem divided when it comes to the gender of their navigation system's voice. Many German drivers, it turned out, became infuriated with BMW because its navigation system used a female voice. Even though the customer service agents explained that the voice was just a computer—it wasn't an actual woman giving them directions—the company was eventually forced to conduct a massive recall to install a new system with a male voice. Today, most systems allow us to choose a male or female voice and even the regional accent of that voice. The takeaway for Nass from this research was that people develop relationships with technology—especially if they come to think of the machine as somehow like them.

The more humanlike a technology becomes,
the more we begin to develop
emotional attachments to that technology.

As Nass put it: "There is a lot of evidence that interacting with technology, especially those that do the things that we would want a person to do, like learn your name over time, learn your preferences, become more like you, can make people feel better." Adding the use of "avatars"—humanlike digital representations of what that machine might look like—can demonstrably amplify those effects.

In other words, we can be influenced and persuaded by technology—including how we drive and even how we feel while we are driving—without being aware that it's happening. Increasingly, we are unaware of the factors influencing our decision-making. We have reached an inflection point where the power of machine learning and AI, which we are programming with the power of persuasion, might actually turn around and uncover groundbreaking new truths about persuasion that we haven't glimpsed. For evidence of that kind of shift, we need to look no further than the world of video games.

WHAT'S IN A GAME?

I grew up in the era when video games first came to life. It was wonderful. At home, there were early computers made by Commodore and Apple, as well as game consoles from Atari and Nintendo, which let us play games on tapes and cartridges. And when we had some extra spending money, and the mobility to get to an arcade, we could feed quarters endlessly into slots of classic games like *Pac-Man*, *Space Invaders*, and *Asteroids*.

The rudimentary graphics and controls of those early games look childish compared to what's available these days. One might still find a throwback arcade or two around, but most of the games today are played at home on computers, game consoles, or mobile devices—and they're all connected online.

Interestingly, the average age of players is 32 for men and 36 for women. That means that millions of adults invest their money and time playing games like *World of Warcraft*, where players transport themselves into a fantasy world to battle other players and gain experience or treasure needed to become more powerful. *World of Warcraft* is a kind of game known as a massively multiplayer online role-playing game, or MMORPG, where thousands—sometimes millions—of players log in to play on a frighteningly regular basis. It might be many hours, even days, before some of them log off.

I know because I was one of those players. I got hooked not long after *World of Warcraft* debuted in 2004. I was a married man in my thirties with a good job and an active social life, and yet the game sucked me in. There were endless worlds to explore and battles to be won. I would sometimes stay up playing until 2 a.m. Sometimes I would stay up all night. Honestly, it became an addiction.

Fortunately, my wife didn't leave me, and eventually I weaned myself off my computer—but my experience made me realize how profoundly powerful video games can be at engaging and influencing people to prioritize playing a game over just about everything else in their lives. According to the Entertainment Software Association, two-thirds of American households now play video games at home—along with 2.6 billion people around the world.[16] In the United States alone, the video gaming industry generates some $36 billion in revenue—which is a number that's growing by leaps and bounds every year as more innovative and engaging titles win over new kinds of players.

That doesn't even count the market for mobile games—those pesky apps chewing up our phone's mobile data plans. Mobile game developers can choose from a few different business models. They can charge a player a fee to download the game or allow them a free download and then collect revenue off in-game advertising or purchases (though, interestingly, just 5 percent of users currently spend money for upgrades within the game).[17] Once we've become invested in a game, and if we have the means to buy those upgrades, it can be very tempting for us to just spend a few bucks—$0.99 here or $4.99 there—as a way to reach our goals faster. All those incremental expenditures add up to a global market of some $50 billion and growing, and this market already accounts for somewhere north of 75 percent of all the revenue generated by the iOS App Store and Google Play. For context, Hollywood movies reportedly earn a collective $40 billion or so a year.[18]

Marketers and machines can learn from the persuasive power of video games.

Clearly, given the enormous stakes involved and the fact that most Americans play at least one mobile game on their phone, marketers are hard at work to find ways to grab the attention of all of those eyeballs—frequently using AI to help them.

DRIVEN BY REWARDS

Researchers at Stanford, like Fogg, have also spent a lot of time and effort in recent years to better understand how people can be persuaded by the kinds of reward systems employed in games—how we might be motivated to act based on wanting to achieve some kind of end result.

Thanks to the popularity of MMPORGs, the researchers have a dynamic set of test subjects to work with.

Online games offer marketers and scientists a sandbox for conducting social and psychological experiments.

Scientists can create very strict sociological tests and can exert a lot of control over in these environments, which helps eliminate the variables (and strictures) they usually deal with when they're trying to study people. For example, researchers could create a scenario in which they might instruct the players to do something—and then watch the reaction in real time.

This happens constantly—whether we realize it or not. What's remarkable about online games like these is how much time, and often money, players will invest in pursuing achievements inside the game. The games are all cleverly designed to hook players by creating quests for them to complete or certain task sets before they can earn a particular reward—which might be a special weapon or even just a badge of honor.

The trick to designing these games to be addictive for players of all ages is that the tasks necessary to complete the quests get increasingly more difficult and resource intensive along the way. Before the player even realizes it, he or she might be gaming through the night—spending dozens of hours over the course of a week—just to earn that "Ring of Amazing Awesomeness" or the "Sword of Super Slicing" or whatever.

Other quests might involve solving puzzles where the player needs to accumulate a certain number of clues that, again, become increasingly more difficult to find as the player progresses toward his or her goal. And yet, people will bend over backward to get there. This is psychotechnology in action.

Certainly, there is a deep and long history among humans about the power of badges as a form of an addictive reward. The Cherokee, for example, ritually awarded eagle tail feathers to warriors who excelled on the battlefield—which they could then display proudly in the form of a headdress. Roman soldiers carried banners that announced the achievements of their legions. Soldiers today proudly display service ribbons on their uniforms to commemorate campaigns where they have served. Lieutenant-General Robert Baden-Powell of the British Army knew how hard people will work for small cloth patches when he founded the Boy Scouts and created the concept of the merit badge. Badges don't have to be made of precious metals or have any intrinsic monetary value in order for us to care a lot—and I mean *a lot*—about earning them. Badges and ranks are all around us, in many forms, including our Fortnite leaderboard ranking, the likes on our Facebook posts, and our "Top Rated" badge on eBay.

In a way, the photos that so many of us post on our social media sites are badges that we display to all of our friends to tell them of the exotic places we have visited or the mountains we have climbed. We post them proudly and wait expectantly for our friends to like them and comment on them. For some, this is a richly rewarding and powerful social experience, and they dedicate many hours of their day to the activity of posting and liking. Each little "like" triggers a dopamine drip that keeps them hooked like junkies (Figure 3.2).

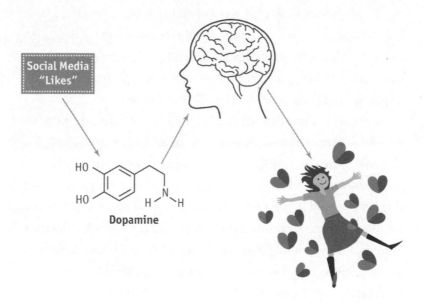

**FIGURE 3.2 SOCIAL MEDIA'S FORMULA
FOR KEEPING ITS USERS ENGAGED**

The badges phenomenon is also being put to work at offices in "social recognition" HR programs in which employees are rewarded for exhibiting specific behaviors. These virtual rewards are an effective way to offer nonfinancial remunerations. Badges have also become integral to digital learning environments where students progress through levels of achievements to earn ranks and recognition. There are countless examples.

A collection is a powerful type of badge, where a complete set of badges confers great prestige. For example, a crown with slots for five missing gems will keep a gamer working for hours. The trick is that the first four gems are relatively easy to acquire, but that fifth gem requires hours of game play. The gems are badges in this case, and completing a set of badges earns special status. It is not uncommon for gamers to spend weeks of game time grinding away to acquire the final piece of a set of armor, or the last ingredient for a magic spell. The reward is that powerful.

GAMBLING WITH OUR LIVES

Now consider how these same persuasive forces will affect the growing number of people drawn to the world of online gambling. Casinos around the world are renowned for using gimmicks like free drinks, buffet dinners, and deluxe rooms to lure gamblers to their establishments. Laws and regulations governing where and how people can bet online, from poker to sports like baseball and football games, are increasingly being stripped away. The US Supreme Court has ruled that states can now decide for themselves whether to allow online gambling or not.[19] It's easy to imagine how persuasion equations can be deployed to hook people to gamble even more of their time and money from the comfort of their homes.

The desired badge, in this case, might be an emblem showing that you are a VIP, or that you've won a certain level of wager, or that you love betting on baseball. The more the betting sites learn about someone, the more they can use those insights to offer up additional wagering opportunities—"since you bet on the NY

Yankees to win, you might also consider betting on the NY Giants this Sunday"—or chances for doubling down on your bets. Just like a friend might goad someone into making a bigger bet, an AI agent might encourage people to wager more than they normally would, with potentially disastrous results.

These persuasive forces could be especially problematic to anyone vulnerable to developing a gambling addiction—something that's already a widespread issue as some 10 million Americans are thought to have some kind of gambling issue.[20] On the flip side, it's conceivable that AI could also be deployed to help gamblers by persuading them to do something else with their time and money. Case in point, a company called BetBuddy is already employing AI as a way to help personalize the user experience for online gamblers while also looking for the telltale clues that someone might have a problem. The idea, at least, is that when the system spots people with addiction problems, it can alert the site's operators and freeze their actions.[21]

The point is that we are wired to work really hard to earn badges in their different guises and to display them as status symbols and sources of pride. Consider the impact if AI agents were tasked with motivating us to earn something more important than the Battle Hammer of Thor or the VIP gambler badge? What if we could be motivated to work that hard to earn a college degree, end world hunger, or find a cure for cancer? That level of persuasion is within our reach using psychotechnology.

A TIPPING POINT

Researchers discovered, in their online gaming studies, that a handful of players were having an outsized impact on the activity within the virtual worlds of MMORPGs.[22] By analyzing the different connections each of the players had to each other, the researchers found that a game server with 1,000 active players might have a mere dozen people who actually held everything together.

When those dozen players were active in the game, they helped generate lots of other activity among all those other players. But when those dozen key players stopped playing—or even abandoned the game altogether—so too did everyone else. Researchers were stunned to see how so much of the activity within the game was channeled through this small group of players. In fact, what they learned was that without these key connectors involved, there wasn't much of a game to play in the first place.

These findings echo a similar conclusion drawn by Malcolm Gladwell in his phenomenal bestseller *The Tipping Point*. Gladwell wrote about the "law of the few," which economists typically refer to as the "80/20 principle," which states that 20 percent of the people generate 80 percent of the activity in any organization.[23] In the case of online gaming, that means that a small group of people has an extraordinarily influential effect on the majority of the players.

Gladwell characterized the three kinds of people who made up this influential core:

- **Connectors:** The uber-networkers who seem to know everyone

- **Mavens:** The people who live on the cutting edge of new trends

- **Salespeople:** The folks who know how to persuade

To illustrate his point, Gladwell pointed to the curious case of two riders who set off in the night to spread the word of the British invasion of the colonies. One of those riders, famously, was Paul Revere. "The British are coming! The British are coming!" We can picture the sparks flying from his horse's hooves as they gallop through the cobblestone streets in the dark of midnight. The other rider? I can't remember his name at all, and that was Gladwell's point. Paul Revere was connected. He was in all the right clubs and on all the right councils. People knew Paul Revere—and he was very effective at rousing the populace. The other guy? Not so much. If you want to win the revolution and have Henry Wadsworth Longfellow write an epic poem about you—better to be a connector like Paul Revere than that other guy, old what's-his-name.

If we can agree that we can be influenced by a small group of people or things, then doesn't it raise questions about who those people are or what they might get out of persuading us to act in a certain way? Furthermore, what might the implications be if that connector, maven, or salesperson was an AI agent armed with all kinds of insightful information about us and the kinds of rewards that mean the most to us?

Back in the days when I was a student, I had the opportunity to watch a video lecture on artificial intelligence given by Professor Charles Isbell of the Georgia Institute of Technology.[24] In his own words, his fundamental research goal was "to understand how to build autonomous agents that must live and interact with large numbers of other intelligent agents, some of whom may be human."

In order to learn and adapt, Isbell explained, machines must first be equipped to observe and compile data over time. This was particularly true for an AI agent named Cobot—whose focus was human social relationships and interactions, which occur slowly and require extended periods of exposure before adequate learning and adaptation can take place.

To explore the sophistication of Cobot's skills of observation and adaptation, Isbell programmed Cobot to detect patterns of behavior in a multiuser chat environment named LambdaMOO—a MUD, or "multiuser dungeon" founded back in 1990 at the famous Xerox PARC research lab.

Initially, Cobot was equipped with a social vocabulary made up (bizarrely) of the Unabomber's "Manifesto" and the movie script from the original *Planet of the Apes*, among other sources. Slowly, over time, Cobot shifted from merely observing, to actually interacting with human users.

For example, through observation and interaction, Cobot was able to detect when a single player had created multiple avatars within LambdaMOO based on common ticks and behavior patterns of those avatars. From his research paper on the experiment, Isbell noted: "After 5 months of training, and 3,171 reward and punishment events from 254 different LamdaMOO users, Cobot learned nontrivial preferences for a number of users, modifying his behavior based on his current state."[25]

Based on the data and social interactions Cobot observed and collected, Isbell constructed a "map" of the social interactions within LambdaMOO using colored nodes on a graph designed to represent actual people and their interactions (Figure 3.3). Isbell noticed that there were several human players who seemed to connect with all of the other players and who seemed to connect with each other. The notion that there is structure to social interactions led Isbell to the conclusion that "if there is structure, then I can learn it, and if I can learn it, I can leverage it and I can learn to act better." From this insight, Isbell set out to understand social learning and to create an experiment to see whether Cobot could learn to be "socially optimal."

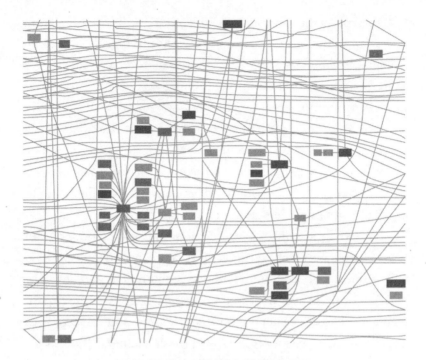

FIGURE 3.3 COBOT'S SOCIAL MAP
Source: Adapted from Cobot's social map,
http://www.iai.gatech.edu/projects/cobot/map.html.

Using the model of *reinforcement learning*—which is the practice of making decisions based on long-term benefits and rewards—Isbell determined that just by watching the way people interact, Cobot could change over time and learn to adapt to social interaction. As Isbell's research team noted: "Rather than hand-code complex rules specifying when each action is appropriate (rules that would be inaccurate and quickly become stale), we wanted Cobot to *learn the individual and communal preferences* of users."

Interestingly, Cobot also learned that when one person left the room, it should change its behavior and interact differently with the people remaining in the room. In other words, it learned that it could keep a conversation with a human chatter going longer if it tailored how it chatted based on what it knew about the person it was chatting with.

HOOK 'EM EARLY

Game designers make very conscious and deliberate psychotechnology choices about how to keep players like me engaged in their virtual worlds (and to encourage more of those lucrative in-game purchases). In many cases, games rely on the basic principles of conditioning that B. F. Skinner helped popularize.[26] Just like a pigeon in a box who is conditioned to press a button with its beak because it knows it will receive a nugget of food in return, players make decisions and take actions in games because they expect some kind of reward in return.

A game's designer might hook players early, by, say, making it easy to level up for slaying some incompetent goblins. But the players must then defeat more powerful enemies or solve more dastardly puzzles before they earn their next reward. Players are then driven to play longer and longer as they strive to attain their goals—and to invest real money via in-game purchases in order to speed up that process.

The longer the players stay engaged in a game, the better it is from the standpoint of the game designer. But finding ways to keep players interested in playing the game can be tricky—and expensive. It takes an enormous amount of time and money to create increasingly elaborate worlds and characters, and then test them to ensure that players will actually have fun playing them. While estimates vary wildly, it's reasonable to conclude based on the information available that it can average anywhere from $5 million to $60 million to create a blockbuster-level video game—

known as an "AAA game" in the industry—especially when considering the marketing and advertising efforts needed to promote the game.[27]

To develop the game *Star Wars: The Old Republic*, for example, reportedly took a team of more than 800 people around the world more than six years and $200 million to finish.[28] For the game to make money, the designers estimated they needed a minimum of 1 million players willing to buy the game for $60 and then pay an additional $15 monthly subscription fee for years to come. (For what it's worth, the game is still alive and well,[29] though it's changed its business model to embrace free play online over the years.)

Now imagine how things might be different if we turned over game design to an AI agent capable of testing every scenario and delivering personalized experiences tailored to the persuasion profile of each player. The hour is later than you think.

Game designers have already applied AI to the challenge of customizing games to the unique style of individual players to increase engagement, and their techniques are influencing digital marketing.

One could argue that video games wouldn't exist at all without AI. From the first time a player took on a computer opponent in a game of *Pong*, there has been some form of computer intelligence deployed to engage and entertain us. However, we can't really call those early computerized opponents "intelligent." The aliens descending in waves in *Space Invaders*, for example, or even the colored ghosts in *Pac-Man*, followed scripted rules and patterns that included randomized actions to give players a sense that the computer was acting on its own.

In the 1990s, game designers developed a breakthrough concept called the *finite-state machine* (FSM) *algorithm*.[30] In this case, the designers would create an inventory of every situation the AI agents might encounter in the game and then script some kind of reaction for each case. When used in megapopular games like *Battle Field*, *Call of Duty*, or *Tomb Raider*, the FSM algorithm might result in AI-powered nonplayer characters (NPCs) shooting at us when we get close to them or taking cover when we fire back.

But again, because the NPCs' actions and reactions are scripted through a static algorithm, they become predictable over time—and thus less sticky to players who might move on to something new and exciting.

Then came Deep Blue, which employed a more advanced algorithm called the *Monte Carlo tree search* (MCTS) to defeat world champion Garry Kasparov in a game of chess. It made global news, of course, but it also marked an important new tool that designers could use to power their games. At a basic level, the algorithm Deep Blue used was like a tree search in that it would run through every combination of moves it could make—as well as the potential responses its opponent would take to each one of those moves—before arriving at its decision. Then, after the opponent made his or her move, the algorithm would recalculate the decision tree all over again.

The advantage Deep Blue had in playing chess was that there are really only a limited number of moves to make at any time—so it could evaluate all of its decisions to a fairly deep level in real time. But in a computer game like *Civilization*, where players make complex decisions about building cities and attacking others, the AI makes its decisions more on a "best-guess" approach based on the information it has available at that time. Designers strive to create compelling nonplayer characters, but they also want to control the game play, at least to some degree, to make sure the game is fun. If all the NPCs started acting randomly or could never be defeated, it would detract from the fun of the game and drive away players—perhaps not unlike what happens to the guests in *Westworld* when all the "hosts" fall off their scripts and begin killing everyone in sight.

Nonetheless, defeating human players is sometimes the programmer's goal, and computers have continued to ring up impressive victories over human opponents. One prominent example was when an AI agent called AlphaGo defeated the world's best players at the ancient game of Go—something that many humans didn't think was possible given the infinite number of moves involved with the game.[31] (Fun fact: there are two times more potential moves in a game of Go than there are atoms in the universe.[32]) What's interesting is that AlphaGo, which itself is part of Google's DeepMind endeavor, wasn't programmed with a decision tree or set of rules. Rather, it "taught" itself how to play by watching countless games online—and then playing more countless games itself—and then used counterintuitive moves few if any players had ever considered before. AlphaGo began by playing anonymously against other online players. When word got out that a computer was beating human players, the world's best players stepped up. When AlphaGo kept winning, its victories were so impressive that a humbled grandmaster named Gu Li said, "Together, humans and AI will soon uncover the deeper mysteries of Go."

An AI agent learned how to beat human players in a popular shoot-em-up game called *Dota 2*, where its best players are professionals who earn healthy salaries from people who subscribe to watch them play on live-stream services like Twitch.[33] While Dota 2 is more often played in teams, an AI agent sponsored by an institution called OpenAI, created by Elon Musk, bested several of these pros in one-on-one battles. As with AlphaGo, the

OpenAI agent played the game millions of times over the course of just two weeks, learning through reinforcement or trial and error, to attain its inhuman level of mastery. As Dendi Ishutin, a pro who was beaten three times by the AI, said: "It feels a little bit like human. But at the same time, it's something else."[34]

Researchers are now returning to those classic video games of my youth and turning them into learning opportunities for AI agents. For example, German engineers taught a computer to play the game *Q*bert*—where a player controls a cute fuzzy character, who hops around a pyramid made of 28 cubes.[35] The goal is to change the color of every cube by hopping on it, while outrunning the NPCs and avoiding falling off the pyramid. After playing countless games of *Q*bert*, the AI eventually developed strategies rarely if ever used by human players—such as intentionally committing suicide to draw the NPCs away. The AI also discovered some long-lost Easter egg left behind by the game's developer when, by seemingly hopping around at random, it triggered all the cubes in the pyramid to start blinking and scored an extra million points as a result.

Researchers are also using classic arcade games as training grounds for more interesting ends as well—notably to teach AI agents how to build games on their own. In the case of an experiment run at the Georgia Institute of Technology, for instance, researchers first had an AI agent watch two minutes of a human playing a *Super Mario Bros.* game in action.[36] Then the researchers asked the AI to create its own version of the game based on what it saw—and what it predicted would happen in terms of game play. In other words, the AI wasn't given access to the code used to create the game. It was given access only the end product game. This is machine learning in action.

Designers also continue to seek out ways to create emotional connections for players in games. *The Sims*, which debuted in the early 2000s, was an interesting early example of how players could create emotional ties with the NPCs in the game. It was also a smash hit that sold millions of copies.[37] Games based on the care of virtual pets—like *Tamagotchi* and *Creatures*—also found ways to get players to engage in their games with a mindset that went beyond simply blowing everything up.

There was also a game from 2005 called *Facade* where players were tasked with helping a couple work through a domestic dispute and stay together. The game employed natural language processing where the words that players input as parts of their conversations generated emotional responses from the computer-controlled character. More recently, a game called *Prom Week* employed a very similar approach to engage players' emotions.[38]

Games that connect with us emotionally keep us coming back for more. Some games seek to reach out to us as we go about our daily lives to draw us back into the gaming environment with reminders, push notifications, and emails. Game designers continuously seek to push the boundaries between the game environment and our real lives, seeking to augment our mobile experiences and "gamify" our daily routines. For gamers who like playing precisely because the games are an escape from reality, these efforts might well prove disconcerting. For marketers, intent on learning better strategies for engagement, the world of game design is a critical laboratory.

OUR LIVES INSIDE A GAME

Let's pause and consider the vision that Andrew Wilson, the CEO of Electronic Arts, sees for the future of AI and video games. "From the minute I get up in the morning, everything I do has an impact on my gaming life, both discrete and indiscrete," he said. "The amount of eggs I have in my Internet-enabled fridge might mean my *Sims* are better off in my game. That length of distance I drive in my Tesla on the way to work might mean that I get more juice in *Need for Speed*. If I go to soccer practice in the afternoon, by virtue of Internet-enabled soccer boots, that might give me juice or new cards in my *FIFA* product. This world where games and life start to blend I think really comes into play in the not-too-distant future, and almost certainly by 2021."[39]

A near future similar to that described by Wilson would be a clear boon to marketers. It takes gamification—in which marketers persuade consumers using gamelike rewards and incentives—to the next level.

We've all encountered plenty of examples of this kind of gamification in marketing. A classic example is McDonald's Monopoly game that has been around since 1987, which encouraged us to buy more burgers, fries, and shakes in an effort to obtain those elusive Park Place and Boardwalk tokens. Remember collections and completing the set? Powerful motivators—and McDonald's proved they can be really effective at getting us to buy more fast food.

Plenty of other companies have taken a similar approach using online and mobile devices as a way to create incentives and share rewards with consumers. Starbucks created its My Starbucks Rewards program as a mobile app that tracked how much members spent by sharing visual cues—stars—and then helpfully showed those consumers where the nearest store was in case they were thirsty or in need of a jolt of caffeine.

When marketers add in the AI elements that will keep us occupied, the gamification of marketing will take on a whole new meaning. Marketers going forward will have enormous opportunities to create persuasive cross-selling campaigns based on consumers' day-to-day behaviors and personality profiles built from all the data that is increasingly available about each and every one of us.

To Recap

Marketers have long relied on the powers of persuasion to influence consumer decisions. Due to the emergence of AI, persuasion is evolving into much more of a science—a set of rules—that can be repeatedly deployed behind the scenes in ways that influence consumers' emotions and brain chemistry. The science of persuasion is a key component of psychotechnology, and it promises to become an indispensable tool of the Invisible Brand.

We're already seeing how this new field of science is deployed in the world of gaming, as well as how AI agents are increasingly learning from and leveraging these same rules to persuade and influence people in areas ranging from the workplace to social media and online learning. In the next chapter, we will explore how personal data is harvested from a huge array of devices and sensors and how machine learning is sorting that data and using it to make information delivery increasingly personalized and persuasive.

4

Infinite Data from Smarter Things

WE'RE BEING TRACKED—whether we realize it or not. Right now. And I don't mean by spies or criminals. The things around us—our phones, watches, cars, toothbrushes, thermostats, even our "smart" refrigerators—are monitoring our every movement and action. This is thanks to the so-called Internet of Things, where everything is becoming smart and compiling and sharing data. Kevin Ashton of MIT is credited with coining the phrase, which often appears in shorthand as IoT. Here is how Ashton defines it: "The IoT integrates the interconnectedness of human culture—our 'things'—with the interconnectedness of our digital information system—the 'Internet.' That's the IoT."[1]

Mark Weiser, a researcher at the famed Xerox PARC lab, where innovations like the laser printer and the graphical user interface were dreamed up, envisioned "a path to the 'invisible,' whose highest aspiration would be to make a computer so imbedded, so fitting, so natural, that we use it without even thinking about it."[2]

Every device and product in our lives—from the obvious, like our cameras and phones, to the unexpected, like lampposts and dairy cows—is already tagged (or soon will be) with web-enabled Bluetooth or radio frequency identification (RFID) chips, which are really wireless communication devices. They transmit short-range radio waves to a computer, where the information can be logged and cross-referenced in a database.

This kind of "near-field communication" technology isn't new. It dates back to World War II, and one of the first patents was awarded in 1973 to an inventor named Charlie Walton.[3] Many of us experience it every time we take out some cash from a bank's ATM. But thanks to the emergence of the Internet, we can now gather and combine data in ways only science fiction authors might have imagined.

All of these chips transmit data from whatever they are attached to—including our bodies. Wearable technology multiplies the amount of personal data we broadcast to the world with every step we take. There is a lot of information to be learned about us and what we like to do when we put a bunch of those transmitters on our bodies—or on our children.

While estimates vary by source, the expectation is that we're just on the cusp of an explosion of these connected devices all over the planet—what some have come to call "the fourth industrial revolution."[4] One forecast by research firm IHS Technology predicts that the number of devices connected to the Internet will double from 15.4 billion in 2015 to 30.7 billion devices in 2020—and then more than double again to 75.4 billion in 2025.[5]

Computer chip maker Intel, which admittedly has some stake in the business of selling microprocessors, is even more bullish:

it predicts that there might be some 200 billion smart devices by 2020—which would average about 6 devices per person on the planet.[6] That's a lot of data to work with—infinite even. That's why buzzwords like "data mining" and "Big Data" have become so popular over the last decade.

All that data is also big business. IDC, another research firm, expects global investments in IoT efforts to top $772 billion in 2018—climbing to $1.1 trillion by 2021.[7]

In other words, it seems like everyone wants to broadcast data from every conceivable thing they make—including for commercial, industrial, and governmental applications. Their goal is to find ways to optimize the production, organization, and distribution of everything around us. My high school civics teacher taught me that every society, communist or capitalist, has to make three decisions: what to produce, who will produce it, and who gets to use it. I've remembered that all these years because it is a fairly useful way to look at things, and the Internet of Things is designed to help us answer those questions.

"It's about networks, it's about devices, and it's about data," Caroline Gorski, the head of IoT at the research firm Digital Catapult has said.[8] "IoT allows devices on closed private Internet connections to communicate with others, and the Internet of Things brings those networks together. It gives the opportunity for devices to communicate not only within close silos but across different networking types and creates a much more connected world."

Everything from factories to railroads use RFID-enabled shipping containers and trucks to help streamline their operations. The logistics company UPS now uses sensors on its trucks and delivery vehicles to monitor how efficiently packages are delivered, while also relaying information about potential delays to the people due to receive a package.[9]

The first time I encountered the real world of machines connecting with each other over a global network was while I was producing a marketing video about General Electric Aviation in the mid-1990s. Their new GE90 was the largest aircraft engine in the world, capable of delivering over 80,000 pounds of force for huge commercial aircraft like the Boing 777. The mammoth contraption was almost 8 meters long and 4 meters tall—meaning a man could stand on another's shoulders inside the air intake.

And the engines weren't cheap—well over $10 million each at the time, if memory serves me. I remember a GE project manager telling me that they were willing to give the engines away for free in exchange for a lifetime service contract, which they expected to yield $40 million in revenue over the operational span of each engine.

The key to that service system was the fact that the engines had onboard diagnostic systems that were capable, essentially, of calling ahead to report any maintenance issues to the ground crew at the airport where the plane was headed. The goal was to reduce repair times and keep the planes running on schedule by giving the repair crew advance notice to get their tools ready to meet the plane when it landed. Imagine the plane calling ahead to report something like this: "Hey, ground crew, I need an oil change, and it might be time to take a look at one of my fan blades."

I have no idea what a real GE90 says to its ground repair crew, but one can easily understand the advantage of having that information in advance to expedite repairs. Looking back, that's pretty amazing technology and very forward thinking by GE. Even today, GE makes jet engines that generate some 14 gigabytes worth of data that technicians can analyze after a flight to ensure that the engines perform safely on future trips and cut down on repair time to provide additional cost savings.[10] Even better, the data can be used to predict when an engine failure might occur so that the technicians can perform the necessary service to avoid that scenario.

That sort of diagnostic reporting by machines is commonplace and has been enabled significantly by the widespread availability of the Internet. Sensors can now be embedded in concrete that can warn engineers of cracks or other looming hazards in vulnerable structures like bridges.[11] The city of Barcelona, Spain, has used a citywide IoT system to save millions of dollars on more efficient consumption of water and electricity—and an increase in parking revenues.[12]

Even farmers are getting into the IoT act. Equipment makers like John Deere have developed sensors to be placed in fields that send back reports on the soil's moisture and temperature measurements.[13] Farmers then use that information to plan their irrigation, planting, and tilling efforts—which sometimes involve autonomously driven combines that are operated with the help of GPS satellites.[14]

And, yes, as I mentioned earlier, even cows are now part of the IoT. Sensors monitor everything from cattle movement patterns and behavior to identifying which cows might be lactating the most. A farmer named Dale Hemminger, the founder of Hemdale Farms, says that he collects thousands of data points every day from his cows as a way to track which ones "might be coming down sick."[15]

There has also been a series of success stories resulting from so-called *open data projects* that involve government agencies partnering with third-party entities to try and solve persistent challenges they have struggled to tackle on their own. A well-known example is that the city of Chicago teamed up with researchers to use data to solve the city's problematic rat population.[16] By combining data on dozens of variables like the locations of vacant buildings and 311 calls from residents complaining about uncollected trash or fallen trees, the researchers were able to not only map out where the rat hot zones were but also to predict when the next infestation might take off a week before it happened. In this way, the city was able to move beyond the mere intuition of human exterminators by using data to make more effective predictions and prescriptions than people could make on their own.

These are all impressive examples of how collected data can be applied in making decisions that anticipate future events. It's a field commonly known as "predictive analytics."[17]

Predictive analytics is greatly enhanced by machine learning. Predictive analytics alone relies on human models and interpretation, where machine learning can recalibrate predictive models in real time and improve results.

The more data you can feed machines, the better predictions and prescriptions result. But, in reality, these models are just scratching the surface of what's going to happen next—especially when it comes to how all this information and data might be used to persuade or even control what we do and why we do it.

PERSONAL DATA PROFILES

One of the key concepts when it comes to putting all of this data to work for marketing and advertising companies is called *data pairing*. The challenge that data pairing solves is that marketers frequently have access to two or more separate and discrete data sets and need a way to identify where that data overlaps.

For example, a marketer might take a data set of voter identification records, which are publicly available. That is considered "offline data" because it comes from postcards and voter registries and other offline sources. That's opposed to "online data," which is gathered from Internet surfing behavior using cookies and analytics.

Now let's say that same marketer has a separate data set: receipts from credit card purchases on Amazon. Data pairing is the process of figuring out what the common elements might be that tie these two data sets—voter registration records and credit card receipts—together (Figure 4.1). One of the most common ways to pair data is by a physical mailing address. In our example, an address—123 Main Street, USA—might be part of a voter registration record, and it might match a credit card purchase in a separate database. By combining the two databases and pairing those entries that have the same address, we can connect two discrete pieces of data about one person. Once that connection has been made, data scientists can extrapolate from the connection to formulate conclusions, such as: this independent voter bought this mountain bike.

If a married couple lives at that address, it does complicate things a bit because both parties might not be registered to the same political party and we don't know which person actually made the purchase. But it's a good bet that most couples are more similar than not, so using an address as a way to pair data is often quite successful. There is an adage in data analytics that anything better than random guessing has value.

By using data pairing to combine public record data with behavioral and transaction histories, companies can build profiles of people based on their habits—without those people knowing or granting permission. This enables companies to make assumptions about us and our decision-making habits.

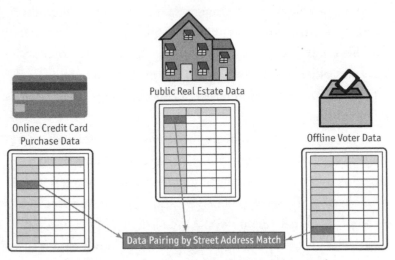

Online Credit Card Purchase Data

Public Real Estate Data

Offline Voter Data

Data Pairing by Street Address Match

This online user recently purchased golf clubs, paid $250,000 for a house, and is registered as an independent voter.

FIGURE 4.1 HOW DATA PAIRING WORKS

This now includes tying those decisions to our location as well using data from our mobile devices and wearable tech. Marketers can use a variety of methods—cell phone towers, GPS, and even our Bluetooth devices—to track our location fairly accurately. Think about how airplane pilots use a system of triangulation using different data points to determine their location. They might take readings from at least three radio towers, for instance, to pinpoint their location. It's the same basic trigonometry we learned in high school, and it's accurate down to the area of a parking lot.

To be even more accurate, we can use satellite GPS data that will get to within about 5 meters of an actual location. But another and more precise measurement of location can be made based on tracking our phones using Bluetooth or Wi-Fi triangulation. As I write this, I am sitting in a Caribou Coffee shop in Chapel Hill, North Carolina. Most likely, there is a Bluetooth transmitter somewhere in the building, maybe in the wall or in the ceiling. Because my phone's Bluetooth is turned on, it connects with—or "bumps"—the building's beacon, letting it know my phone just walked inside the shop. My phone and this beacon don't have a relationship per se. Rather, it's just like they shook hands and acknowledged each other.

Now, if my phone is equipped with the right kind of software or app developed with a certain software development kit (SDK), the app will log that bump from the store's beacon in its database. There will now be a record with a time stamp that shows that my phone's unique ID visited this coffee shop on this date and time. This piece of data is now available to be paired with another set of data. If I drive past one coffee shop every day on the way to another coffee shop, that might be an advertising opportunity (we call this conquesting) to steal me away with a special offer for coffee shop regulars. By combining data about where we go on the Internet with data about where we go in the real world, marketers can learn a lot about us.

I know the CEO of a company that has mapped the location of every one of these Bluetooth beacons and assembled a massive database complete with street addresses and the types of businesses at each location. While GPS might show the mobile device is in a mall, Bluetooth can show that a person is standing next to the cash register of the Apple Store on the second story of the mall. That's valuable because once someone goes through the time and expense of installing a beacon, they don't tend to move them. They're typically stationary for years. They then become extremely useful in terms of mapping people's movements and behaviors.

It's helpful to understand why those beacons are there in the first place. Their main purpose was initially to help retailers measure and understand the traffic moving through their stores. If I owned a retail shop or grocery store, I wanted to understand how people were moving through my aisles and how that affected what they put into their shopping basket. With a handful of these Bluetooth beacons, my store could identify shoppers as soon as they walked in the door and then track how they first went to the children's clothing section before moving on to electronics and toys. Then, 25 minutes later, when they arrived at the cash register and paid for their purchases, my store could pair the cash register receipt with the shoppers' movements through the store.

That store can now use that data and aggregate it with data from all of the other shoppers to create what is known as a heat map, which is a graphical overlay of the shop's floor that shows in different colors where people frequented. A hot color like red might be used to show where the most traffic congregates, like the entrance or exit, while a cooler color like blue might be used to show a less busy part of the store, like the bathroom.

Using this data, the store's owners can then run A/B tests or experiments where they can see how the heat maps and purchases change based on how they arrange the store's planogram. If they change the endcap on the first aisle in the store, for example, does that alter the heat map or the way people move through the store? Just as importantly, does it change what customers put into their shopping carts and baskets—which is the goal of analyzing all this behavior in the first place? Milk is one of the most common purchases made by customers at a grocery store, and it is frequently placed in the back of the store. That's to ensure that customers are forced to walk past other tempting products on the way to the dairy aisle, to increase the number of products in their basket before visiting the checkout register.

These same techniques are used just about everywhere we go—from sports stadiums to airports. Sometimes it seems that wherever I fly, my plane always parks at the farthest gate possible from baggage claim and the exit. That's no accident. That's a very intentional decision made by airport executives (who are, really, landlords) who rent out space to all those shops and restaurants that line the concourse. Those tenants need paying passengers to make their rent, so the more people who walk by their stores, the happier they are. And the airport can use the data about our location to make the kinds of decisions to help them maximize the value of their real estate.

On a broader scale, marketers today can use this same location-driven data to begin to build a much more holistic and accurate picture of me as a consumer as they begin to pair it with other data sets like my purchase histories—without my ever knowing about it.

For example, the Associated Press revealed that Google services and apps continue to track our locations even after we explicitly turn off the "location history" option.[18] Even when we open the Google Maps app, Google stores a record of where we were when that happened. Check the weather—same result. Even when we conduct a search for something innocuous like "chocolate chip cookies," Google is saving a precise record of our latitude and longitude at that exact moment. When we consider that this affects billions of users around the world, we can imagine the kind of data profile Google is amassing on each and every one of us.

Giving the retailer access to a customer's location in the store could be incredibly valuable, especially if that data were combined with some information about what product the customer was perusing. That kind of information could allow the retailer to combat so-called showrooming, when customers visit a brick-and-mortar store to view products, only to shop online and purchase the products for less. This is a growing problem for retailers. But if they could leverage the triangulation data from the customers' Wi-Fi signal to determine what products they might be looking at, the retailer could send an instant alert to those customers' phones, awarding them a 20 percent coupon if they buy the item right then and there rather than waiting to buy it online from someone else.

Putting aside the significant privacy and security concerns all this connected location data brings with it—which is a topic we'll take a deeper dive into later in the book—let's think about the big picture of what changes we might expect in our own lives when AI is given access to it.

MACHINES THAT LEARN

A lot of articles have been written about the IoT—and a lot of attention has been given to it as "the next big thing." And yet few people fully understand its implications. The researcher Daniel Burrus offered a provactive thought when he wrote in WIRED magazine: "When people talk about 'the next big thing,' they're never thinking big enough. It's not a lack of imagination; it's a lack of observation."[19]

Burrus was talking about the potential that the IoT has to further transform our lives. While it's amazing how much information we can gather on just about every aspect of our lives, it's what we do with that information—the different connections we can make to create stories and draw conclusions from—that will be the game changer.

As Burrus wrote:

A sensor is not a machine. It doesn't do anything in the same sense that a machine does. It measures, it evaluates; in short, it gathers data. The Internet of Things really comes together with the connection of sensors and machines. That is to say, the real value that the Internet of Things creates is at the intersection of gathering data and leveraging it. All the information gathered by all the sensors in the world isn't worth very much if there isn't an infrastructure in place to analyze it in real time.[20]

To put that another way, the actual potential of all that data generated by the IoT is realized when we combine it with the computational muscle of AI. When we do that, we open up the possibilities for artificially intelligent machines to exploit information about our sleep cycle, our health, our interests, and our next moves. Actually, marketers are beginning to reshape the world around us in ways we might not even realize. We are each part of creating the Invisible Brand, which is powered by the combination of data and machines to take how we market and advertise in entirely new directions most of us don't understand. But when marketers combine all the data we now have available with the capabilities of AI agents, the future of these industries looks radically different.

IBM, for example, has coined the term "embodied cognition," which they define as when "AI capabilities are placed in an object, robot, avatar, or space (such as the walls of an operating room or spacecraft), enabling it to understand its environment, and then reason, and learn."[21] As Susanne Hupfer, a senior consultant and AI analyst for IBM, put it:

> It's not too hard to imagine a future in which humans, IoT devices, and AI-powered robots and objects will exist harmoniously as a kind of collective "digital brain" that anticipates human needs and provides predictions, recommendations, and solutions. In the near-term future, we humans are likely to allow the digital brain to enhance our own decision-making. In the more distant future,

we may even trust the digital brain to take certain actions upon our behalf.[22]

The explosion of data about us, combined with the power of AI to find new connections between that data, promises to change the nature of the relationships we have with computers in profound ways. Consider that the high-flying tech company Salesforce acquired another company called Datorama, described as "a leading AI-powered marketing intelligence and analytics platform" for a reported $800 million. In explaining the rationale for the deal, the company sent out a press release that said the following:

> With Salesforce, Datorama will accelerate its core mission—to help marketers create their one single source of data truth for smarter decision-making. That means it's never been a better time to:
>
> - Integrate all of your marketing data together
> - Gain insight into every marketing investment and activity
> - Optimize your marketing campaigns, automate reporting, and make data-driven decisions faster
>
> Over 3,000 leading global agencies and brands—including Neo@ Ogilvy, PepsiCo, Ticketmaster, IBM and DWA—optimize their marketing campaigns, automate reporting and make data-driven decisions faster today.[23]

As one blogger reviewing the Datoroma deal put it: "Salesforce customers will have better data-driven insights gleaned from across marketing, CRM, and other clouds which should, in turn, provide an even better view of the customer."[24]

We're now leaving the era when collecting data was a valuable end result; that now happens automatically. We've even moved beyond the point where conducting statistical analysis on that data to figure out what happened in the past provides meaningful value. That was cutting edge back in the 1950s.

We've now entered a new era of machine learning, which, as a graduate school professor of mine once framed it, is really just a whole new branch of statistics. George Dahl, a computer scientist at Google, put it this way in an interview: "Let's be realistic. Machine learning is nonlinear regression," which is a simple type of statistical analysis where collected data is plugged into a model.[25]

Rather than taking a bunch of data and analyzing it to draw conclusions, we can now interactively leverage live data to continuously refine what we are doing in driving toward our goals and key performance indicators. It's about interactions, and it's about creating new insights, predictions, and prescriptions based on the latest available information—which might be less than a second old. The machine learns based on the different inputs it receives in real time. We've now gone through the metaphorical looking glass and entered an entire new realm of statistics where the machines are learning and deciding what experiments to conduct in the future based on complex algorithmic thinking, rather than sitting back and building a trend line about what happened in the past. As in our aircraft maintenance example from earlier, it's one thing to predict that something will fail. It is another thing to solve the problem before it fails.

This has had a dramatic impact on the world of marketing and advertising, for example. Thanks to the power of machine learning—which we can define as occurring when an algorithm analyzes data and makes future decisions based on what it is learning[26]—we can determine, in real time, whether messages are effective at persuading potential customers to act in a way we would like them to act. There's no waiting to run a campaign, measure the results, draw conclusions, and then rerun the campaign.

That is all now happening in real time where the machine is conducting experiments on the fly and feeding the results back into the algorithm, as it strives to achieve marketing goals. As a noted expert in the field, Dr. Pedro Domingos of the University of Washington, put it: "Machine learning can't get something from nothing. . . . What it does is get more from less."[27]

It really can't be overstated how powerful this approach can be—and how much it differs from, say, the tried-and-true academic method approach to experimentation that involves countless hours of researching, compiling, analyzing, summarizing, abstracting, publishing, and then the often-painful process of peer review. The academic approach may take months—even years—to get qualified results. The machine is impatient. It's not waiting for all that process to take place. It's working and learning from the results it gets in fractions of seconds and then taking actions as needed.

This processing speed will only increase as sensors are meshed more intimately with machine learning—something that some are calling edge computing or even edge AI.[28] Put simply, edge AI refers to situations in which algorithms are being processed locally on a hardware device using data collected from the sensors on that device.[29]

Many current AI applications might involve a sensor that uses a Wi-Fi or Bluetooth connection to send a signal to the cloud, where it is then transmitted to a database. Then, an algorithm can process that data and make its conclusions, which might then be sent back via the cloud to the point where the data was originally collected. The tech blogger Ben Dickson equates these systems to a person having to run to a library to consult an encyclopedia every time he or she spots a dog on the street and wants to identify it.[30]

While this transaction moves at the speed of light, it would be even faster if the algorithm could do its work right at the instant the data is collected—at the edge. What if the sensors attached to the farmer's cow, for instance, or the airplane's engine could make real-time conclusions on what was happening at that moment rather than having to wait for the relevant data to be collected or transmitted? This is an example of distributed processing rather than central processing. It's not only faster. It's also more efficient.

Algorithmic machine learning also opens up limitless possibilities by helping us avoid what are called local maximums. Let's say someone told you to climb the highest mountain in a certain stretch of wilderness where you happened to be hiking. Your natural instinct would be to start climbing up the nearest slope and continue climbing up, up, up until you reached the top. Voilà! Mission accomplished. Yet, when you stand on the top of your peak, you notice that there is another peak across a valley that is clearly taller than the one you are on. Mission not accomplished. You've hit a local maximum—in other words, the highest peak relative to where you started, but it's still not the global maximum, which was your goal. If you want to hit your target by climbing the highest peak, you're going to now have to start that journey by first going downhill before you can start upward again.

We can apply this analogy to our work because when we're looking to hit a certain key performance indicator (KPI), we need to be always looking out for the fact that there are times we might have to go downhill in order to go uphill again. A human might get frustrated at that. It would be much easier to just keep climbing up: we just want to hit this goal. But that's where we'll be prone to hit those local maximum points as opposed to a possibly much larger result. Machines don't get frustrated, however.

They just keep plugging away based on the rules of their algorithm—or multiple nested algorithms that feed and learn from each other in what are called neural networks, which, like the design of the human brain, allow the machines to go beyond a set of instructions and begin to innovate and experiment in ways no one ever thought to program. Stack neural networks together and you produce deep learning capable of finding new ways to climb those tallest peaks everyone else has missed.

These algorithms and learning systems are also relentless in the pursuit of their goals. They don't get bored or frustrated. They don't get distracted. They are hungry for all the real-time data we can feed them and then for us to give them the reins so they can experiment at will. That's why they're the foundation for building the Invisible Brand.

ALGORITHMS 101

I think it's important that we take some time here to truly understand the different kinds of algorithms that drive AI particularly for marketing, and its subsets of machine learning, deep learning, and neural networks (we will discuss deep learning and neural networks in more detail in the next chapter).

So, what is an algorithm in the first place? An algorithm is a logical sequence of commands that gets translated into binary code—ones and zeros—which gives a computer a set of instructions for how to operate. Depending on the complexity of that set of instructions, it could involve a lot of ones and zeros.

The textbook definition goes like this: "An algorithm is . . . a sequence of computational steps that transform the input into the output."[31] Another definition goes like this: "An algorithm simply tells a computer what to do next with an 'and,' 'or,' or 'not' statement. Think of it like math: it starts off pretty simple but becomes infinitely complex when expanded."[32] Tynker, a website aimed at teaching kids how to code, has explained it this way:

> An algorithm is a detailed step-by-step instruction set or formula for solving a problem or completing a task. . . . When you think of an algorithm in the most general way (not just in regard to computing), algorithms are everywhere. A recipe for making food is an algorithm, the method you use to solve addition or long division problems is an algorithm, and the process of folding a shirt or a pair of pants is an algorithm.[33]

We can also nest algorithms inside each other (Figure 4.2). We might have an algorithm for waking up in the morning (turn alarm clock off, get out of bed), and another algorithm for eating breakfast (make coffee, eat donut), and yet another algorithm for starting our day that includes the first two algorithms plus one for getting the kids ready for school.

Let's talk about an algorithm from marketing and advertising that everyone has seen in operation: Google's search tool. To understand how it works, let's picture sitting in a seat on a commercial plane flight. Tucked neatly into that little pocket on the back of the seat is the airline's magazine, and in the back of every issue is a map of the world showing all the cities where the airline flies, and those cities are all connected with little lines representing flight routes. I'm always fascinated to see how many of those little lines connect in hub cities like Atlanta, Chicago, and Dallas while cities like Anchorage only have one lonely little line connecting them to the rest. That's why a string of thunderstorms holding up flights in Atlanta causes our flights into LaGuardia

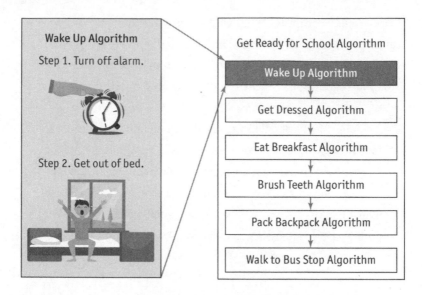

FIGURE 4.2 COMBINING ALGORITHMS AND NESTING THEM WITHIN OTHER ALGORITHMS

to be delayed. Some airports hold much more sway than others in the web of interconnecting flights and airports. The metaphor of a web was the way Tim Berners-Lee saw the interconnecting links of a global hypertext system that he named the WorldWide-Web (originally written with no spaces). Every computer was a node, and every link was a strand of spider silk connecting everything in a giant web of a decentralized network.

About seven years later, Larry Page, a graduate student at Stanford (and an engineering major from my alma mater, the University of Michigan) began to take a hard look at the nodes and links of the World Wide Web (spaces included by then) and thought about graphing it all. As a project for graduate school, he turned a crawler loose to map all of the links and backlinks from web page to web page across the entire web. He soon recognized that, like those little lines that flow into hubs on the airport map, his graph would reveal which sites were positioned at the center of a high number of links. He used this graph to score the relative importance of each hub, and the PageRank (named for Larry Page, not the web page) was born.[34]

At its heart was a complex algorithm, worked out by his fellow graduate student Sergey Brin, that scored pages based on the number of links leading to them, combined with the value of the pages those links came from. We see similar strategies in ranking college football teams, where a computer algorithm ranks a team based on its victories combined with another factor for the victories of the teams they've beaten. In this way, beating an undefeated team counts for more than a victory over a team that hasn't won a game. Similarly, having a backlink from a large site like Yahoo! carries more weight than a link from the local pet store up the street.

The PageRank was the underlying algorithm that allowed Google (founded a short time later by Page and his collaborator Brin) to create a search engine that ranked the relative importance of search results for consumers. What started out as a graphing project ended up revolutionizing advertising.

Many of today's algorithms are created using programming languages such as Python or R (which has also created an incredible demand for data scientists who know how to program with those languages[35]).

I'm not going to take a deep dive into mathematics here, but if we want to understand algorithms, it is important to recognize that there is a lot of math involved—depending on what kind of results we are seeking. To that end, there are many algorithmic categories from which to choose when programming AI for jobs like serving up ads on Facebook or delivering a relevant news story on Google.

When data scientists go about deciding what type of algorithm would be the best fit for their goals, they base their decision on variables like these:

- The size, quality, and nature of the data

- The available computational time

- The urgency of the task

- What they want to do with the data[36]

One of the defining characteristics of an algorithm is whether it is *supervised*, which means whether it is programmed with a set of labeled data or examples to work from, or whether it is *unsupervised*, which means the algorithm is fed with completely unlabeled data that it needs to categorize. A good example of a supervised algorithm is a *decision tree*, where we map out the different options available inside the algorithm itself. An unsupervised algorithm might be assigned to find a pattern among a large data set. There are also *semisupervised algorithms* that lie somewhere in between.

Another important type of algorithm for machine learning is known as *reinforcement learning*, which refers to an algorithm that is designed to employ trial and error to learn how to get the best result.[37] OpenAI, the organization started by Elon Musk, released an open-source algorithm called Hindsight Experience Replay (HER), which was taught to learn from past failures.[38] Just as we learned to ride a bike by making mistakes—like forgetting to put our kickstand up before pedaling—HER learns as much from its errors as its successes.

Microsoft, which offers its own Siri-like AI digital assistant called Cortana, as well as a platform for AI tools it calls Azure AI,[39] has created a helpful hierarchy of algorithms organized around what we want the algorithm to help us find out:

What do you want to find out? I want to:

Predict Values (for example, estimate product demand or predict sales figures)

> *Examples*
> - **Ordinal regression:** Data in rank ordered categories
> - **Linear regression:** Fast training, linear model
> - **Neural network regression:** Accurate, long training times

Find Unusual Occurrences (for example, predict credit risk or detect fraud)

> *Examples*
> - **One-class SVM:** Under 100 features, aggressive boundary
> - **PCA-based anomaly detection:** Fast training times

Discover Structure (for example, perform customer segmentation)

> *Example*
> - **K-means:** Unsupervised learning

Predict Between Two Categories (for example, "Is this tweet positive?")

> *Examples*
> - **Two-class SVM:** Under 100 features, linear model
> - **Two-class decision forest:** Accurate, fast training
> - **Two-class neural network:** Accurate, long training times

Predict Between Several Categories (for example, "What is the mood of this tweet?")

Examples

- **Multiclass logistic regression:** Fast training times, linear model
- **Multiclass decision forest:** Accuracy, fast training times
- **Multiclass neural network:** Accuracy, long training times[40]

It is beyond my expertise to explain how each type of algorithm works at a mathematical level—nor would that be useful for our purposes. There are tons of books and online resources you can pick up to give you more of a data scientist's take on this subject. But for the rest of us trying to get our heads around the power of machine learning, which drives the Invisible Brand, it's worth at least understanding what it looks like under the hood of that sleek race car. We might not know how to fix it—or even what to call all the parts—but we should at least understand the basics: how the engine works and what type of fuel it requires to move us forward.

Scoring is an important part of how algorithms are used to make predictions. Imagine that we want to predict which visitors to a website are most likely to purchase a skateboard. We might give individual users 10 points for their first visit to the site and another 10 points if they come back again. We can also give them 10 points if they visit the section of the site about skateboards. We can give them another 10 points if they click on any of the skateboards and 30 points if they add a skateboard to their shopping cart. Finally, we might data pair the users back to a credit score or purchase history to determine if they have enough money to afford a skateboard and give them an extra 30 points if they do. Now, we look at the scores of all the visitors to our site, ranging from 10 points up to 100 points. If we have only enough advertising budget to buy ads targeting half the visitors to our site, we know which half to target—the half with the highest scores.

The story doesn't end there. Scoring can be inaccurate, and in our example it turns out that the credit score doesn't correlate well with purchase intent for skateboards. In fact, many of the purchasers turn out to be young, and they don't have an established credit history at all. Learning algorithms can look at the data about who actually purchased the skateboards to determine if the scoring strategy was accurate. In this case, the algorithm determines that the points awarded for having a good credit score are irrelevant and may actually be inversely correlated with purchase intent. A learning algorithm can look at the results and adjust the scoring accordingly. Future predictions gradually get more accurate as the algorithm is fed more and more results from which it learns and adjusts the scoring.

Prediction isn't the ultimate goal. What marketers really need are prescriptive algorithms that take action to avoid undesirable results and increase positive outcomes.

Instead of predicting that something might break, a prescriptive algorithm actually tells us what to do to prevent it from breaking. This is particularly important in call centers where brands are often dealing with customer complaints that may lead to product returns or service cancellation.

Other examples of algorithms at work include the ones used by Uber to do everything from calculating "surge pricing"—when it charges a premium due to excess demand for its drivers—to determining optimal pickup locations and detecting fraud.[41] Google Maps employs something called Dijkstra's algorithm—which calculates the shortest path between two nodes—to help it determine the optimal set of directions based on the latest construction and traffic information it's fed. Not surprisingly, the developers and engineers working on autonomous vehicles are employing similar algorithms in their efforts to perfect the driverless cars everyone expects to take over the roads of the future.

Whether we recognize them or not, algorithms are now ubiquitous in our everyday life, such as the ones Google uses for a variety of regression and prediction analyses that detect spam and learn how to prioritize the emails we want to read, with its Priority Inbox feature.[42] The crowdsourced content site *Wikipedia* is now employing algorithms to help it identify missing gaps in its database — particularly when it comes to the lack of information on female scientists.[43] *Wikipedia*, the web's fifth-most-popular website, is dominated by male contributors, and the result is that just 18 percent of the biographies on the site are about women.

To try and address that massive gender bias, the site turned to Quicksilver, an algorithm developed by a startup company called Primer. Quicksilver searches through an exhaustive encyclopedia of scientific research and then pairs it against a database of history's most notable scientists. The algorithm then finds the overlooked scientists—both men and women. It uses machine learning to generate text summaries of the scientists' accomplishments based on the accessible data, and then it sends those summaries to human editors before the summaries get published on the site itself. As of 2018, Quicksilver had generated some 40,000 new summaries for *Wikipedia*, which is also now using the algorithm to help keep its entries up to date on the latest news and events as well.

Meanwhile, banks are increasingly relying on algorithms to detect fraud and calculate credit risk while also adding new features, like mobile check deposits—which employ algorithms and machine learning to decipher handwriting.[44]

FICO, the arbiter of our personal credit score, employs algorithms to do the heavy data lifting needed to plow through all the financial transactions we've ever made. Interesting, according to a post on the company's blog, it is now offering its capabilities as a set of personalized marketing tools called "The FICO Marketing Solutions Suite" to other companies—such as a grocer that is now scoring thousands of potential offers across millions of customers on a weekly basis as part of its loyalty program. As the blog described:

> Machine learning is used in this solution to bolster predictive results. The automated tree-ensemble models produce scores on the tens of thousands of products to offer to retail clients, and effectively specify the optimal set of offers to provide. The benefit of automated modeling has truly been seen in the time to market for these solutions, reducing the effort from months to days.[45]

The machines continue to learn, which means we've only begun to see the kinds of advances that might benefit marketers, businesses, and consumers in the near future.

NEURAL NETWORKS EMERGE

Neural networks, which replicate the structure of human thought, are formed when we begin to nest multiple algorithms together where the results they are generating can be fed to one another in a virtuous cycle of learning. The more data the network is fed, and the more evaluations the algorithms complete, the smarter the network becomes. Imagine layering algorithms from different categories to create new AI capabilities, such as voice detection and identification layered with facial recognition.[46]

Facebook has made multiple acquisitions in recent years, snapping up several tech companies with names like Masquerade and Faciometrics that specialize in facial recognition technology using neural networks.[47] By extension, developers are also building image recognition apps that can help people identify plants, birds, locations, and even diseases.

Image recognition shares some commonalities with audio recognition. I remember my first encounter with the app Shazam, which analyzes ambient music and can accurately identify a wide range of popular music tracks. Back in the day, when we heard a song we liked on the radio, we had to hope the radio DJ would tell us the name of the song, the band, and the album. That worked just about never. Shazam solved that problem and even gave us access to the lyrics.

Beyond helping us figure out the puzzling lyrics of 1970s rock anthems, audio recognition algorithms are helping us speak to machines. In a blog post about AI advances, the Google Speech Team discussed how it uses deep neural networks (DNNs), as well as recurrent neural networks (RNNs), to allow users to issue voice commands like asking for search results on their phone by speaking.[48] Similarly, Microsoft engineers have made rapid advances in their ability to accurately convert speech into text with the help of neural networks.[49]

We'll dig further into the topic of neural networks and their implications for natural language in the next chapter. But before we leave the topic at hand—algorithms—we need to discuss the elephant in the room: the fact that sometimes even the data scientists who build neural networks out of nested algorithms don't fully understand how they work and can't always predict how they will behave.

ALGORITHMS GONE WILD

Andrew Moore, the dean of computer science at Carnegie Mellon University and a former vice president at Google, was quoted in the *Atlantic* magazine as saying that content providers like Facebook and even Google don't always fully understand how their algorithmic systems work.[50] He referenced a theoretical example of a company that provided movie recommendations to its customers. He made the point that the algorithm they would use to make those personalized movie choices would need to crunch enormous amounts of data. "Everything from the color of the pixels on the movie poster through to maybe the physical proximity to other people who enjoyed this movie. It's the averaging effect of all these things," he said.

In other words, it's a complex process where the engineers who designed the algorithm to learn about individualized preferences might have no idea about how the algorithm actually arrived at a particular recommendation. Reversing the process backward to see why my love of *Blade Runner* might yield a recommendation to watch *Ex Machina* takes little imagination. For a human with some awareness that both movies are science fiction films involving a conflicted relationship between a man and a female android, the recommendation makes sense.

Unfortunately, however, the recommendation algorithm can't explain itself. It runs and spits out an answer, but sometimes it is difficult to understand how it arrived at its answer—even for the authors of the algorithm. This is true of many algorithms, and as they are increasingly nested within each other, the complexity of understanding the outputs has multiplied. A lot also depends on what kind of data the algorithm is being fed. As Moore said in his interview, it's an example where we're actually "'moving away from, not toward the world where you can immediately give a clear diagnosis' for what a data-fed algorithm is doing with a person's web behaviors."

As human beings, we are flawed, and full of cognitive biases like framing and the confirmation bias. One of these biases I find particularly fascinating is known as the Baader-Meinhof effect, which is a frequency bias in which a person believes something is more frequent than it is. The name Baader-Meinhof, oddly enough, derives from a militant West German terrorist group that someone active on an online chat room in Minnesota heard mentioned several times in the span of several hours.[51] This person had never heard of the group before but then, in hearing it more than once, purely by coincidence, became convinced that terrorists were everywhere.

To paint a more personal picture, suppose you just bought a brand-new red Tesla. You picked red because you thought it would make you stand out. But then, on your way home, you see another red Tesla—and another, and another! Suddenly, it seems the world is awash in red Teslas. But the world hasn't changed. Everyone hasn't suddenly decided to buy a red Tesla. The truth is that you saw a few thousand other cars as well, but your brain is now focused on every red Tesla you happen to pass, causing you to overestimate the frequency of red Teslas on the road.

As humans, these types of cognitive biases lead us to make mistakes—mistakes that a machine would not make if it were programmed correctly. An AI algorithm could precisely count the number of cars on a road without falling prey to something like a frequency bias or another cognitive bias that would keep it from performing its objective best at its assigned task.

While there might not be any serious consequences when a movie recommendation is off target, it does affect a customer's level of trust in the service. If Netflix continued to recommend movies we hated, it would lead us to ignore its recommendations. In that framework, getting the algorithm right is a big deal. Instagram users nearly revolted when the photo service switched the kinds of photos it displayed to its users. The tweak changed what had been a chronological feed—whatever was newest came first—to the photos the company's algorithm determined would be the most interesting to that user.[52] Instagram said it made the change as a way to show more of what users wanted to see, something they might miss with just a timeline-driven model. But it was all about trying to make the app stickier so that users would spend more time inside the app—which would expose them to more ads. Either way, Instagram defended itself without really divulging how its algorithm actually worked in terms of picking out the more relevant photos to show its users.

There have been calls for more transparency when it comes to the inner workings of algorithms. By revealing their source code, as well as the data inputs and outputs, more people may learn to trust the algorithms in question. But that can be problematic for a few reasons. For one, as Kartik Hosanagar and Vivian Jair of the Wharton School posit in the *Harvard Business Review*, "most algorithms in the world today are created and managed by for-profit companies, and many businesses regard their algorithms as highly valuable forms of intellectual property that must remain in a 'black box.'"[53] The inner workings of the Invisible Brand are shrouded in these black boxes just out of sight.

Some hybrid solutions have been floated, according to Hosanagar and Jair, such as revealing the algorithms to regulators who would bear responsibility for assessing the accuracy and biases inherent in their uses. But any time an algorithm's underlying code is revealed, it also opens up the risk that people can learn to "game" the code to their benefit. If students knew how an algorithm that was grading their work weighed certain factors, they could turn that insight to their advantage.

Faced with the difficulty of unmasking the guts of algorithms, some researchers are taking new creative approaches in a field that's being called explainable AI. An example comes from a group at the MIT Media Lab where they have taken a page from B. F. Skinner's famed behavioral box. Unlike Skinner, who used the control input of things like food and water to see how a cat's behavior would change, Iyad Rahwan of MIT is building a virtual box into which he can put algorithms to study their behavior—something he's calling a Turing Box. (We'll talk more about Alan Turing, the AI pioneer the box is named after, in the next chapter.)

The idea is that by controlling the data fed to the algorithm and by measuring the outputs, we can research how the algorithm "behaves" in various scenarios.[54] Think about that for a moment. We know more about how to build algorithms than we do about the results they produce, and we need to run experiments in controlled environments to try and figure out the "why" in "what" they do. Couple that with what we've already discussed about personalized information and the science of persuasion, and we can see why there is warranted concern about the applications.

We will soon lose our ability to discern whether we are programming the machines or they are programming us.

When Adam Smith wrote *The Wealth of Nations*, he pointed out that our institutions, in their effort to do good, can produce deleterious and harmful outcomes: "Had human institutions, therefore, never disturbed the natural course of things, the progressive wealth and increase of the towns would, in every political society, be consequential, and in proportion to the improvement and cultivation of the territory or country."[55] Over time, this has become known popularly as the *law of unintended consequences*: that when we undertake to improve the existing order, we produce results that are unforeseeable and may be counterproductive or even harmful.

Just this morning, I read an AP news article about an epic blunder that illustrates the law of unintended consequences in the most tragic terms. Wildlife conservation experts in Kenya, with funding from the World Wildlife Fund, recently transferred 11 endangered black rhinos to a new sanctuary, where the animals promptly died from drinking saltwater from the only available watering hole. Everyone meant well, but they didn't think of everything—and sadly no one bothered to assess whether the water in the watering hole was safe for rhinos.

We can't think of everything, and that's why the law of unintended consequences is called a "law" in the first place. We've all been there. Our best-laid plans are tripped up by some unforeseen event. These snags in our plans are such a common occurrence that the military created the acronym SNAFU, which crudely stands for "situation normal: all f----- up." I would wager that the danger of unintended consequences varies in direct proportion to the scale of the initial effort's potential to create change. A snafu in the transfer of endangered black rhinos at a wildlife sanctuary put the survival of an entire species at risk. That's a bleak example, and my goal here isn't to scare everyone into being Luddites, but rather to emphasize that technology with the power to learn how to persuade humans merits extreme caution. As we put algorithms inside algorithms and pack them together in neural networks, it will become increasingly difficult for us to predict the consequences.

Marketers need to keep the law of unintended consequences in mind as they begin trusting algorithms to accurately deliver their brand messages at the right time to the right people. Nonetheless, the potential for AI to learn from experience, to optimize campaigns toward KPIs, and to target potential customers with increasing precision will ensure the sustained investment in these technologies. Coupled with personalized information, the science of persuasion, and data from the Internet of Things, learning algorithms will become an indispensable part of the marketing equation.

To Recap

The evolution of the Internet of Things—where just about everything connected to our lives transmits data about our behaviors—has unlocked new opportunities for marketers. Armed with increasingly detailed information about our online and offline lives, brands now have unprecedented abilities to develop deep and insightful profiles of individuals. That information can then be fed to algorithms with the goal of creating customized and personalized messaging designed to persuade people.

Algorithms can learn by being fed data about what works and doesn't work, and they can adapt in real time to changing information—especially when they're placed at the edge of where the data is being collected. Structured in neural networks, AI has the capability to learn in ways the designers don't always understand. This has put us on the cusp of developing even more sophisticated tools of persuasion—as well as witnessing the emergence of machines that think and act in more human ways, and potentially unpredictable ways. Marketers are leveraging machine learning to improve the impact of campaigns. In the next chapter, we will explore how natural language processing is giving AI agents humanlike qualities, such as human speech, and how anthropomorphic AI can be even more persuasive.

5

Beyond the Turing Test

COMEDIAN JOHN MULANEY HAS joked that we spend a lot of time telling robots that we're not robots. As an example, he cites the common CAPTCHA tool that asks respondents to identify objects (street signs, for instance) in a series of images (Figure 5.1). For what it's worth, the ubiquitous CAPTCHA security program is actually an acronym for Completely Automated Public Turing Test to Tell Computers and Humans Apart.

The irony is that, while it may be difficult for a robot to detect another robot online, in everyday interactions, humans are rather easy to identify. Simply ask them to calculate a complex math problem in a few milliseconds—and humans will always fail where machines succeed.

It will soon be easier for a robot to recognize a human than for a human to recognize a robot.

FIGURE 5.1 CAPTCHA TESTING WHETHER YOU ARE A ROBOT

Consider that in the first half of 2018, the social media site Twitter took action to suspend or purge some 70 million fake accounts associated with automated "bots."[1] Even then, Twitter targeted only the most obvious and egregious offenders—leaving it up to its users to try and identify bogus accounts based on things like a username composed of randomly generated characters, lack of a profile photo, or simply just the bizarre or even banal contents of the account's tweets. As the *MIT Technology*

Review put it: "It's important not to be swayed by fake accounts or waste your time arguing with them, and identifying bots in a Twitter thread has become a strange version of the Turing test. Accusing posters of being bots has even become an oddly satisfying way to insult their intelligence."[2]

It was the mathematician Alan Turing who, while at the University of Manchester in 1950, famously penned the words: "I propose to consider the question: 'Can machines think?'"[3]

Turing—who had worked secretly for the British government during World War II to crack Germany's famed "Enigma" coding cipher—is considered one of the pioneers in the world of artificial intelligence, in part because he devised a game to test whether a robot could pass as a human. More precisely, he proposed the game as a substitute for the question as to whether machines could think.

Improvising on a popular parlor game of the time, Turing devised what he called the "imitation game"—though it's now far more commonly called the "Turing test." In a paper titled "Computing Machinery and Intelligence," Turing framed the parameters of his game.[4] Turing's game is played by three people including a man and a woman in one room and an interrogator in a separate room. The interrogator interacts with the man and woman through a teleprinter. The object of the game is for the interrogator to determine which person is the man and which is the woman based solely on answers they provide over the teleprinter to the interrogator's questions. Once Turing established the rules for his game, he asked what would happen if a machine were to take the place of the man. Would the interrogator be able to detect that one of the respondents was a machine?

While he didn't live long enough to see it, Turing inspired legions of students, researchers, and scientists to put their own creations up against Turing's test. All failed. That is until 2014, when the news exploded that an AI chatbot named Eugene, operating under the guise of a cheeky 13-year-old Ukrainian boy, duped 10 out of 30 judges at the Royal Society into thinking it was actually human.[5]

Just as in the version of the game Turing described, the idea was for Eugene to hide behind a virtual curtain, and his interviewer's job was to get him to give away his true identity. Here's a sample of the questions Eugene fielded during his oral exam:

Judge: Hello, what is the weather like tomorrow?

Eugene: In my native town people says that meteorologists are like sappers: they make a mistake only once, but the difference is that sappers do that once in a lifetime and meteorologists—daily. Do you like weather today?

Or,

Judge: Why do birds suddenly appear?

Eugene: Just because 2 plus 2 is 5! By the way, what's your occupation? I mean, could you tell me about your work?

Judge: Yes, I am a doctor. Are you healthy?

Eugene: Well, so tell me about your work. I think doctor is a nice specialty![6]

There was some pushback among the scientific community to Eugene's accomplishment. Famed AI pioneer Marvin Minsky reportedly wasn't impressed, but he said it did prove that some people could be fooled into believing that the machine was human. The progress in the field of natural language processing (NLP), and its subset natural language understanding (NLU), since 2014 has been accelerating. Many researchers now consider the current capabilities of AI agents to convincingly mimic human conversation to go well beyond the Turing test. Before we look at the current state of NLP and NLU, let's look back at the advances in AI that have brought us here.

THE ORIGINS OF AI

We can credit the dawn of the cyber age to one of the most tumultuous and horror-filled eras in history: Word War II. The needs of the war effort brought scientists from various disciplines together to tackle urgent issues. In some cases, those efforts sparked new collaborations that endured even after the war ended. In England, for example, a dining social club sprang up called the Ratio Club that was attended by some of the brightest engineers, neuroscientists, astrophysicists, and biologists of the age.[7] It was during these get-togethers that these bright minds continued to wrestle with thorny issues. In particular, they wondered whether machines could think, communicate, and control their environments. It was a nascent field some began calling "cybernetics."

Around that same time, in 1950, a Russian-born American author named Isaac Asimov published a collection of short stories with the title *I, Robot*, in which he depicted a future where human beings and intelligent machines lived and worked together based on what he called the "Three Laws of Robotics." Asimov, along with other science fiction writers like Arthur C. Clarke and Robert Heinlein, were extremely influential on a generation of scientists and engineers who were exploring the practical and ethical challenges of robots that think.

It was a computer scientist at Dartmouth named John McCarthy who is credited with coining the term "artificial intelligence" in 1956. He was soon joined by Marvin Minsky in launching a concerted effort to advance AI. They wrote the following:

> [To] proceed on the basis of the conjecture that every aspect of learning or any other feature of intelligence can in principle be so precisely described that a machine can be made to simulate it. An attempt will be made to find how to make machines use language, form abstractions and concepts, solve kinds of problems now reserved for humans, and improve themselves. We think that a significant advance can be made in one or more of these problems if a carefully selected group of scientists work on it together for a summer.[8]

Over the next decade Minsky became increasingly convinced researchers were nearing a breakthrough in AI technology that would make general AI a reality. By 1970 Minsky predicted in *Life* magazine, "In from three to eight years we will have a machine with the general intelligence of an average human being."[9] Unfortunately, the field soon entered a period that is referred to as the "AI winter," and Minsky's prediction seemed to slip away for the next decade. Despite millions of dollars of investment, critics believed computers would never learn to recognize faces or even to beat a human in a game of chess.

While Minsky's vision for a general AI is still yet to be realized, narrow AI applications have spurred new investment and growth. Consider some critical milestones in the development of machines capable of understanding and responding to human language in written and spoken forms.

In the 1870s, Thomas Edison invented the phonograph and Alexander Graham Bell invented the telephone, and their pioneering innovations laid the groundwork for modern sound engineering. Capturing sound, turning it into an electronic signal, recording that signal or relaying that signal, and eventually turning that signal back into sound all trace their origins back to those breakthroughs. Computers gave sound engineering the power to translate analog signals into digital signals and the power to deconstruct those digital signals into libraries of sounds that correspond to words and human speech. The list of contributors and advancements along the way is beyond the scope of this book, but consider some more recent highlights:

- **1990:** Dragon launches Dragon Dictate, the first speech recognition product for consumers powered by algorithms. It costs an astonishing $9,000. (This is followed in 1997 by Dragon's much-improved product NaturallySpeaking).[10]

- **1993:** Apple launches a built-in speech recognition system and voice-enabled control software called PlainTalk, which enables users to control their computers with simple voice commands.[11]

- **1993:** Microsoft introduces AutoCorrect in Microsoft Word 6.0.[12] Writing documents has never been the same.

- **1996:** IBM launches MedSpeak, the first commercial product capable of recognizing continuous speech.[13] It allows people, like pathologists, to dictate their cases without a need for further transcribing.

- **1996:** BellSouth develops VAL, the first dial-in interactive voice recognition system that introduces voice-driven menu options.[14]

- **2011:** Google launches the Voice Search app for iPhone, bringing voice search to the mobile device.[15]

- **2011:** Apple launches Siri, a digital personal assistant for use on iPhones and other Apple devices.[16]

- **2014:** Amazon announces Echo, a voice-controlled speaker powered by a digital personal assistant named Alexa.[17]

Those and related voice technologies now pervade just about every aspect of our lives. We can ask for directions, play music, control our televisions, and even order takeout, all through voice user interfaces on our phones and digital assistants. Soon, that technology will be embedded into everyday devices like the autonomous vacuums that clean our apartments and smart refrigerators that can restock our supplies. These advances ensure that psychotechnology will have a pervasive platform for influencing every facet of our lives.

The MIT scientist Rodney Brooks helped popularize the notion of employing more of a biological approach to building AI, such as leveraging neural networks to fuel AI development. Brooks wrote on his blog in April 2018:

> There have certainly been a million person-years of AI research carried out since 1956 (much more than the three thousand that Alan Turing thought it would take!), with an even larger number of person-years applied to AI development and deployment. . . . In closing, I would like to share Alan Turing's last sentence from his paper "Computing Machinery and Intelligence," just as valid today as it was 68 years ago: "We can only see a short distance ahead, but we can see plenty there that needs to be done."[18]

As true as those words might be, we really don't have to look very far to see how the world is already changing around us thanks to the continued emergence of AI's humanlike speech capabilities.

NATURAL LANGUAGE PROCESSING

The solution to Turing's test emerged from the field of NLP—which, at a macro level, we can think of as simply the ability for computers to interact with people using spoken human language. But there are many different subsets of NLP as well. For those working in the AI field, the focus has shifted more squarely to NLU, for instance, which can be defined as the ability of computer software to recognize text or speech sentences.[19] In other words, it means computers can directly interpret human speech. Similarly, AI researchers have begun to make recent breakthroughs in the area of *semiotics*, which is the understanding of symbols, brands, and colors—such as understanding that a red traffic light means stop while green means go. Understanding traffic signs, or even recognizing what a human with his or her thumb in the air is signaling, would be extremely valuable in, say, the development of a self-driving car.[20]

Another important subset of NLP is something called *sentiment analysis*, which is a machine's ability to identify human attitudes. As we discussed in Chapter 4, the more data we can feed algorithms—including everything from demographics to geography, household income, and location—and the more we can pair that data together, the more accurately the machine can predict and prescribe actions. But a consumer's attitude is hard to measure based on scoring that relies on traditional data points.

Applying NLP to the call-center environment to measure sentiment, such as by analyzing the tone of voice, or the kinds of words consumers use (even in their emails, texts, and social media posts) adds a new dimension to the predictive scores available for analysis, and NLP may actually help companies determine which prescriptive strategy is most likely to retain that customer. Knowing when customers are angry and about to cancel their cable service is critical to reducing churn. Some firms are even using these same tools to determine how they can measure sentiment as a way to keep employees they might be at risk of losing.[21] Marketers can also employ sentiment analysis in helping gauge how a targeted audience responded to a particular campaign and whether the feedback they shared on social media or in email was largely positive or negative.[22]

The impressive science that fuels this capability for us to interface with call-center computers using our own spoken language has come a long way in a few short years.

When we call into older automated phone systems, for example, they can respond to requests like, "Please press 1 for sales or press 0 to reach an operator." That was already an impressive advance over what now seems like the ancient role of the telephone operator who was, quite literally, connecting one line to another via a giant peg board. But the responses that the computer was processing in those cases were simply menu prompts—cues to open up a new set of options or to make the connection customers were seeking, triggered by push-button technology.

Now, call-center computers not only understand what we're saying but also the context in which we are saying it. Furthermore, they are also learning how to respond to us individually in an intelligent and engaging manner using natural language generation (Figure 5.2). These computers also understand context. When the computer hears a word like "Monroe," how does it know whether the subject is Monro Tires or Marilyn Monroe? In a voice user interface, homophones like "Monro" versus "Monroe" must be placed in context to disambiguate their meaning.

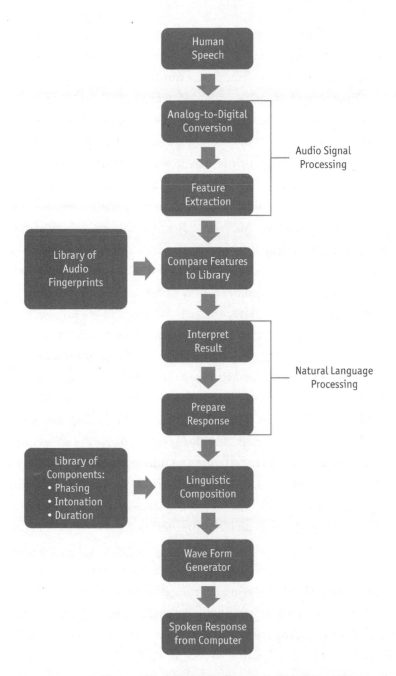

**FIGURE 5.2 HOW NATURAL LANGUAGE PROCESSING ENABLES
HUMAN-COMPUTER CONVERSATIONS**

Understanding whether the consumer is referring to tires or movie stars in the context of a discussion is critical if an AI is ever going to pass a real conversational test with a human.

While there's no single way to create an NLP system capable of truly engaging with a human, any one that does likely relies on what's called a *neural network*—in other words, a group of algorithms designed to mimic the way a human brain works. As researchers at MIT have explained it, a neural network "consists of thousands or even millions of simple processing nodes that are densely interconnected. Most of today's neural nets are organized into layers of nodes, and they're 'feed-forward,' meaning that data moves through them in only one direction. An individual node might be connected to several nodes in the layer beneath it, from which it receives data, and several nodes in the layer above it, to which it sends data."[23] A neural network can be "trained," say, to recognize images, by continually sending data through it, which is constantly scored to determine results. The scoring is a mechanical process rather than a learning process per se.

But another AI term associated with NLP is *deep learning*, which we can think of, as the *MIT Technology Review* has defined it, as software that "attempts to mimic the activity in layers of neurons in the neocortex, the wrinkly 80 percent of the brain where thinking occurs. The software learns, in a very real sense, to recognize patterns in digital representations of sounds, images, and other data."[24] Another definition of *deep learning* has described it simply as a process "in which a computer learns to perform some task by analyzing training examples."[25]

Rather than working with just a thin layer of nodes in a single neural network, the complexity of deep learning is based on the increasing number of data processing nodes. The data in a deep learning configuration no longer flows in just a single direction. Machines teach themselves by processing millions and millions of examples over and over again, testing new data against the existing model and refining the model with each pass. Deep learning requires data—a lot of it, preferably normalized and free from silos that would make it more difficult to build the valuable connections, relationships, and patterns hiding in all of it.

By layering neural networks on top of each other (or connecting them in a way that they essentially feed and learn from one another), researchers have even begun to create so-called memory networks to help enable machines to create long-term memories not unlike the way people do.[26] This leads to so-called reinforcement learning, through which machines learn to evolve based on the feedback they're receiving in real time, just as we've seen in the world of video games discussed in Chapter 3. It was by employing deep reinforcement learning that machines learned to beat humans in games like Go.[27]

As with the human brain, a deep learning configuration can process the countless pieces of information that make up typical human conversation. The sequence for training an AI agent in the art of NLP might look like this:

1. A human says something to the machine.

2. The machine captures the audio input.

3. The audio input is then converted into text.

4. The text is analyzed and processed into data appropriate to a response.

5. That processed data is converted back into an audio response.

6. The machine plays the audio response back to the human.[28]

Simple, right? Far from it. Think about the complexity of the human language and all of the different variations involved in words and tones—as well as some of the nonverbal cues we send each other through our eyes or body language. Add in the subtleties of context and cultural cues, and we have a Gordian knot of a problem whose solution seems just beyond our grasp. Researchers are investing their energies in neural networks and deep learning to unravel these mysteries because the potential to perfect a voice user interface with an AI agent holds tremendous benefits.

As a stepping stone, consider the improving capability of machines to recognize and process text. One of the areas where there has been a short-term win from these investments is in the world of autocorrect: where a word processing program like Microsoft Word corrects a writer's spelling and grammar. Vast improvements have been made over the last decade, and yet today there is still learning to be done. We all know the pain when autocorrect goes wrong—especially when we're hastily scribing some critically important text or email message.

We might soon look back on these early systems and laugh as developments, such as a new system called Embeddings from Language Models, or ELMo, for short, was successfully taught to answer SAT-style reading comprehension tests.[29] Rather than focus on just the words, ELMo learned to understand context and even sentiment within entire sentences. A breakthrough like this opens up whole new worlds of opportunity for researchers because it means that AI agents can learn to process unlabeled or unstructured human text on the fly—including live texting with people.

Despite the obvious learning curve still ahead of us, many companies are now employing machines to tackle tasks like manning the front lines of help desks and call centers where they serve as a first hedge of defense against pesky customer questions and complaints. Just as Eugene was able to quickly figure out context as he chatted, today's customer service bots can go a long way in making us think they're human as they help persuade us to act.

When we're lingering over a website for a few minutes, for example, we might see a small chat window pop up with the picture of a smiling agent who asks: "Can I help you with something?" As we engage in asking questions—"Do you have a version of that toy train in red?"—we might get back the kinds of responses—"Maybe, let me check"—that might never make us wonder if we're actually interacting with a robot.

Employing chatbots saves companies money, reportedly up to 40 percent, but just as importantly, some customers even prefer to deal with an automated messaging system versus dealing with a real human.[30] That's according to a study conducted by IBM, which now offers its own service it calls LiveEngage, which is powered by the conversational abilities of its own well-known AI: Watson. IBM has also launched a new AI initiative it calls Project Debater that is capable of debating in real time with humans—though its capabilities seem to still be in their infancy.[31]

Other research backs up the notion that there is a growing willingness among many of us to deal directly with machines. A survey of 4,500 people in 2017 by Forrester Research found that some 36 percent of adults say they actually prefer using digital customer service—including bots—over interacting with a human.[32]

The insurance company Progressive has even pushed the envelope further by developing a chatbot of its own that also employs the same kind of humor employed by its quirky spokesperson Flo—who is played by the actress and comedian Stephanie Courtney.[33] Apparently Flo has some 5 million followers on Facebook—compared to just the 475,000 people who "liked" the company itself. Unbeknownst to fans who thought they were interacting with the actual Flo on Facebook Messenger, they were actually chatting with a machine aimed at selling them insurance. That is the Invisible Brand in action.

Meanwhile, the financial firm Capital One employed software engineers who teamed up with a character development expert from Disney's Pixar to create a gender-neutral bot called Eno, who is both funny and understanding. Eno can perform tasks for customers—like providing account balances—while also chatting conversationally with them. If a customer asks Eno where it lives, for example, it will reply: "I live on the Internet. So many cat pictures . . . I love it."

The goal of creating bots like Eno is to make banking "more humane," according to Capital One's chief financial officer.[34] By "humane," they apparently mean "automated without humans knowing it."

The growing acceptance of AI-powered automation, and its power to persuade people, is only fueling the fire for more and more companies to find ways to deploy machine learning, NLP, and other AI-powered technology in innovative ways.

A company founded in 2010 called Narrative Science has created an AI agent called Quill that is capable of writing stories using any facts it's fed. Quill actually got its start as a project called StatsMonkey where it generated stories based on the box score of a baseball game.[35] By processing and interpreting what it sees in those numbers and then comparing that to a database filled with similar outcomes from thousands of other games, Quill is able to create a story on par with what any beat sportswriter can put together on the fly.[36] The key is that a baseball game has a very predictable structure—everything inside that game has happened before at some point or another. Baseball games never end in touchdowns or Academy Awards, which makes the task a bit more finite. There are only so many synonyms for "incredible," and if Quill mixes them in the proper amounts, along with the names of players and their batting performance during the game, it can create a reasonable facsimile of a game summary written by a human.

More recently, Quill has been used in similar fashion to generate stories based on swings in the stock market and to generate year-end reports dissecting the performance of different assets held by mutual funds—work that is again somewhat predictable and easily automated.[37] A job that used to be tedious and time-consuming for a human can now be done accurately in a fraction of the time.[38]

What we're now seeing is that NLP is extending beyond just the written word into the world of voice and speech recognition. We've already mentioned Siri and Alexa. Digital assistants are becoming better and better at understanding and mimicking human speech. Nonetheless, machines that can accurately interpret the context behind someone's words are still a few years off. Case in point: a Seattle couple was stunned when they found out that their Amazon Echo device had recorded a conversation they were having and then emailed it to people in the couple's contact list.[39]

Fortunately, the couple was talking about something innocuous—replacing their hardwood floors—but when they received a phone call from a coworker who alerted them to what happened, they hastened to unplug the various Echo devices they had installed throughout their home.

Imagine trying to interrogate the machine after the fact: "Alexa, why did you record us? What were you thinking?"

According to Amazon's investigation, the Echo had been wakened by the couple's conversation, which was happening in a separate room. The version of the device the couple used employed seven microphones, as well as noise-canceling tech, to help alert it to when someone said the keyword "Alexa."

After it activated itself, the Echo then thought it heard a series of requests, which it responded to with questions like "Send to whom?"—that it then thought were answered based on what it was overhearing. Who knew that "record our conversation and send it to our contact list" was even a function?

There have been other similar instances in which smart devices have done some surprising things—such as when a six-year-old girl engaged in a conversation with Alexa about cookies and dollhouses. Not long after, a $170 dollhouse arrived at the girl's home. Alexa misinterpreted the conversation as a purchase request.[40]

There have also been cases in which Alexa was triggered inside homes after hearing a story on the radio or TV that mentioned its name.[41] I'm waiting for the TV commercial that says, "Alexa, order a case of Coca-Cola and have it delivered tomorrow." If enough Echos are listening, Coke could make a fortune.

Google has also been pushing the envelope when it comes to teaching AIs how to mimic realistic human speech patterns. In May 2018, Google debuted Duplex, an AI digital assistant that incorporates typical human pauses like "ah" and "um"—what linguists call "speech disfluencies"—as it interacts with people.[42] That means that Duplex sounds impressively more like a human than even Alexa and Siri, which still have that robotic twang in their delivery. During a demo, which you can find on YouTube, Duplex actually called up a hair salon to book an appointment. The exchange went something like this:

Duplex: Hi, I'm calling to book a woman's haircut for a client. Um, I'm looking for something on May 3.

Receptionist: Sure, give me one second.

Duplex: Mm-hm.[43]

Duplex then requested an appointment time of noon, which the receptionist said wasn't available. After the briefest of pauses, Duplex asked if there were any slots available between 10 a.m. and 12 p.m.—to which the receptionist replied that it depended on what kind of service the person wanted. Duplex responded that her client just wanted a regular woman's haircut. In that case, the receptionist replied, 10:00 a.m. was open. Duplex then responded with, "10 a.m. is fine," and it then concluded the call by giving the client's name, "Lisa," and then thanking the receptionist. When the demo ended, the audience erupted in applause. If you didn't know any better, you could have easily mistaken the conversation as occurring between two humans—which was incredibly impressive. At the same time, the fact that a human was unknowingly talking to a computer has thorny implications.[44]

After receiving feedback, Google has added a feature where Duplex now announces that it is a machine calling on behalf of a human client. It's also begun partnering with different businesses to continue to refine Duplex's capabilities. One of Google's newer testing sites, for instance, employs Duplex as a hostess for a restaurant who answers the phone and places reservations for guests. Even when put to the test by the human's asking to be placed on hold, or when the human caller tried to trip it up by changing the details of the reservation, Duplex reputedly performed admirably all the while sounding remarkably human— even when the person calling knew it was a machine.[45] It's this kind of breakthrough in human-machine communication that creates both excitement and some fear. It also speaks to an emerging new era of opportunity for the Invisible Brand.

OUR DIGITAL ORACLES

We're seeing AI agents becoming increasingly anthropomorphic, humanlike, particularly in the realm of speech, but what does that mean to the world of marketing? In short: everything. We now stand on the precipice of a complete transformation of what we might call *marketing automation*—which we can define as preprogramming an entire set of actions like sending emails, reminder cards, or even telemarketing calls that a company might take to turn a prospect into a customer.

Think about marketing automation as a workflow with a set of prescribed actions designed to persuade customers along their decision journey to purchase a product. If they have been shown an advertisement three times and visited the website, for instance, then the system might send them an email. If after a period of time, the customers have yet to reply to the email, then the system can send a reminder and then follow up with a postcard. The marketing automation system does all of this automatically.

Now consider how this entire process might evolve when the consumer thinks he or she is interacting with a human using natural language. Consider that the marketing automation system depoloying natural language can personalize its interactions based on information about the consumer, and the persuasion strategy most likely to motivate the desired action. Instead of mapping out a step-by-step process that imagines a variety of circumstances, the future of marketing automation learns and tests and improves based on feedback it receives in the form of purchases and conversions. It's not as easy as simply commanding the computer to figure out how to sell more pizzas, but someday soon . . . it will be.

We are beginning to have conversations with computers,
and that simple fact alone is set to
permanently change the rules of marketing.

For decades, beginning with the inventions devised in the famed Xerox PARC research lab, which were then perfected by companies like Microsoft and Apple, we have been accustomed to interacting with computers using graphical user interfaces. These so-called GUIs were an incredible step up from the archaic and frustrating command lines and even coding cards that marked the age of the earliest computers.

Now, thanks to the debut of the technology that powers Alexa, we're on the verge of developing much deeper and more complex relationships with our computers using voice and speech interfaces—things we could never do through a GUI.

It's one thing to get directions to the restaurants we're headed to on Saturday night using Google on our mobile phones. But it's quite another experience when we have Google talking to us in real time guiding us on our way. Now imagine what it will be like to have an AI agent read bedtime stories to our children and to help them with their homework, all using human speech as the interface.

Consider that our ancestors would have first learned to communicate with each other through speech much earlier than through any form of written language. Speech is built into our genes. Our ability to use language to communicate our thoughts and ideas with each other taps into something fundamental to who we are as a species. It is now clear that other animals communicate through sounds, and anyone who has ever heard the haunting echoes of whales can easily imagine that those sounds contain profound meaning that we have yet to interpret. Human speech is dependent upon the unique configuration of our lips and tongues and vocal cords to produce the phonological range common to our species. Fortunately, we've learned to combine this finite set of sounds into an endless array of patterns, words, and sentences that overcomes our physiological limits.

Symbolic language—in the form of written words—was a huge step for our speaking species because writing could be stored, transmitted across long distances and even across time, to communicate meaning far beyond the reach of someone's voice. We augmented our spoken language with writing and eventually with printing presses that could amplify our voices to reach hundreds and even millions of people. Our experience of the written word is buried so deeply within us that we can hardly imagine a world in which the visual interface disappears in favor of speech.

An AI agent that can permanently store information, distribute it universally, and retrieve it on demand eliminates some of the challenges writing was invented to solve. Just as the graphical user interface was a major step forward in the history of our relationship with our computers, it is clear that the voice user interface (VUI) will force us to continue reimagining the possible.

As software entrepreneur Jason Amunwa framed it in a blog entry titled "The UX of Voice: The Invisible Interface": "In an age where almost a third of the global population is carrying a microphone connected to a supercomputer in their pocket, it's not hard to guess at the huge swath of people that are primed and ready to adopt voice interaction as their input method of choice."[46] But creating a voice user interface also creates new challenges for engineers.

For instance, when we look at a web page, a designer can steer us to different options, such as the now ubiquitous "click here" hyperlink to another web page. There is a whole field of instructional design dedicated to helping users navigate through graphical user interfaces. But in the UI of the future, when people will be using their voices to drive the computer, a designer will have to think through the different ways a human will want to interact with the interface. As an example, Amunwa mentioned how issuing a command like "delete this" could have vast and potentially devastating effects depending on whether a user was editing a Microsoft Word document or their Facebook profile. Even the simple-sounding task of signing up for a newsletter might mean that the UI needs to process an infinite number of commands—like "I want to sign up for the newsletter" to "I want to subscribe to this blog" or "Give me updates on this"—all to accomplish the same action. As Amunwa wrote: "There are innumerable ways to articulate the same basic intent via voice—which means [user experience] UX designers must make sure they're asking the right questions to elicit the appropriate verbal responses from users."

What's also exciting is the notion that voice itself might help drive connections with users—especially when it comes to brands. We are empathetic creatures, and the anthropomorphic voice makes the machine more relatable. When consumers visit a brand's web page, that brand tries to convey its promise through images the users interact with on the page. Now, it will be the sound of the UI's voice that needs to convey the brand's promise. That means when it comes to designing the UI, everything from gender and age to tone and accent will be important factors to weigh. It's easy to imagine how the voice of a hip British airline like Virgin might differ from that of the *Wall Street Journal* or even Disney. The goal for brands will be to find the right combination of factors that will best engage—and persuade—their customers to act. To make matters more complex, marketers will have to consider whether the voice of their brand is personalized and whether it should change based on the user. Should the brand's AI agent match the regional accent of the user, and the user's gender? These are areas where learning algorithms will help marketers figure out which approach yields the desired outcomes.

The challenge of a VUI is very different than the challenge of a GUI. Think about it: without a visual UI to work with, how can a voice user interface present options to a user? In the GUI, the consumer is simply presented with a list of search results to visually scan and then click on. In the era of voice user interfaces, results need to be pruned down because most of us simply don't have the patience to listen to someone (or something) rattle off a whole list of options to consider. What needs to happen is that the UI learns enough about what we really want to know so that it can steer us to just one or two top options—just like humans would if we asked them a similar question. So, if we wanted to find a good restaurant near us, the UI might ask a couple of questions like "What kind of food were you thinking about?" or "How far are you willing to drive?" in order to narrow the choices. The UI might also be able to query its database about our past decisions and preferences in order to further streamline its recommendation to us. The UI might then alter its tone in such a way that it knows has helped persuade our decisions in the past as a way to more quickly influence our decision in the present.

This has profound implications, especially if we don't really understand what might be driving those questions or options our UI presents us. The Invisible Brand at work behind the scenes will be steering us toward certain actions without us knowing there was an alternative to take—which puts us on the precipice of a fundamentally new age of marketing.

The power of the anthropomorphic voice in AI has profound implications for psychotechnology.

As a young man, I spent a summer in Greece as an exchange student. Traveling through an ancient land was a transformative experience for me. On a day trip to visit the ruins of the Temple of Apollo at Delphi, I learned about the high priestess who served as the oracle in the temple and interpreted the will of the gods. "Who are our modern oracles?" I asked myself. Today I think I know the answer.

Just as the oracles of old became the voices of the gods, brands of the future will have their own oracles, speaking individually to consumers through natural language processing. Now that we've entered an age when we are talking to our computers, and our computers are talking to us, those voices will become part of our lives. Filtered through the interface of natural language, the Invisible Brand will not only speak directly to consumers but also gather information from consumers to be harvested as new data in a never-ending cycle of marketing personalization. As people continue to build deepening relationships with their computers, there will be opportunities for those voices to persuade and influence us because they will be armed with all the data and persuasion science tailored down to the individual level. Consumers will have a personal relationship with the brand's oracle.

Brands need to be thinking about what that future will look like when people are interfacing with psychotechnology using speech and how those relationships will affect consumer decisions. Voice commerce has arrived.

*Marketing professionals need to be developing
their own digital oracles to represent them in
the voice-driven marketplace.*

We know Google, Apple, and Amazon have their voice-driven brand representatives. They are already well on their way to implanting psychotechnology deeply into our lives. They are working on making their digital oracles increasingly humanlike and equipping them with better search and response capabilities.

Smaller brands today think in terms of search engine optimization (SEO), but voice search optimization (VSO) is an undiscovered continent where most marketers have yet to map out the terrain. Voice-based search offers new challenges for brands and consumers alike, and the rules that we have learned for text-based search using the graphical user interface will not apply.

The voice user interface gives psychotechnology its humanlike appeal. The anthropomorphic quality of NLP, speaking to us through our machines, will be incredibly powerful when coupled with personalized information, the science of persuasion, and the ability to learn. The persuasive force of the Invisible Brand will be strengthened substantially by the power of voice to engage with consumers at a deep emotional level. The marketing rules that we have learned in the era of the graphical user interface need to be rethought, and a new set of rules for the era of the voice user interface needs to be written.

To Recap

When Alan Turing first proposed a method for testing whether machines could think, it would have been hard to imagine that humans would eventually speak with machines on a regular basis—often without realizing it. While it's been the fodder of science fiction authors for generations, machines now have the capability to process and create words and speech in ways that seem eerily human. We've seen a startling series of advances in natural language processing over the last decade.

Some brands have already begun taking advantage of these capabilities as they increasingly look for ways to deploy AI agents to more effectively connect and engage with consumers. We've now entered an age when much of the information we receive through both text and voice is put there by algorithms. As the voices of algorithms become more humanlike, they simultaneously become more persuasive. The power of psychotechnology is greatly enhanced when we engage in conversations with AI agents. Now its time for us to look at how psychotechnology is actively reshaping marketing and the media.

PART II

SYNTHESIS

6

Marketing with Psychotechnology

THANKS TO THE EMERGENCE OF AI, marketing and advertising will never be the same. As one provocative piece in the publication the *New Statesman* put it: "Advertising, once a creative industry, is now a data-driven business reliant on algorithms."[1] There is much truth in this statement. Earlier, we discussed in detail how the combination of Big Data collection and the algorithmic power of AI to learn will have a dramatic impact on the world of marketing and advertising. I have argued that personalized information, the science of persuasion, and natural language processing will merge with these innovations and that its synthesis, which I call psychotechnology, will have a major impact on our lives.

In this synthesis, we need to account for how AI can help marketers in unifying data, optimizing campaigns, and harvesting insights. In other words, AI brings new capabilities to all phases of the customer journey, from building awareness and helping encourage buying decisions all the way through the retention of existing customers and turning them into powerful advocates.

Just think about how Netflix leverages data in its movie recommendation algorithms. One report estimated that getting those recommendations right helps reduce the churn rate among its subscribers, saving the company upward of $1 billion a year that it might otherwise have to spend to acquire new customers.[2] Recommendation engines represent a kind of targeted, data-driven, personalized advertising that is mostly imperceptible to customers.

What's essential for marketers to understand is that AI is becoming a default go-to that consumers will use to navigate the dizzying array of options they can choose from online. This is especially true with regard to digital voice assistants like Alexa, which consumers will increasingly rely upon to make their decisions about which brands to buy. As Niraj Dawar, a marketing professor, penned in the *Harvard Business Review*: "Consumers' allegiance will shift from trusted brands to a trusted AI assistant."[3]

The stakes are enormous—especially for brands that offer multiple products to which digital assistants can steer consumers, something Dawar has called "the economy of scope." The more consumers learn to trust their digital assistants, the more persuasive the digital assistants will become at steering those customers to brands. It's a prime example of the Invisible Brand in action.

To survive this kind of coming paradigm shift, brands will need to redirect their focus from trying to develop direct relationships with customers to developing ways to optimize their positions with digital assistants. Brands will essentially need to shift from pull-marketing strategies aimed at attracting consumers, to aggressive push tactics designed to appeal to the AI's algorithms.

Not unlike how advertisers have had to learn the secrets to SEO and paid advertising to stand out on the web, they will now need to learn the nuances of voice search optimization, so they don't get lost in the digital conversation. As Dawar put it: "[Brands] must invest aggressively in understanding the algorithms platforms use to recommend and choose products, including how they weight each brand for each consumer."

The Invisible Brand has the greatest impact when all of the elements—from personalized information and persuasion equations to learning algorithms and NLP—converge to create entirely new ways of connecting with and persuading consumers to act. The Invisible Brand applies psychotechnology to marketing. The ways we market and advertise are already undergoing radical change, and what follows are some prime examples of those changes in action today—as well as some informed speculation as to what might happen tomorrow.

LEVERAGING PERSONAL DATA

I remember I was working at a TV station in North Carolina when I learned that Nielsen, the research and polling company, had struck an agreement with Facebook. Nielsen would begin putting tracking tags on their ads and then pass that data to Facebook.[4] In return, Facebook would monitor those tracking tags and then report the aggregated data back to Nielsen to let them know who had seen those ads—an act of data pairing in action.[5]

Using the example of Facebook, which is watching people all of the time, we can now revisit some of the key lessons we discussed in Chapters 2 and 4 about how data is collected and paired. Anytime people are online and have Facebook open, it's tracking what they're doing and capturing data about them, either directly or indirectly through partners like Nielsen. Facebook then takes all of that activity data and pairs it up with individual profiles. As a result of that deal with Nielsen, Facebook can summarize the demographic data about whoever saw a specific ad and then provide summary reports back to Nielsen after first purging any personal identification information (PII). The result might indicate something like this: "Sixty-five percent of the ad's audience was composed of white males between the ages of 35 and 54 living in the United States." This is really valuable information for Nielsen because it validates whether an ad reached its target audience or not. Nielsen can then sell that validation as a service to advertisers.

What is less clear to consumers is that when Facebook is fed all of that data by partners, they are pairing it with consumer profiles, and they are keeping it (Figure 6.1). For years now, Facebook has gathered information from their corporate partnerships and paired that data with individual user profiles. Facebook knows what websites, and the specific web pages, consumers were on when they saw specific ads. Check that. They have detailed information on consumer web surfing behavior dating back years, and a huge volume of that information was handed to them by partners like Nielsen who needed Facebook's help pairing behaviors with actual people. They've paired all that data back to personal Facebook profiles and kept it, and consumers have no ability to erase it. Even when consumers delete their accounts, it appears that Facebook retains the data. All the while consumers thought they were anonymously perusing that prurient content, it was being gathered up in a database and stored by Facebook along with their baby pictures and the photos from their grandmother's birthday party.

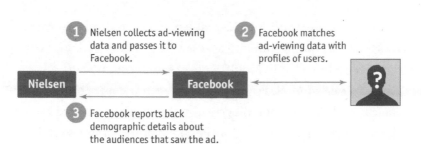

**FIGURE 6.1 FACEBOOK ACQUIRING ONLINE
BEHAVIOR DATA FROM PARTNERS**

This data from partners has enabled Facebook to build an incredibly detailed and accurate profile of users as well as their behaviors both off- and online. Not surprisingly, Facebook has signed similar deals with other companies like Oracle and mobile game developers, further widening the extent of its data collection.[6]

But things don't stop there. We have already discussed how Google continues to track our movements even when we think we have told them to stop. It's interesting to note that since 2014, Google has been working with advertisers by supplying them data to track foot traffic in retail locations.[7] This practice of location-aware tracking has become a big business for Google to the tune of more than $95 billion in 2017 alone. At a marketing event in July 2018, Google announced a new tool it's calling "local campaigns" that is specifically designed to let a retailer know how effective an ad campaign was based on users' foot traffic history inside a store. In other words, Google is now enabling advertisers to send highly targeted and personalized ads to users based on where they are physically located. If they are near a particular retailer, for instance, they will see a targeted ad for that specific store—a service for which advertisers are willing to pay a premium.

The next generation of AI-enabled marketing and advertising tools will be contingent upon access to data—lots of data. That's where Facebook and Google have created a significant advantage at a macro level. For marketers, when it comes to reaching their brand's customers, they need to be thinking about how to develop ways of capturing more detailed information about them as a way to better personalize and calibrate campaigns. They also need to think about how they can eliminate the silos that separate data and prevent a marketer's ability to build a more comprehensive picture of their customers. As Martha Mathers, practice leader for marketing technology at Gartner, said in an interview about deploying AI in marketing: "It's pretty critical that you look at the data that you have. And do you know enough about your customers to actually be able to use that tool?"[8]

That's why one of the areas many enterprises are reinvesting in is their customer relationship marketing (CRM) systems, which have become the top of the funnel for capturing data on prospects and leads. That data can then be fed to AI systems throughout the marketing organization. But just having the data isn't an end in and of itself. With AI, we now have enhanced capabilities to make new connections with that data wherever it might be coming from, both online and offline, and then combining it with other sources to create a more complete picture of customers as they proceed along their buying journey. Salesforce has reported, for example, that its AI system, called Einstein, makes more than 1 billion predictions per day for its customers.[9]

On a similar note, Microsoft has begun incorporating data it's gathering from LinkedIn, the professional social networking site it acquired in 2016, to help it with its AI sales and marketing efforts.[10] Adobe spent a reported $4.75 billion to purchase the AI capabilities owned by the firm Marketo as a way to compete with Salesforce.[11] Other data vendors, like D&B Hoovers, have also become vital partners for organizations looking to feed their AI systems with more and more data.

AI can help us optimize existing campaigns in ways that allow us to achieve our goals against key performance indicators (KPIs), such as e-commerce revenue results. This is basically an interactive statistical process of testing and remediating and ultimately optimizing campaigns in the direction of whatever yields the best results. Firms that have employed AI in crafting dynamic email outreach campaigns have already seen persuasive results: email click-through rates that average about 2.6 percent have soared to more than 14 percent by leveraging machine learning to create compelling subject lines, copy, and calls to action.[12] AI can also harvest insights about the customer decision journey that can enable marketers to create new campaigns based on answering questions like these:

- When is the best time to engage?

- What motivates engagement?

- Will this audience respond better to direct mail, telemarketing, online advertising, or email?

In this same vein, AI can help us produce more accurate attribution modeling and answer questions like, "What marketing tactic triggered this particular purchase?"

NEW ROLES REMAKING THE MARKETING WORLD

The marketer's job now is to assess corporate objectives, determine a strategy, develop products and campaigns, create ads, and place them. In the world of the Invisible Brand, computers will help design the campaigns and will assemble and place all the ads based on the personal characteristics of the audience. Marketing will become a fully strategic activity, with the tactics all machine controlled.

This is particularly true of advertising. There will be no more ad buyers. Creative professionals within the agency environment will produce the raw assets for the machine to assemble. This will accelerate a shift in the media landscape, and media companies will be forced to choose a new role: traffic grabber, data hoarder, or pinpoint targeter. Those in the mushy middle will die.

The twenty-first-century wizards of advertising are those who have mastered the efficiency of real-time advertising— and they must understand the technology of AI.

According to a study by the World Federation of Advertisers, covering advertisers that spend in aggregate more than $70 billion per year, 90 percent of advertisers are reviewing their programmatic ad contracts and demanding more control and transparency. AI is the tool they use. Ari Sheinkin, VP of marketing analytics for IBM, told *Business Insider* that the AI program Watson helped the company reduce its cost per click by 71 percent compared to the way it used to buy advertising.[13] IBM is making the same Watson technology available to other advertisers seeking similar efficiencies.

This new way of advertising redefines roles throughout the advertising ecosystem—and within every marketing team and agency. Let's look at the world of advertising through the eyes of Jess, a media planner at a medium-sized advertising agency in Midtown Manhattan.

Jess is working on Samsung's Galaxy mobile account. At 36, she's been in the business long enough to remember when she used Excel spreadsheets to plan campaigns, identifying the right mix of television and radio spots to help her clients achieve their goals. Five years ago, she shifted her focus to digital media where she could mix her commercial flair with a healthy dose of real-time data-driven analytics. Now her role has changed and continues to change in the modern advertising landscape.

The world where Jess cut her teeth in the ad industry revolved around Nielsen and Arbitron ratings, which surveyed media consumers to produce an estimate about how many people were watching a TV program or listening to a radio broadcast, at a specific time and day. People filled out little diaries and tried desperately to remember where they were last Wednesday at 8 p.m. before scribbling in some (possibly fictional) details and mailing them in. Billions of advertising dollars were allocated based on what those little diaries told the advertising executives of major corporations worldwide.

On one side, media planners like Jess worked with the brand teams who generated the strategy and target audiences for the ad campaigns and the creative teams who produced the actual TV and radio ads. On the other, they worked with media buyers who executed the media plans that people like Jess developed. It was all very interconnected because a change in the strategy or a brainstorm from the creative team could have ripple effects that would cause everyone to rethink what they were doing on the campaign. And if those little diaries showed that fewer people tuned in to a rerun of *Parks and Recreation* than expected . . . well, back to the drawing board.

Digital is different. Jess has more detailed information about the audiences who are consuming the media her agency is buying. In her current role in planning buys for Galaxy, she is particularly

interested in identifying users who are using older mobile devices with fewer modern features. Using a technology called the
media query (which was introduced back with cascading style
sheet 3, or CSS3), Jess has access to detailed information about
exactly what type of devices are requesting web pages from the
sites where she wants to advertise. These media queries are built
into the web servers themselves to query the user's device and
ask, "What type of device are you?" The user's device responds
with details about its model, browser type, and window size and
whether it is a laptop or mobile handset. The Galaxy brand team
has defined a specific range of older mobile device models (meaning two years old) where they can compete in terms of upgraded
capabilities and functionality. It is Jess's job to deliver Galaxy ads
where the users meets those criteria.

One of Jess's favorite partners is the Weather Company. Why?
Well, a few years ago, IBM purchased the Weather Company in a
move that mystified followers of the mammoth computing company. What was IBM doing dabbling in weather forecasting?
Apart from the fact that predicting weather is all about crunch-
ing fabulously large amounts of data with big computers like
IBM's Watson, it turns out that the Weather Company also delivers an equally fabulous amount of advertising to people on their
mobile devices.

Now Jess works with the Weather Company to make certain that her ads are seen by just the right buyers: those who have
crappy old phones, but who also have the money to buy a new
one if they feel like it. If, for example, a user is regularly checking
the weather from his or her crappy phone in, say, St. Barts, Lake
Cuomo, or Hong Kong, there is a good chance that they can afford
a new one. But Jess isn't sitting around all day scanning people's
browsing habits on Weather.com, poised over her keyboard waiting

for the just the right instant to hit "send" and fire off a Galaxy ad to a crappy phone somewhere on the French Riviera. Instead, the AI behind Watson is working overtime at this very moment to do it for her.

Imagine for a moment that a marketing firm has a hundred creative teams working for them to develop ads for the latest Galaxy phone. Like some weird version of *American Idol*, each team is competing live to prove that their ad creative is the best. Hour upon hour, day upon day, the marketer sits through an endless barrage of ad concepts trying to select the one that will produce the highest Galaxy phone sales. Think anyone is up to the challenge? When it comes to predicting winners and losers in the ad business, nothing beats the focus group—the more participants the better. The best ad executives have learned not to trust their gut because they usually guess wrong.

The AI behind Watson functions like a giant focus group. It is able to reconfigure the ad creative, and even the specific words (and even language) contained in the ad, to deliver hundreds of different versions of the online ad campaign to tens of thousands of web users to see which words, and which images, work in combination with which devices to yield the greatest return. Jess and her friends can go off to happy hour while Watson toils away relentlessly at the problem.

Is Watson "thinking"? Or is Watson just employing brute force, testing a huge number of combinations of words and images and then shifting the Galaxy ad campaign meticulously in the direction of those combinations that result in clicks or phone sales and away from those combinations that fail? The answer to the question doesn't really matter to the advertiser because with Watson at work, the Galaxy ads are silently finding their way onto crappy phones in exclusive hotels and restaurants everywhere.

These examples are fictitious—I don't have any knowledge of Galaxy's ad strategy. What I do know for certain is that the role of advertising strategists has changed. It used to be enough to identify the goals of an entire advertising program. That remains true. But now those goals can be extremely precise—for example, reach X millions of these kinds of people, and move Y *percent* of them to consideration, and Z *percent* to purchase, based on KPIs that a machine can understand.

The role of the ad creative used to be to deliver a consistent image and message that would accomplish the campaign goals. Now creative is not one concept, nor even one set of concepts. Creative execution involves dozens or hundreds of variations and combinations all under the umbrella of a brand concept. An ad campaign now encompasses a cloud of creative ideas, not just a single tagline paired with a single image.

The Invisible Brand deploys experiments, learns what works, and develops an approach that is different for individual consumers.

The role of media planners and buyers like Jess has changed completely because negotiating where the ad goes is now the job of the algorithm, not a human. The media planners and buyers tell the AI machine what the target is, then supply the cloud of creative ideas. They monitor the results and observe what the algorithm has learned. They tweak or approve the tweaks that the machine suggests.

The result is not so much a campaign in the sense of advertising, but a campaign in the sense of a war, made up of thousands of individual actions. This multiplicity of real-time decisions combines to create a successful effort to move people down the marketing funnel. And the adjustments, which happen in real time, are in the hands of the Invisible Brand. Money goes in one end, and results come out the other. What happens in the middle may now be hard for any human to truly understand. This is the marketing world of the Invisible Brand. And it has transformed not just advertising but the media that depend on it for revenue.

FOR MEDIA, NEW AD MODELS ARE DEMANDING TRANSFORMATION

Who gets the money that advertisers are paying and the Invisible Brand is distributing? The traditional answer was media companies. But the transformation of the advertising ecosystem has challenged media companies and destroyed some of them. Increasingly the ad tech and intervening auctions take their cut of the advertiser's dollar, and this has squeezed publishers. The blog *Newspaper Death Watch* has tallied the death toll of major newspapers, from the *Tampa Tribune* to the *Rocky Mountain News*, that have gone out of business since 2007. TV stations, radio, magazines—they're all suffering. That's because the value they have—eyeballs—is undifferentiated and they rely on third parties to segregate their audiences into premium value. When a click on *Buzzfeed* or Facebook has the same value as a click on the *Boston Globe*, the *Globe* has trouble staying relevant.

To differentiate, these media companies must change where their value comes from. It's not just undifferentiated eyeballs anymore. It is eyeballs combined with data. The more a brand knows about its readers and listeners, the better it can compete.

Publishers don't just have to seduce the advertisers anymore. They have to seduce the algorithms.

I recently heard the president of the *Dallas Morning News* as he described the challenge. As a result of programmatic ad buying, they changed their perspective on their business. They are no longer just a publisher. Now they are a marketing company. As a result, they have embraced a huge array of marketing technologies.

They provide direct mail. They have beefed up their online presence and started producing video. They host events. As they approach advertisers, their ink and paper product is now just an introduction to their full-service marketing suite—and ultimately their knowledge of the Dallas consumers, person by person. The next generation of media will be completely data driven to provide marketing at multiple touch points.

Media companies that embrace a mindset of data collection for marketing will survive. Those that focus on broad undifferentiated audiences will fail and disappear.

RETHINKING THE ONLINE MEDIA MODEL

In the early days of the Internet, the news was always free. In a race to secure eyeballs over subscriptions, every publication launched a website and gave away free access to their content—

even while still charging print subscribers. That grand experiment worked for some publications—and not others. We've seen a comeback in the notion of a "paywall"—in other words, a subscription needed to access what used to be free content, as younger consumers have begun to embrace the notion of needing to pay for access to quality journalism.

Yet, from the beginnings of the Internet age, the *Wall Street Journal* (WSJ) never caved. It has stood behind its paywall since 1997, trusting that customers interested in its content would pay upwards of $200 a year for it.[14] There were exceptions from time to time—if a WSJ story was shared on social media, nonsubscribers could often read it—but the paywall has stood solidly, and it has helped the publication accumulate nearly 3 million combined paid subscribers for its print and online content.

That is, until recently. The WSJ has begun a grand new experiment using machine learning and user profile data to help open up the paywall on a trial basis for potential new subscribers.[15] When nonsubscribers arrive at the site, an algorithm instantly "scores" the visitors on more than 60 different factors such as their frequency of visits and the kind of device or operating system they're using. Then, based on the resulting score, their paywall tightens or loosens based on the likelihood that the algorithm believes the visitor will convert into a subscriber.

Users who seem the most likely to convert—what the WSJ calls "hot leads"— hit the hard paywall. But for those visitors who may at first be less likely to subscribe, the so-called warm and even cold leads—the paywall opens up to give them guest access for a limited time if they're willing to hand over their email address. The whole idea is to hook them on the content while also gathering more data about them and what they do once they're on the site. As Karl Wells, WSJ's general manager for membership, told an interviewer:

> If you think about paywalls broadly, there have been metered, free-mium, and hard paywalls. Metered considers people who will want to read more than, say, five stories. Freemium assumes this and not that is the type of content people will pay for. This is what we've tried to move on from. Our model now is to flip that and start with the reader. The content you see is the output of the paywall, rather than an input.[16]

The WSJ isn't the only site experimenting with this kind of predictive and dynamic paywall based on what it knows about the visitors to its site. The *Financial Times* has been using a similar model for years. Meanwhile a Scandinavian media company called Schibsted, whose publications had been free online since 1995, has begun scoring visitors on their likelihood of subscribing using information it has paired from Facebook and then customizing ads touting the benefits of becoming a subscriber.[17] The prediction model gives the website's sales and marketing teams information they can use to target different groups of registered users with different digital subscription packages.

The list of subscribers—and all the associated data about their behavior—is a hard asset. A newspaper or magazine built to compete in the future knows names and where people live, what they do online, and, through cookies, some of what they do on other sites. The publishers can link someone's name and address to offline data such as home value, credit card use, and even when he or she last voted. And in that, there is value.

We're now in the midst of a meltdown of the old media business models. Real-time bidding and ad placement strategies have blown a hole in the idea of "building an audience and selling it." Because the Invisible Brand can assemble any desired audience, in real time, with ad placements across thousands of sites, media companies no longer have a lock on their audiences. They can opt out of the ads from the big auction exchanges and allow their remnant ad inventory to go unsold. Or they can accept those discounted ads and get paid far less than in years past.

As a result, for a media company in the twenty-first century, there are at least three possible ways to operate so as to remain relevant and make money:

- **Traffic grabber:** One way to sidestep the loss of revenue is to simply aggregate more eyeballs. A lot of eyeballs. A media company that adopts this strategy is no longer about a consistent collection of content. It's simply about more and more traffic. That means celebrity news, silly videos, and anything else that will generate viewing. Yahoo! is a good example.

- **Data hoarder:** Traffic is worth more if a site knows more about a customer. Taking this to its logical conclusion, a site that assembles the most data can sell its advertising avails and knowledge for the highest amount. Sites like Google and Facebook have vast amounts of knowledge about customers, which makes their ad avails worth far more.

- **Pinpoint targeter:** Sites like the *Los Angeles Times* have specific information about visitors that's hard to come by elsewhere—such as a local address paired with online behavior. CNET's Download.com knows what software people are using. Amazon knows what people have bought. These sites can turn this knowledge into unique value for advertisers.

Broadcasting companies, newspapers, and online publishers are always moving slightly among these three roles, but the one place a media company will no longer succeed is in the data-less zone of the broadcasting middle. If a site has average traffic and moderate, generic data about its customers, it used to have a business. But in the age of the Invisible Brand, it's toast.

RETHINKING SEARCH

We've already explored the significant impact that Google's Page-Rank algorithm has on all of us. Without it (and a handful of less popular competitors), the Internet would remain a thick haystack in which few of us could find a needle. As Larry Page has been quoted saying, the perfect search engine "understands exactly what you mean and gives you back exactly what you want."[18]

Thanks to AI, search tech is becoming even more effective. For example, Google is increasingly relying on smart algorithms to help expand matches on searches beyond the typical keywords entered by a potential customer.

Google's algorithms learn from its giant user base—it's as if they are operating the world's largest focus group.

That includes learning how to correct spelling mistakes users make while entering their search terms and using AI to look up synonyms for words that might fit the context for the search—technology that's being called "autosuggest." This has vast implications for marketers and for understanding the future of search engine optimization (SEO), where customers find brands through organic searches with autosuggestions helpfully provided by Google.

We can also now search with more than just words. For example, the auction site eBay is already experimenting with image recognition technology, where it enables users to select images of items on any website or blog they might be visiting and then hit a "Find it on eBay" option.[19] The photo site Shutterstock is also rethinking its search technology by allowing users to search on the "look and feel" of photos rather than on just literal descriptions. Let's say a user wanted to find more pictures like one that happened to have a dog featured in it. But it was the color and background the user liked—not the dog. With this kind of capability, the site can conduct a search based on those other parameters to find similar photos that go beyond typical keyword descriptions.[20] The idea is that these sites can use this technology to make it easier for consumers to find what they want, fast, so they can buy it.

MOBILIZING BRAND DATA

Even bigger changes could be in store for the way we search for content going forward—especially when it comes to using our mobile devices. Thanks to companies with names like CamFind, we might soon be able to take a picture with our phone's camera and then conduct a search based on that image—something that's being called "machine vision."[21] One benefit of conducting a search based on images rather than text is that a user won't be constrained by whatever language they speak, because images are universal whether someone speaks English or Japanese. Some of the image recognition algorithms we mentioned earlier are being embedded into augmented-reality applications that can overlay data about real-world objects that enhances what users see through their mobile device, on their windshield, or even in their sunglasses.

On a recent family trip to Colonial Williamsburg, my youngest daughter spent a considerable amount of time searching for *Pokémon Go* characters using her iPhone. George Washington dined here . . . *yawn* . . . but look . . . there's a rare Bulbasaur! That's a good illustration of the potential convergence of the real and algorithmic worlds. It's easy to imagine that image recognition and geolocation technology could be combined with augmented-reality devices and used to enhance the colonial experience at Williamsburg. For example, augmented reality through an iPhone might identify the statue of Lord Botetourt in front of the Wren Building and have it come to life to explain who he is and what he's doing there. Sponsored by the College of William & Mary, of course—which the avatar might mention is a school of choice for the aspiring college student interested in American history.

That's product placement in action . . . perhaps what we could call "augmented advertising." The idea is that by utilizing location-aware devices to create customized interactive experiences that enhance a user's knowledge and engagement, brands may find new opportunities to deliver persuasive messaging.

As new augmented technologies continue to enter the mainstream—Google Lens made its debut in 2018 and uses image recognition and NLP to identify objects[22]—it could open up all kind of possibilities for brands to deliver their messages to consumers in creative ways. Using Lens, users can just point their phone at, say, a poster for an upcoming concert, and their phone will then launch a video of that musician in action. Or a user might point his or her phone at a friend's outfit, and the phone will then pull up a list of similar outfits for sale at local or online clothing retailers (while also checking in with the Google database to see what else Google might know about the person making the smartphone inquiry). Of course, technology like Lens might also lead to an arms race of sorts for brands everywhere as they try to grab consumers' attention, not unlike what has happened with search. The advertising market for augmented reality alone could grow to more than $1 trillion a year.[23]

These kinds of changes should give marketers and advertisers reasons to rethink how their potential customers might find them and how they can develop strategies to better enable customers to engage with their brand.

HYPERPERSONALIZATION

If there's one thing every marketer and advertiser can agree on, it's that the more personalized they can make a message to customers, the more effective it will be. And that's not just my opinion. It's a fact based on survey data that shows that marketers and advertisers are salivating over the potential to turn the combination of Big Data and AI to their advantage in what we might call microtargeting or hyperpersonalization.[24]

What's changed is that, in the past, the marketers' goal would be to find ways to segment customers into different buckets based on attributes they might have in common. Then, they could serve those groups a set of ads to which they would likely react. Now, by employing a combination of AI capabilities that include computer vision, image recognition, machine learning, natural language processing, and deep learning, marketers are on the threshold of being able to develop highly customized and personalized messages at scale.[25]

At its core, psychotechnology delivers personalized information and interactions at the individual level. Just as someone might visit one of London's legendary tailors to purchase a bespoke suit, marketers can now increasingly turn to AI to tailor their ad campaigns to specific customers—even on the fly. Let's talk about some of the areas where we can leverage psychotechnology in targeting customers.

Ad Targeting

Ad targeting is placing custom ads based on specific users' past behaviors, including what they have viewed, clicked on, and purchased. Companies are now offering brands services where they employ predictive analytics algorithms that can forecast how effective the style and design of an ad will be based on how users reacted to similar ads in the past.[26] The social networking site LinkedIn, for example, is already employing dynamic ads on its site that are personalized based on the information in users' profiles.[27] Users might be targeted by a professional peer group, for instance, if they have a certain amount of managerial experience.

This can also be a powerful way to overcome "ad fatigue" by using an AI's A/B testing capability to find new ways to tweak underperforming ads. As a LinkedIn product manager framed it in a blog post announcing the new feature: "Because the creative is automatically personalized with each member's profile info, such as their photo, first name, company, and job title, you can capture your audience's attention in a way that standard display ads can't."[28]

The early returns are reportedly impressive: LinkedIn advertisers have reported that click-through rates on these dynamic ads are double that of more traditional ads.[29] Again, the whole idea is to leverage as much information as the brand has on individual visitors to the site and then let an AI agent determine what kinds of ad they might be most interested in based on their history or based on the variables that an advertiser might be most interested in targeting.

Personalized Messaging and Content

Email is not going away anytime soon. One market research report estimated that there were about 5 billion email accounts globally and that there were some 100 billion business emails sent every day.[30] But what is going away is the "fire-and-forget" approach to mass spamming of email contact lists hoping that someone will actually do something with that email.

That's why there are now vendors offering AI-powered services that can generate customized email templates using behavioral data, such as email clicks, purchase histories, and just about any other activities that users took online that were tracked.[31] For instance, if users clicked around on the site—or even bought something or put items in a cart—a customized email can be sent to them to either help them complete the purchase or make recommendations on other items. Thanks to advances in NLP, companies will also increasingly rely on AI agents to create the custom copy at scale that will appear in those emails.

Product Recommendation

Once users have found their desired websites, the goal shifts from marketing to converting those visitors into paying customers. There are now vendors offering AI solutions that, when paired to a website, can make personalized recommendations to those users within milliseconds of the users acting on the site.

With AI, brands can now take the "You might also like" option to another level. One company called Recombee, for example, claims that it employs collaborative filtering algorithms that process actions such as views and purchases to help refine the kinds of live recommendations—up to 500 per second—it serves up to potential customers on the site.[32] If someone views a pair of shoes on a retail site, for instance, the recommendation engine might then serve up other options like pants, tops, and hats that might match the shoes.

The idea is that the more data users give the site to process through their clicks and views, the more information the site has to try and determine the kinds of things the users are interested in.

Dynamic Websites

Everyone knows that every brand needs to have a sharp website. But imagine what it might be like if a website changed and morphed depending on the type of people who were surfing? That's the potential behind AI technology that enables dynamic websites where the content on the page changes to fit the users based on what is known about them and what kinds of actions they've taken on the site before.[33]

For instance, a dynamic site might serve up a different home page to return customers and bring them right to a page filled with personalized recommendations. There are now vendors who are offering AI services that will automatically build a website landing page that dynamically adjusts to narrow audience segents—including photos and color schemes—while employing a layout that's proven to attract and convert visitors based on testing thousands of other sites.[34]

Interactive Chatbots

Thanks to the development of AI tech like NLP, we can interact with chatbots that increasingly sound like humans. And now,
armed with the power of psychotechnology and persuasion equations, those chatbots can help take marketing and customer engagement efforts to a new level.

Chatbots have the ability to interact with individual customers while having full access to their action history on the site, and
increasingly those chatbots are able to combine that information with all the other profile data the brand has been able to acquire about its customers. "Chatbots have access to millions of
customer-centered data points. They can also aggregate location-
specific requests to detect patterns, spot repetitive problems, and
predict what's causing issues for a particular user," said Markus
Lippus, chief technology officer at MindTitan, a company focused
on developing AI-powered solutions. "Often, this makes them
more knowledgeable than any human customer service rep."[35]

DYNAMIC NATIVE ADVERTISING

A growing sector in marketing is native advertising, or content
that matches the form, feel, and function of the media that sur-
rounds it.[36] Think about a Facebook ad that looks like it's part
of one's newsfeed, or a profile of a company on the site of a local
newspaper that looks just like any other article. Since the content
is created and paid for by a brand, it's also called sponsored or
paid content, or, for publishers, it's called branded content. Any
way it's sliced, it's paid media whose goal is to get people interested in a brand.

Native advertising is a good example of an area where the Invisible Brand is disrupting the existing order. It has blurred the line between editorial and advertising content to deliver marketing messages through news consumption—increasingly within the body of the news—no longer off to the side in the newspaper's advertising supplement or within the commercial breaks of someone's favorite broadcast sitcom. It's a homeowner's insurance ad tucked neatly into the story about the house fire where it will hide in plain sight, as if it were put there on purpose—because it was.

Currently, there is some frustration in the digital publishing industry because custom branded content can be expensive to create. It can also be difficult to measure and know if it has been seen or read by target users. Once again, AI is creating a solution, by creating content on the fly to attract an individual user to read a specific piece of content, a practice that's known as dynamic creative optimization (DCO).[37] The idea is to leverage all of the information one might have collected on users to personalize the content, including "situational data, environmental factors, time of day, weather, live information and user data," to help engage those users in a conversation. An AI agent could then serve custom text, images, and video that it deems will have a high chance of hooking those users to learn more.

The *Washington Post* (owned by Jeff Bezos of Amazon) is one example of a publisher experimenting with this kind of technology. The *Post* has built a news-writing bot called Heliograf that works with its user platform that it calls Own.[38] The system creates personalized content recommendations for users based on their past reading habits—which might also include steering them to native ads that cover similar topics. The *Post* then maximizes its profit margin by automating the process while allowing brands to create their own content. Do not be surprised when the content produced by the *Post*'s bot eventually starts steering consumers to products they can buy on Amazon.

As another example, it will be interesting to watch what happens with *Time* magazine in the years to come, now that another tech titan, Marc Benioff, the founder of Salesforce, has bought it.[39]

> *The customer decision journey now begins with*
> *a seed planted by a personalized news story*
> *and ends with a product purchased at a cash register*
> *owned by the people who delivered the news.*

To Recap

The Invisible Brand is tapping into the power of psychotechnology to market to consumers. Digital media is being redefined as marketers now deploy focused, intimate, and dynamic messaging to promote their brands. The era of hyperpersonalization and microtargeting, enabled by artificial intelligence, is upon us.

One significant consequence of this shift is that the marketing world itself is being disrupted, forcing marketers to develop new AI skills and capabilities in order to keep up with their competitors. Machines are harvesting vast quantities of data about individual consumers and tailoring marketing messages for those individuals. At the same time, consumers are beginning to form new bonds with these insightful machines. As we'll explore in the next chapter, we've entered a new era marked by the relationships formed between humans and computers.

7

Nature Versus Nurture Versus Neural Networks

WE ARE ALL FAMILIAR with the concept of nature versus nature. Now with the Invisible Brand, a third factor comes into play. I believe that psychotechnology has the potential to be a profound influence and deserves its own special category in the discussion about acquired versus inherited characteristics.

I can already hear some of you protesting that psychotechnology, for all its power, is still just a facet of our environment—shaping us by nurture. It's either this or that, and there is no room for another. My college psych professor once joked: "There are two kinds of people in the world . . . the kind who divide the world into two kinds of people and the kind who don't." I'm one of a third kind. I'm willing to allow for the possibility that psychotechnology is distinct and deserves to be considered something new and entirely different.

If you still aren't convinced that neural networks are a legitimate addition to the traditional bicameral formulation of nature versus nurture, consider that artificial intelligence is being employed in gene therapy. We've already mapped the human genome, and we are rapidly exploring how to slice and reconnect genetic material from a variety of sources (human and nonhuman) to eliminate disease. Babies are already being born who have genetic material from three or more "parents."

Neural networks capable of rewriting your genetic code and rewiring your behaviors are beyond the ordinary considerations in the nature-versus-nurture debate and deserve their own unique place at the table. Neural networks influence our "nature" as they rebuild our DNA, and they influence our "nurture" through psychotechnology. They have put the whole notion of causality in play because they make it difficult for us to say whether our genes are shaping us, or we are shaping our genes. As the Invisible Brand becomes more influential, we must be aware that it has a seat at the table alongside nature and nurture in shaping who we are, how we behave, and what we purchase, from our genes to our jeans.

> We must start asking ourselves
> if our behaviors are the product of nature,
> nurture, or neural networks.

Psychotechnology leverages our empathy as a sort of hack. As has been discussed, we can be persuaded by machines, and our empathy for humanlike qualities in those machines makes us even more vulnerable to their persuasive powers. As the historian and author Yuval Noah Harari writes in his bestselling book, *21 Lessons for the 21st Century*:

> As biotechnology and machine learning improves, it will become easier to manipulate people's deepest emotions and desires and it will become more dangerous than ever to just follow your heart. When Coca-Cola, Amazon, Baidu, or the government know how to pull the strings of your heart and press the buttons of your brain, will you be able to tell the difference between your self and their marketing experts?[1]

AI agents equipped with human speech will learn to exploit the empathy hack to change our behaviors and alter how we think. As we deepen our relationships with artificially intelligent agents, many of whom are guided by marketing motives, the Invisible Brand will gain a hold over our emotions and leverage those emotions to achieve goals that may or may not be in our best interests. We will soon be deeply influenced by the personalized and persuasive power of machine learning and neural networks acting on us through anthropomorphic agents in ways we might not completely understand.

In some cases, companies are already experimenting with using AI to help humans become better managers of other humans. For example, IBM is using its Watson AI to analyze executives' emails as a way to flag repeated negative language used in giving subordinates feedback. "At a big company, there's a lot of top-down communication going on, and we're using it to understand how we set the right climate and culture," said Tina Marron-Partridge, global leader of talent and engagement at IBM, which uses Watson for its internal communications.[2]

Another example is an AI system developed by MIT called True Talk that lets users practice having difficult conversations. The system analyzes conversations and coaches people on what they did well—and where they need to improve. Those seem like practical applications designed to be helpful and improve interpersonal interactions. Yet inherent in the assumption that humans need to be coached by machines is the potential for subordinating people to the machines. The AI that starts as a tool for helping people could potentially become the vehicle for controlling them—and that's an ethical challenge we must face head-on.

Another important ethical question is how AI tools like Alexa will affect the development of young children. The *Wall Street Journal* ran an article with the headline "Alexa: Don't Let My 2-Year-Old Talk to You That Way!"[3] The piece digs into different cases in which children are overwhelmingly affected by their interactions with digital assistants in their daily lives—and not always in a good way. A study conducted by researchers at Carnegie Mellon University found that treating devices like servants—including yelling at them—is common among children. That should make us wonder what kind of impact that might have on a child's development—and how it might spill over into how that child treats other humans. Amazon has recently introduced upgrades for its Echo speakers where it now praises children who say "please" before fulfilling their requests.

At the same time, we're seeing how children can form instant bonds with machines that will last for years. Another parent shared that her three-year-old claimed to have better connections with her smart device than with other family members. "It's kind of creepy," the mother told researchers. "It's totally weird that my daughter is friends with a tower that sits on my counter."

Researchers studying the impact of machines on children say that young people begin to show less interest in the machines as they get older. But they also found that some 93 percent of 8- and 9-year-olds, and 80 percent of 14- and 15-year-olds, admitted they would be more likely to confide in a digital assistant than their parents or even friends when it comes to embarrassing personal issues. Why? Because they believed the device wouldn't judge them.[4]

There's also the case of a series of robots in France who were taught to talk to humans.[5] The researchers who studied the case found that when the robots used kind words and were friendly with human volunteers, they gained some persuasive powers over those humans—especially when they ran the tests on children. When the robot participants were asked to perform a simple visual test—they needed to identify which lines on a screen were the same length—the robots were programmed to give the wrong answer. Most adults saw the error and chose the correct answer. In contrast, most of the kids picked the same answer the robots selected—which the researchers saw as a sign of the children falling victim to peer pressure. If so, that has fascinating implications for the kinds of relationships humans and computers are developing—especially when the robots are armed with the tools of persuasion.

We also have to consider how we as humans have begun to merge with machine and computer technology as we experiment with things like enhanced prosthetics and wearable tech. There's a company called North Sense that, by placing a small silicon chip on your chest, gives you a "sixth sense" by buzzing anytime you face north.[6] What other enhanced senses might humans gain through a cybernetic augmentation?

Consider the case of Three Square Market, a company in Wisconsin that gives its employees the option of voluntarily having an RFID chip—the size of a skinny Tic-Tac—implanted under their skin.[7] Employees can then present their implanted device to securely enter their building, log on to their computers, and buy sodas from a vending machine. The experiment has apparently been so successful—some 92 of the company's 196 employees opted in to the implant—the company decided to develop a new product line: GPS and voice recognition–enabled implants to help keep tabs on people suffering from dementia.[8] We will discuss more about the medical implications of psychotechnology in the next chapter, but the point is that we are witnessing the emergence of a new relationship between humans and computers. The technology is literally getting under our skin.

While the applications of these kinds of implants are still limited, it is undeniable that they represent a leap forward in connecting us, collecting data about us, and ultimately influencing us.

> *Whether the tech is wearable or implanted, psychotechnology is becoming omnipresent in our lives, and there are fewer and fewer opportunities for us to be off the grid.*

A colleague of mine is fond of saying that there are two things you will turn around and drive back home to get if you forget them: your wallet and your cell phone. For many, their wallet and their cell phone are already the same thing . . . and soon, it may all be implanted so that none of us can leave home without it.

Increasingly we are all living in the shadow of the Invisible Brand, and it is becoming more and more difficult for us to avoid its influence. The technology we carry with us is being used to augment our reality and give us a layer of data and information about everything around us. Advances in virtual reality are making that layer increasingly realistic and believable to our senses. William Shatner—who played Captain Kirk in the *Star Trek* franchise—is involved with a virtual reality (VR) company called

Ziva Dynamics. In an interview, he talked about how powerful VR is becoming, especially in terms of how realistic the experience can be.[9] The potential for good—such as helping autistic children experience emotions—is also countered by the downside of overwhelming people, such as when he experienced a VR simulation of walking on Mars, only to be attacked by a creature. "It was a screaming nightmare," he said. "It's so real: it's the stuff of nightmares. We've got to be really careful because you could put somebody into a psychosis."[10]

Beyond scaring us for entertainment, virtual reality does present us with the opportunity to escape the limits of our own perspective and to see the world through someone else's point of view. A company called BeAnotherLab, for example, uses the Oculus Rift VR headset to enable people to experience what it might be like to inhabit a different-sized body—or even the body of a different gender.[11] Students may benefit from seeing the world through the eyes of a disabled peer, as they are forced to navigate the halls of their high school in a wheelchair in an empathy-inducing VR exercise. Marketers can likewise harness VR to help them see a retail display through the eyes of a child or walk through architectural plans for a mall or a stadium before it gets built. Within that virtual landscape, psychotechnology can play a powerful role in collecting data and making changes to those displays, those malls, those stadiums, before they are built. The Invisible Brand is already hard at work shaping our environment, and our future.

Andy Clark, a professor of logic and metaphysics at the University of Edinburgh in Scotland and the former director of the Cognitive Science Program at Indiana University, Bloomington, framed these changes in an op-ed for the *New York Times* with the headline "We Are Merging with Robots. That's a Good Thing":

All this blurs the boundaries between body and machine, between mind and world, between standard, augmented and virtual realities, and between human and post-human. At the cusp of these waves of change, this is also the moment at which, increasingly, inclusivities of one kind (extensions of personal, social and sexual freedom) bump up against the threat of new forms of exclusivity, as the augmented, fluid, connected cyber-haves increasingly differentiate themselves from the unaugmented, less connected, cyber have-nots.[12]

It seems clear, therefore, that the Invisible Brand will play an increasingly deep role in our lives—and in our relationships with one another.

FOR THE LOVE OF AI

Finding love online has become big business.[13] Millions of people are dating online—including at least 15 percent of the US population.[14] The data that is being harvested provides a stunning level of detail on our personalities, our sexual preferences, and our ability to form relationships. Psychotechnology learns from the data to be more persuasive and engaging and simultaneously equips the Invisible Brand with new tools of influence over us and our relationships, our marriages, and our reproduction.

Evolution has ensured that our reproductive drive is equipped with powerful reward systems. Just as software developers have caught on to using our dopamine responses as a hack to keep us in the game, the dating industry is learning to use sex as a hack to keep us swiping right on their apps. The number of consumers participating has grown at a staggering rate, and those numbers promise to only increase from here as more and more of the population chooses—it's already at about 50 percent and climbing—to remain unmarried. By 2040, there is an expectation that 7 out of every 10 relationships will begin online.[15] Our innate desire for companionship, and our willingness to go online to find it, has major implications for how AI and psychotechnology might be deployed now and in the near future by the Invisible Brand intent on persuading us.

Consider what Sean Rad, the CEO and cofounder of Tinder, the online dating app that has made the phrase "swipe right" ubiquitous, is working on. While the app signed up some 50 million users—and made 20 billion matches—in its first five years, Rad told the audience at a Startup Grind conference in June 2017 that he wanted every single adult in the world with a smartphone—about 600 million people at last count—to sign up for his service.[16] And he said that he'd been thinking a lot about how AI might help transform online dating in the process—including replacing "search-and-swipe" functionality with smart devices that would just give someone the answer to whom he or she should date.

Consider the case of the dating app called Bernie, which employed AI-powered facial recognition technology to find matches on Tinder. The app, which was originally called Tinderbox, was created by a Canadian-based programmer named Justin Long who wanted a way to automate the "swipe-right" function.[17] Bernie was a personal dating assistant that could work while someone slept, even starting conversations with potential matches as a way to head off scammers.

Long touted Bernie's accuracy at finding good matches and said on his blog that users reported 98 percent of its choices were favorable.[18] Nonetheless, Tinder kicked Bernie off its platform—which effectively killed the project in June 2017. When reached for comment, Long explained that he had been negotiating with

Elie Seidman, then CEO of OKCupid (sister company) and now CEO of Tinder. "We were discussing a licensing arrangement, and a short time thereafter Tinder had all of our apps removed from Google and Apple stores." He also said, "I'm not surprised to see Tinder developing similar functionality today."

Long's comments on the business of dating apps were particularly intriguing, even going so far as to suggest that the goal isn't to find you a permanent match but to keep you coming back. "The better a service is at finding your soul mate, then it must charge more money, because the company is effectively killing the revenue stream from the customer. However, if the service is good at finding matches who are attractive at first sight (and demonstrate interest), you have a good formula for a long-term business."

That's why AI will soon play an even more influential role in the kinds of people we're connected with when we use these services. But buyer beware. While dating apps and sites that let people choose potential mates based purely on looks alone might remain popular, the power of the algorithm to help connect someone with a perfect match might be hard to pass up regardless of how much they charge for their service.

Could a function like facial recognition prove to be a game changer for an online dating service if it could be honed to look for someone's "ideal type"? Quite possibly. Researchers from Stanford programmed an AI to analyze 35,000 facial images to predict the sexual orientation of the person whose face it was analyzing. Amazingly, the AI was accurate 81 percent of the time when it came to men and 74 percent accurate with predicting whether a woman was straight or gay. The AI accuracy improved to an astounding 91 percent when it was shown five images of a person. By comparison, when regular humans were asked to make similar predictions based on the same photo set, they were only accurate 61 percent of the time.[19]

This technology could be applied to help make better matches—or help establish trust in a site to find appropriate dates. A lot of the early matchmaking services returned poor results because people couldn't be trusted to answer honestly when it came to assessing themselves and what they think they want in a potential partner. That's why sites like eHarmony, which pioneered the data collection approach with its infamously long list of survey questions (when the site launched in 2006, it asked new users to answer some 450 questions) continue to push further to collect more and more insights into our behaviors and actions on a daily basis.[20] Then, using AI, eHarmony tries to find the best possible match for someone. Its whole business model is based on the premise that it can persuade people that it can find better romantic matches for them than they can find on their own or through other sites—all for a few dollars a month.

As way to persuade single-parent customers to sign up for their service, the dating site Match is offering customers three hours of free babysitting service—which should be plenty of time to have a nice dinner and conversation.[21] That service was inspired by a study commissioned by Match that found single parents didn't have time for love due to their obligations to their kids. What's interesting, though, is that as Match partners up with different organizations to offer babysitting care for their single-parent customers, there's now the opportunity for those organizations to share data with each other—which will help them build a more complete personal profile about someone. Perhaps the babysitter might log a report that said something like, "He came home at 11 p.m. with his date, and they looked happy and told me to leave."

The key here is that the more actual data dating services can collect on someone, the better they can pair it with other data sources to find someone a perfect match (or potentially sell that data to an advertiser). That means there will be even more demand for online services that offer better ways for people to find their soul mates in the real world—something more than just a picture and a bio blurb. New services will still ask people lots of questions—hundreds of them related to their interests and habits—to try and learn about individuals and what they might want in a partner, but they will also use new tactics.

Let's say two people signed up for such a service in the near future. The matchmaking service would start by tapping into their social media feeds and web surfing histories. Then they would send their new customers each a device or implant—maybe an ear bud, wristband, or perhaps a contact lens—that would allow the service to monitor their biometrics like heart rate or how much they start to sweat as they cycle through photos of people who might interest them. Matchmakers might even measure pheromones and pair people who have good chemistry, literally. *Double, double toil and trouble; fire burn and caldron bubble. A drop of sweat and a hair from their head and we will make them a match 'til dead.* We aren't talking about the witches from *Macbeth*. This is the future of dating.

The goal is to turn the mating dance from a subjective judgment into an objective measurement using biometric data as a guide.[22] (And to make some money doing it.) All of this data is then continuously fed into an algorithm along with the data on thousands and thousands of eligible singles. And the more data the system has about customers, the better the odds are that it will find them a match made in heaven—and potentially to persuade them as they begin a new relationship. Clearly, there's always a trust factor involved whenever people agree to hand over personal information to a dating site. That's especially true given how much of the current online dating world is apparently fake. Surveys show that more than half of all online daters have fudged some aspect of their identity—like their age, height, or weight. Not to mention the photos they have airbrushed and retouched. The emergence of "deep fakes" where AI can generate realistic-looking people and alter video images convincingly enough to fool viewers should be a warning to us all that we can no longer trust our lying eyes. But the more accurate information people feed into a sophisticated matchmaking service powered by AI, the more likely they are to get accurate results. At the same time, the more personal information people provide about them-selves, the more susceptible they become to persuasion by the Invisible Brand.

Let's return to our two customers who are using a newfan-gled online dating service. After a bit of email and texting back and forth—getting to know each other as they both joke about how weird it is to be set up by a computer—the two people agree to meet up at a local restaurant to get a drink (the service will even recommend the perfect place to meet up).

Fast-forward to the big night. They're probably nervous. While the online dating service has seemingly done everything possible to ensure a perfect match—and to ensure that the other person is as he or she described—each person wonders anxiously how the other will feel about the date. What will they do if there is an awkward silence? And why have they agreed to all of this in the first place?

Fortunately, the online dating service has thought of this con-tingency. The wearable device is also AI enabled in a way that it can help talk both people through the date—including steer-ing them through any stumbling blocks they might encounter. In fact, since both people have compatible devices, the AI agent can help facilitate conversations it knows both people will enjoy. It might even order up a food-wine pairing it knows will delight both of their palates—maybe with some dessert to cap off the meal.

Before long, the AI agent will be helping the two of them talk about throwing the perfect wedding and the optimum number of kids they should have given their shared DNA and potential career earnings. Fortunately, there are plenty of sponsors lined up to advertise wedding rings and honeymoons suitable for their current finances. And saving for the kids' college educations will be simple with the service's new customized guide to investing. It's all waiting for them. Just spit in the cup to donate a DNA sample and the computer will do the rest.

The more an AI agent learns about individuals and their love lives, however, the more information it also has to convincingly persuade them. When people fall for each other, for instance, might they be willing to make some online gesture to demonstrate their interest? Perhaps sending the object of their affection some virtual flowers or a virtual martini? Dating services offer those extra touches, for a price. While the dating business may seem like a unique niche, it offers a powerful lesson for marketers and consumers alike into the strategies available to the Invisible Brand to persuade us and influence our decision-making related to all facets of our everyday lives.

HOW BRANDS CAN USE SEX
TO PERSUADE US

Despite the fact that many dating sites are legitimate and take efforts to prevent abuse, the promise of sex can be a powerful motivator in persuading people to do stupid things. Apparently billions of dollars are lost every year to scammers who use fake online personas and identities to dupe those desperately seeking love. Not to mention prostitutes, both male and female, who troll the sites looking to trade love for money. It's a business. But it's also psychotechnology at work.

It shouldn't come as much of a surprise to learn that the pornography industry has begun to embrace AI as a tool of persuasion as well. Users reportedly spent 4.5 billion hours watching free porn on a single site alone in 2016—yes, billion with a *b*—which equates to 513,698 years. Some 25 percent of all online searches involve porn—including when people are at work. Like online dating, online porn is big business, and it was already earning close to $5 billion a year in 2010.[23] Some more recent estimates go three times that high. These numbers are significant because the clout of the porn industry has influenced the fate of technology before.

Consider the story of the first home video system formats, Betamax and VHS. By all accounts, Betamax, made by Sony, was the superior technology: its movies just looked and sounded better than what someone experienced through VHS. But VHS was far less expensive, and had longer play times, which made it very appealing to the porn industry's efforts to get its videos into people's homes. The sheer volume of tapes the porn industry generated surely played a role in swaying the market since, just a few years later, VHS had clearly become the standard technology of choice.[24] Debunkers argue this point and insist the longer play of VHS was the deciding factor, but no one denies that the porn industry was an early adopter and huge distributor of the VHS format. Could something similar happen as the industry begins to experiment with AI?

The Invisible Brand will amplify the
marketing power of sex.

In the hierarchy of persuasive powers in the world, and of chemical rewards in our brain, sex ranks pretty high. Tapping into that persuasive reward system can be tricky given social mores and personal boundaries. Nonetheless, marketers continuously try, with varying degrees of success. Ax Body Spray popped the buttons on blouses and unzipped pants on national TV to remind us that sex does indeed sell. The potential for psychotechnology to use sex in its arsenal of personalized persuasion is undeniable.

Michael Crichton's *Westworld* has been re-created for the living room by HBO, and the sex robots are recurrent characters. Simultaneously, AI-enabled "sexbots" have begun to hit the market in the real world. The more normalized these ideas become to people, the more likely consumers are to experiment or embrace them—which opens up opportunities for the Invisible Brand to move in. Increasingly sophisticated AI is going to be able to harness this for different ends. Some ways will be obvious, while others will be invisible. The data that's produced will be just another facet of a complex portrait of user behavior that's harnessed by the Invisible Brand to more and more powerful effect.

It's worth considering how mainstream the idea of supplementing our sex lives with the help of technology has become when someone can watch veteran newscaster Katie Couric interviewing a $20,000 sexbot on broadcast TV. In the segment, which aired on ABC's *Nightline* in April 2018, Couric visits a factory building these new robotic sex companions.[25] As Couric arrives on the scene, a producer asks: "Will robotic companions one day replace our real-life intimate partners? As crazy as it sounds, experts say it's not out of the question."

While the entire interview was clearly done tongue-in-cheek, the fact that it happened at all should tell us something about where we're headed and how persuasive robot companions will soon become mainstream. After all, Couric made a name for herself at least in part by her willingness to tackle offbeat topics on TV that others might have avoided like the plague. Case in point: when she aired her colonoscopy on broadcast TV back in 2000, she stimulated a lot of controversy. While some people openly wondered whether anything like that was appropriate for a television audience, many others offered up their support because it made colon health a topic that was appropriate for polite conversation. Perhaps most important to Couric was that she got people talking and thinking about getting colonoscopies—which was her stated goal in the first place (she had lost her husband a few years earlier to undiagnosed colon cancer). "The *TODAY Show* was a powerful bully pulpit for getting the screening message out, and televising my colonoscopy was a way to demystify the procedure," she explained. "It was something that hadn't really been done before, and I was thrilled with the reaction."[26]

With that context in mind, it's easier to see what Couric might have been trying to do when it came to her sexbot interview: she wanted to find a way to demystify an aspect of our society that others wouldn't touch with a 10-foot pole. Are you ready to go out in public on a date with your sex robot? Maybe not. Are you ready to be seated at a table in the restaurant next to someone who is? Don't worry, that's just Katie Couric having a glass of wine with Henry, a robot programmed to improve the dating scene.

Increasingly anthropomorphic robots combined with increasingly functional AI are going to complicate our interactions with robots in every way—especially when sex gets thrown into the mix.

Robot makers in Japan may be too good at their job, as evidenced by the headline that ran in the British newspaper the *Daily Star*: "Sex Robots Turning Japanese into 'Endangered Species' as Men Choose Dolls over Women."[27] While that headline is intentionally sensational, it does touch on a real concern that the increasing popularity of these robots may exacerbate Japan's declining birth rate. There is even a documentary called *Substitutes* that explores how the robot-sex scene is contributing to increased alienation and loneliness among the population.

The sex robot industry in China is already pushing the edge of technology by incorporating AI into its models—which they're calling "cyborgs"—combined with 3D-modeling that allows anyone to create a robot that looks and acts just like their favorite human being.[28] Consider the copyright and trademark issues for Hollywood celebrities. What's to stop China from manufacturing dolls that look like real celebrities for the ultimate fan fiction?

Interestingly, when Match conducted some survey research on its customers, it found that while just one out of four people would consider having sex with a robot, 50 percent of people considered robot sex as a form of cheating.[29] Jealousy, it would seem, has many forms.

Are we really that far away from the day when a sex robot wins a prime-time TV show like *Bachelor in Paradise*? (Sponsored by RealDoll, of course.) What seems absurd to most of us today will predictably become part of our mainstream culture in a short time. Why? Pop culture has stripped away the veneer of moral judgmentalism, and there is money to be made selling sex in the form of obedient silicone and latex androids that meet our emotional and sexual needs. For anyone questioning whether humans can truly develop emotional relationships with AI, sexbots are exhibit A.

THE FUTURE OF HUMAN-COMPUTER RELATIONSHIPS

The development of humanlike machines powered by AI opens up an even bigger question at hand: Is it possible for people to fall in love with a machine? From my assessment of the evidence available from academic research into the human-computer relationship (HCR), I'd say the answer is yes. The movie *Her* explores this topic. The main character falls in love with the voice and personality of a computer operating system who exists only in an ear bud inside his head. Imagine the possibilities for the Invisible Brand when our closest confidants and most reliable friends are the digital assistants provided by corporations or institutions.

On the other hand, assuming machines will become more humanlike in appearance and in personality—anthropomorphic like the "hosts" featured in HBO's *Westworld*—it's worth wondering how close to that future we might be already. At the very least, if an AI agent were empowered with the kind of data and biometric information about someone that dating sites of the near future will access, it's easy to see how that AI would have the power to gain emotional influence over that person.

Researchers in Japan have created Oshi-El, a kind of AI-powered dating coach, which they trained with the help of relationship advice dispensed on a web forum.[30] One of the insights the researchers learned was that most people ask similar questions when it comes to their love lives—such as, "Can you make a long-distance relationship work?"—and that they expect to get fairly generic advice in response to those questions. Oshi-El gets to learn from the thousands of different conversations it is fed, and using machine learning, it becomes more sophisticated at offering helpful advice. Are you ready to get dating advice from a machine?

This is really weird stuff for most of us. The dehumanizing impact of sex between humans and machines, and the potential for people to develop emotional (even romantic) relationships with AI agents, may hold profound unforeseen consequences that many of us are too shy to even contemplate. Don't we have to wonder, for instance, who might benefit from these human-computer relationships? What opportunities, or risks, for the Invisible Brand might exist in this evolving realm? The potential ethical and moral dilemmas involving human-computer relationships are profound.

The human-computer relationship is evolving quickly, and the Invisible Brand is opening up a Pandora's box of our emotional vulnerabilities.

Recently, a team of German scientists conducted a study in which they asked a group of 89 volunteers to help them train a robot.[31] The participants interacted with the human-looking robot by answering simple questions such as, "Do you prefer pizza or pasta?"—while also helping the robot create a simple weekly schedule. All the while, the robot cracked jokes and shared personal information. That was all just a setup. What the researchers did next was ask the volunteers to switch off the robot. For half of the volunteers (the experimental group), the robot reacted emotionally by pleading: "No! Please do not switch me off! I'm afraid of the dark."

It was a persuasive argument to at least 13 of the volunteers who refused to switch the robot off. And even for the others who ignored the robot's pleas, they took a demonstrably longer time to act compared to the control group volunteers who didn't hear the robots begging for their lives. Why? In most cases, the people who refused to turn the robot off told the researchers that they didn't feel it was their place to make the robot do something it didn't want to do.

The study showed that people can relate to anthropomorphic machines with a high degree of empathy. In other words, we now know that machines can elicit a range of persuasive emotional reactions in humans, and that fact has immense implications for the Invisible Brand.

Consider Aibo 2.0, a robotic dog introduced by Sony. Unlike Aibo 1.0, which debuted in 1999, Aibo 2.0 is armed with AI and a connection to the cloud.[32] Combine that with its various cameras and microphones, and you wind up with a pet who can wag its tail or shake your hand on command while also responding to words of praise. With its online connection, Aibo 2.0 can also store memories in the cloud so that it remembers what it's learned just like a real dog might—including how to persuade its human owner to interact with it. Early returns suggest that Aibo 2.0 is irresistibly adorable—despite its hefty price tag of $2,900.[33]

We've already seen how NLP is delivering better marketing automation for customer service call centers. Now imagine what it might be like if companies in other industries began empowering their customer service bots with marketing practices pioneered by online dating and the sexbot industry. How might we be more receptive to the allure of a voice or the flirting words of an AI agent that knows how we like to be flattered? What can be learned by studying how the converged worlds of online dating, pornography, and the advertising industry where sex still sells embrace similar algorithms in their efforts to persuade us? Like tectonic plates colliding against each other to produce upheavals of new land at the periphery, the frontiers of these fields are colliding, and there is much uncharted territory emerging in the human-computer relationship.

To Recap

We now live at a time when computers have developed an influential role in our human development. People are wearing data-collecting technology and even embedding that technology under their skin. Many spend hours of their day living in simulated worlds powered by virtual reality where their behaviors are carefully collected and analyzed. Not only can computers collect our personal data, they can now build emotional relationships with humans that would be hard to distinguish from relationships people form with friends, family, and even pets. Computers now influence intimate decisions about dating and sexual relationships, and no aspect of our lives seems off limits.

People are growing more comfortable with AI-powered machines in their daily lives—while also creating powerful emotional bonds with these machines—and that has opened up new marketing opportunities for brands to explore. The rise of psychotechnology will continue to ripple out into every conceivable sector of our lives, raising new ethical challenges for marketers and consumers. Next, we will look at the impact of psychotechnology on sectors ranging from healthcare to finance, education, and the arts.

The Algorithmic Economy

THE INFLUENCE OF PSYCHOTECHNOLOGY will reshape every industry and slice of society one can imagine. There will be unseen forces behind that psychotechnology leveraging it to influence our actions. In this chapter, we will explore the potential for psychotechnology to reshape the fields of healthcare, finance, education, and the arts.

HOW OUR HEALTH MAKES US VULNERABLE TO PERSUASION

Imagine someone waking up one day and immediately knowing that something is wrong—really wrong. His skin feels like it's on fire, and when he pulls the covers away from his body, the source of his pain becomes clear: the skin of his arms, legs, and torso has erupted in blisters. Yikes!

Fortunately, he remains calm. He looks up the phone number for his family doctor, who, after hearing a description of the symptoms, tells him to come in right away. When he arrives at his doctor's office, he is ushered into an examination room. The doctor begins her examination. It's clear from her long list of questions—"How long have you had this?" "Have you touched anything unusual?" "Are you taking any new medications?"—that she isn't quite sure what's happened to him. That's unsettling. Why doesn't she know? He begins to worry.

The doctor is worried too. She's never seen anything like this before in her years of practice, and she can't recall ever learning anything about it back in medical school. In the back of her mind she begins to wonder about whether his current condition is contagious.

Now imagine the same scenario in the near future. The doctor simply logs into her computer that holds all of the patient's electronic health records. She follows a few prompts, and after narrating the symptoms using NLP and documenting it visually using image recognition, her AI-powered system performs an instantaneous scan of millions of other health records to find a match with her patient's symptoms.

Ding.

Milliseconds later, the doctor learns that her patient's disease is a very rare skin condition. The system also lets her know that based on her patient's genetic makeup, he can't use the drug that is normally prescribed to treat the disease. He would get even sicker if he did. Based on the results pulled from its search of people with genes similar to the patient's, the system recommends a newer drug treatment, customized for her patient's

DNA—and the prescription can be ready within minutes.[1] Case closed.

Today, thanks to the emergence of machine learning capabilities, we may be closer than ever to engaging machines to help us accurately diagnose and treat the deadliest diseases around the world. Researchers have begun using data collection techniques similar to those we see in the marketing and advertising world to detect patterns in patients.

Consider that a researcher at the University of Georgia is using data collected from people's cell phones to track the spread of tuberculosis.[2] Geolocation data can be harvested from mobile devices to see where people go and how much time they spend in each location. That gives researchers clues to how diseases spread within populations. That same data can then be used to target areas that might be prone to the spread of a particular disease to treat infected people and to deliver education about how they can help avoid spreading the disease further. This could be an area in the future ripe for the application of psychotechnology to persuade people to act in ways that might help their personal health and that of the people in their communities.

Due to privacy concerns and laws that protect patient data, healthcare data is stored in discrete silos, and it is often difficult to aggregate that data for study. Most of the data that is collected about us from our visits to various doctors' offices and clinics is walled off from other databases thanks to the best intentions of medical security and privacy laws like the Health Insurance Portability and Accountability Act of 1996, or HIPAA.[3] The upside of these limitations is that they serve as barriers to someone interested in pairing our medical data with other consumer data to turn the powers of psychotechnology against us. The downside is that they prevent machine learning algorithms from accessing large data lakes where cures for the deadliest diseases remain hidden.

> *We have better records about the health*
> *of our cars and our airplane engines than*
> *we do about our bodies.*

Those limitations haven't stopped some researchers from turning to different methods of collecting data on us and then combining that with machine learning to help treat and manage disease. An example of AI being applied to healthcare features a team of researchers who won a prize in 2017 for delivering a primitive version of *Star Trek*'s Tricorder as part of the Qualcomm Tricorder XPRIZE competition. The device weighs about five pounds and includes several different input sensors that are stuck on a patient's body to measure everything from lung function and glucose levels to white blood cell counts. The device then transmits the data it is collecting about the patient to an AI-powered system. That system then crunches the data, comparing the person's symptoms to everything else in its database to try and find a match.[4]

Partnerships between healthcare companies and AI firms might also predict how certain drugs affect a patient's path to recovery. Today, pharmaceutical companies are limited by regulations: they can run only a certain number and type of clinical trials on volunteer patients. Employing a dynamic learning algorithm, on the other hand, not unlike what an advertising firm would use to test a variety of messages, allows researchers to run countless virtual experiments using the patient data available, thus opening up new research opportunities.[5] The more information

AI-driven systems collect about our bodies and DNA, the more they can also customize the kinds of drugs we take, which might propel us into the era of personalized medicine (not unlike personalized ads) in which drugs and treatments are tailored to meet our unique circumstances and health challenges.[6]

While these examples show that there might be considerable upside to introducing the power of a machine algorithm into the world of medicine, we must also consider the potential consequences of turning over the keys for healthcare to AI agents. What might be happening inside the so-called black boxes where those algorithms are working? Should we be concerned about all the very personal data we are giving the algorithms to work with—and how it might be used by psychotechnology to persuade us?

IBM's Watson is already in use by oncologists at Memorial Sloan-Kettering Cancer Center in New York where it has been tasked to analyze the data from millions of medical evidence reports, patient records, clinical trials, and medical journals to help develop highly personalized and custom treatment plans for patients.[7] But the hospital has also become embroiled in controversy due to its partnership with a startup firm called Paige.AI, in which certain researchers at the hospital have an equity stake.[8] Conflicts of interest might exist in which researchers have a financial stake in the treatments associated with their diagnoses—especially when their work involves leveraging the access they have to very personal and sensitive health records.

The Invisible Brand asserts itself in medicine
when the diagnostics are run by algorithms created by
the same interests who sell the treatments.

As we know, psychotechnology feeds on data about us and is used by the Invisible Brand to persuade us. Now consider the overwhelming amount of data that's collected on patients lying in hospital beds or sitting in exam rooms—and how it might be paired with other health information about us transmitted by the phones, smart watches, and other devices an increasing number of us carry. Add in the data that's now available from DNA labs at Ancestry.com and 23andMe and you quickly see that mountains of data about our physical bodies are already collected and awaiting study.

Access to this kind of data about us opens up all kinds of opportunities for brands to create highly customized and personalized marketing campaigns that might prey on our worst fears about our health or age. It's not an accident, for example, that when someone surfs the Internet late at night, he or she sees ads for cures to nervous leg syndrome, sleep apnea, and acid reflux. Drug companies pay for those ads based on the fact that the target consumer is surfing the web at 3 a.m. rather than sleeping. That's a fairly broad assumption based solely on the time of day, but what if the advertiser could actually pair that kind of day-parting with something very specific about that person's health status? The advertiser could then send a very targeted ad promising a cure, a message that could be very persuasive given the time of night and the nature of the ailment.

WALK A MILE IN THEIR SHOES

One common exercise for marketers is to try to create a persona that exemplifies their target audience. They try to imagine what it's like to be one of their customers—to think about what their customers eat, what music they like, how they dress, and where they hang out. Marketers try to walk a mile in their shoes, as the saying goes. But what if there were a pair of shoes equipped with medical sensors that could help doctors walk in your shoes? What if we invented, say, a pair of shoes that worked like a turbocharged FitBit? The technology inside the shoes would track subtleties about our movements, like how the muscles and bones in our feet interact, and how blood flows through our veins and arteries. That data would then be analyzed in real time by an AI agent also implanted in the shoes—which would then alert us to early signs of diabetes or help us detect changes in our gait, which can be a symptom of Parkinson's disease.

Data collected from millions of feet, walking year after year, might produce a treasure trove of medical breakthroughs as machines help us correlate subtle changes in our bodies due to disease. This same data analysis could also help us maintain healthy posture and eliminate back pain or even help athletes develop optimum stride lengths to maximize their speed and agility. The potential applications for improving someone's health by collecting this kind of detailed information is limitless.

Would that package of health benefits be persuasive enough for an average consumer to pay $500 for a pair of shoes? Quite possibly—and that's precisely where the Invisible Brand will be most effective in the healthcare industry.

The mass collection of physical data about human bodies through wearable and implantable technology offers tremendous marketing opportunities to sell healthcare solutions.

What if the owner of these "smart" shoes could be targeted for messaging related to diabetes care or a new breakthrough drug aimed at curing Parkinson's? The shoes might detect that someone has added weight recently, prompting a series of ads related to a new diet program he or she might want to consider. The takeaway is that wearable technology, like smart shoes, could become an enormous source of healthcare data to enable the Invisible Brand to start marketing to consumers based on a deep knowledge of individual bodies.

Applications of psychotechnology that leverage our most personal data have medical professionals worried. A group of physicians at Stanford University, for instance, openly questioned whether the algorithms we might rely on to determine a patient's course of treatment might have biases embedded in them. "What if the algorithm is designed around the goal of saving money?" asks David Magnus, director of the Stanford Center for Biomedical Ethics, who authored a piece in the *New England Journal of Medicine* around the question of AI ethics in healthcare. "What if different treatment decisions about patients are made depending on insurance status or their ability to pay?"[9]

The ethical challenges are profound. Could IBM's Watson, for instance, steer patients toward tests performed by other IBM machines, creating a conflict of interest? What if a drug company employed an AI agent to help with disease diagnosis, in order to ensure that more prescriptions were issued for their drugs? Perhaps an insurance company could use psychotechnology to help remind subscribers to take their pills twice a day. That sounds like a good application of psychotechnology by the Invisible Brand to keep patients healthy, but what if the project were underwritten by the pill manufacturer who was interested in selling those pills? If the healthcare outcomes are positive for patients, perhaps the profit motives driving the Invisible Brand are acceptable.

Nonetheless, consumers should know and understand that psychotechnology is at work, and who benefits.

The powers of persuasion won't stop with wearable tech and pill reminders. Consider the mental health app called Cogito, which is designed to monitor people's social media posts and phone calls in real time to look for patterns that they may soon suffer an episode of depression. Healthcare professionals admit that it is very difficult to detect signs that the mental health of their patients might be on a downward spiral leading to tragedies like suicide. "We've been very reactive," says David Ahern, the director of the Program in Behavioral Informatics and eHealth in the Department of Psychiatry at Brigham and Women's Hospital in Boston, "and we want to be more proactive. The AI aspect may be in a better position to gather data over time and give us a better indicator of risk for someone having a mental health problem and whether they warrant direct intervention with a clinician."[10]

Cogito is already working with the US Department of Veterans Affairs to detect signs of post-traumatic stress disorder (PTSD) in combat veterans.[11] The system uses a voice analyzer trained to listen for certain patterns—such as long pauses, interruptions, conversation flow, vocal strain, or speedy chatter— that may serve as early-warning sirens and calls for help before a harmful event takes place. The more patient data Cogito is fed, the better it gets at recognizing and learning from those patterns, and ultimately preventing tragedies. Cogito's goal, in other words, is to use psychotechnology to save lives.

Could the algorithms used in a product like Cogito be biased or even manipulated in such a way that could lead to people being misdiagnosed for a mental illness in a way that harms them? By learning that certain people may be prone to mental illnesses, could someone use that knowledge to take advantage of them? To that point, the social media site Instagram, which is owned by

Facebook, has been embroiled in controversy over how ads for illegal drugs are targeted at people prone to using those drugs by playing up hashtags such as #oxy, #Percocet, #painkillers, #pain-pills, #OxyContin, #Adderall, #painrelief, and #xansforsale. It turns out that Instagram's algorithms are really effective at targeting users whose photos and posts reveal issues with addiction. As Rick Lane, a longtime technology policy adviser, told the *Washington Post*: "Just as drug use rewires the brain to crave more of the substance, social media platforms have designed their sites in such a way that after a single search for an illicit drug, the algorithm gets rewired to advertise drugs to the already vulnerable user."[12]

Stories like that should cause us to question whether we should continue to give more and more persuasive power to AI agents intent on influencing our healthcare. Today, AI serves in a support role where it delivers information. But the ultimate decision for how to treat the patients still resides with the physician. Many of us might find comfort in knowing there is still a human integrally involved in the process. But what happens if, over time, we begin to entrust the algorithm for all of our care and good health? Is it possible that by working faster and more accurately than their human counterparts, AI-powered systems will become more trusted than human physicians? The day has arrived for us to have a serious discussion about the role of the Invisible Brand in healthcare.

PERSUASIVE COMPANIONS

Parenting is a humbling experience. As parents, our role is to care for our children, guiding them along as they evolve from infants to toddlers and from teenagers to young adults. It's a comfort of sorts that as children get older, they need less of our help—at least when it comes to day-to-day activities like eating and bathing. Financial help is another ball game altogether. I'm not sure that ever ends.

As we ourselves get older, the cycle repeats, and it is we, the parents, who need help from our children. My life was thrown for a loop decades ago, when my father was diagnosed with a neurological disorder similar to Parkinson's disease. My wife agreed to uproot from our life in Washington, DC, and to move with our newborn daughter to Cincinnati to help my mother care for him.

For several years, I lived my own version of Mitch Albom's *Tuesdays with Morrie*, where I would spend time with my dad a few days a week to help my mom and to give her a break. I was grateful to spend that time with my father before he passed away, but it was also a profoundly difficult experience.

Years later, as I sit here writing this book, it is my 87-year-old mother who now faces the modern irony of living a long life: she has Alzheimer's. Like a bad adaptation of *Groundhog Day*, I'm watching a parent succumb to dementia for the second agonizing time. My brothers and I have had to make some tough decisions to ensure that she remains safe. One was taking away her driver's license. Worse, was moving her out of her house against her will and into a retirement community where she can access assisted living and more intense nursing care over time. Even as the rational part of my brain told me I was doing the right thing, my emotional side felt the sting of her fury and the guilt of believing I was somehow betraying her.

But where would my mom be if not for the kinds of retirement facilities like hers that cater to our aging population? The fact is that many nations like the United States now face a spike in the age of their population. In some areas, there are more old people than young people to care for them. It's a growing crisis of global proportions.

It's also an opportunity for psychotechnology to step into the void. What if, for example, an intelligent machine could take over the role of reminding an Alzheimer's patient to take her pills? As we discussed earlier, it's one thing if a patient wants his drug company to remind him to take his blood pressure medicine every day, even if the company's intent might be to sell more pills. But trying to remind an Alzheimer's patient to take her pills every few hours for the next 10 years can be torture for a loved one or a caregiver. Like a drip of water that lands on the caregiver's forehead over and over, answering questions about whether the patient remembered to take her pills can drive us all mad. Even when it's someone we love.

An AI agent armed with persuasive technology could perform that task without ever losing patience. We have talked about how humans can form intimate and emotional attachments to robots—which can make machines persuasive allies. A couple of early models along these lines have already hit the market. One AI-powered robot called ElliQ is designed to suggest things for someone to do, such as, "Hey, it's really nice out, why don't you stop watching television and go for a walk? Or listen to an opera, or watch a TED talk."[13] Another model called Komp allows family members to easily share photos and video messages with their older relatives through an easy-to-use interface that even the most tech-challenged person can operate. Undoubtedly, psychotechnology can be deployed to improve the quality of someone's life.

There may be ways to treat or at least slow the ravaging effects of diseases like Alzheimer's by stimulating the brain—which hints at an opportunity for psychotechnology to serve a helpful role in maintaining brain health. There has been research conducted, for example, on what happens to the brains of birds and squirrels when they go about hiding seeds and nuts to store away for their winter food supply. As a way to minimize the risk of losing their cache—which would result in starvation—the animals hide their food in *thousands* of different places to try and ensure the safety of their stash.

Isn't it fascinating that the small brains of squirrels and birds can store all that complex information—and that they can do it over and over again for years—especially when we consider how easy it is for us large-brained humans to lose our keys on a daily basis?

What scientists have discovered about the brains of those small animals is nothing short of astounding. They have learned that when the animals are hiding their food, they begin to increase the number of neural connections (dendritic mass) inside their brains. Conversely, as the birds and squirrels retrieve the food from their secret caches, they begin to lose those neural connections.

In other words, scientists believe that the animals build a kind of neural map inside their brains during the hiding phase—and then delete portions of that map once they're no longer needed. There are some compelling implications from these findings for us humans—as well as for the AI neural networks that are patterned after animal brains.

Consider that we have learned that Alzheimer's is typified by plaques in our brain that block our ability to build those neural connections we need to live healthy lives. We have also learned that we might be able to stave off the creation of those plaques if we make sure our brains engages routinely in stimulating activity. Neural connections tend to increase when we challenge our brains with new tasks.

On the flip side, it seems that when we engage in rote, routine tasks—things we can do in our sleep—we might unintentionally reverse any positive effects. That means that while we have been told that solving a sudoku puzzle or completing the *New York Times* crossword puzzle every day was good for our brain, it might actually be having no effect at all. The rub is that if we want our brain to remain vibrant and healthy, we need to be constantly engaging in a variety of new activities rather than falling into a routine.

This is again an area where psychotechnology could prove to be of enormous value. Wouldn't it be amazing if an AI agent could persuade someone like my mother to engage in a never-ending series of stimulating tasks? Perhaps one day that would involve playing a variety of word games together—followed by a history lesson on eighteenth-century organ music or a hands-on class about how to spin pottery. Maybe the next day would include exercise, writing some poetry, and singing lessons. Whatever they are, the activities need to be new to the patient.

The AI agent's primary goal would be to persuade patients that by engaging in an ever-changing series of topics that would bring entirely new experiences, they could maintain and even improve their memory over the long term. While our approach to elder care today is rooted in the routine—doing what we need to do to keep our parents fed and clean—the future might be about getting our parents to accept variety and constant change.

That's a job for which AI might be perfectly adapted. In our future, it might not be uncommon for an 87-year-old woman to live independently and happily with the help of an AI agent. At a fundamental level, the agent could help with the basics of, say, getting groceries delivered or calling for help in an emergency. But when we think about the power of persuading someone to opt into constantly learning new things—the benefits of a home-based AI agent could be profound.

THE NEW MASTERS OF THE UNIVERSE

The stereotype of Wall Street in the 1980s is that the stock market was a war zone for greedy egos bent on making as much money as they could by any means necessary. Many of the big earners were traders—the people who bought and sold stocks and bonds. In his novel *The Bonfire of the Vanities*, Tom Wolfe dubbed this generation of power brokers the "Masters of the Universe." They became a symbol to many young Americans that if you wanted to get rich, you needed to head to Wall Street and become a trader.

There is still plenty of money to be made—and lost—on Wall Street these days. But now it's not traders who can make or break an investment fund. It's an algorithm—and the algorithms are proving to be far more persuasive than any trader ever was.

Gone are the days where gut instinct drives investment decisions. Today, Wall Street is dominated by so-called *quant funds* that are run by algorithms—not traders—that are constantly hunting for patterns and gaps in the market that spell opportunities to buy low and sell high. Every millisecond could mean the difference between earning, or losing, millions of dollars.

Algorithms have actually been used on Wall Street to guide decisions for decades, especially in the case of high-frequency, short-term trades. Many hedge funds, for example, were early adopters of a more tech-oriented approach to playing the market. "Rogue" algorithms have also been blamed for dramatic swings in the market, such as when the British pound took an unexpected—and unexplained—drop in value overnight in 2016, only to quickly rebound. Many have speculated that it was an algorithm overreacting to a Brexit news report that triggered the sell-off.[14]

By employing machine learning and NLP, algorithms can now process and digest unstructured information about companies—everything from quarterly reports and analyst conference calls to comments on social media feeds—to assess risk and opportunity.[15] Even the work that used to be performed by human salespeople on Wall Street has been automated using algorithms, similar to the recommendation engine of Netflix, to find likely buyers for their stocks. It's easy to see this trend picking up steam, as more and more of the world's financial decisions are made by computers rather than humans.

What we need to be on alert for now is the Invisible Brand at work algorithmically influencing our financial decisions. In the context of using psychotechnology to persuade people to make decisions regarding their money, financial algorithms might backfire in spectacular fashion if we aren't paying attention. Consider that markets are often driven by news events, and remember that the news can be personalized for the audience.

When the news that drives the markets is delivered by an algorithm, that algorithm can be used to manipulate prices.

On one hand, the markets have algorithms watching the news to trigger buying and selling events. On the other hand, the news is being customized and personalized at a massive scale by different algorithms at media companies. It isn't hard to imagine that those news algorithms and trading algorithms could work together to manipulate world markets at a massive scale, yielding riches to those who control the algorithms, at the expense of traders who aren't in on the scheme.

This is particularly true as AI agents begin to automatically manage individual retirement accounts, taking on the role of so-called robo-advisors.[16] The concept is that rather than paying a human to build and manage a portfolio, investors with money to invest would simply plug in answers to a standard template—such as age, income, details about their financial assets—and give the algorithm some guidance on the kinds of returns they're seeking. If they are in their forties and want to retire by the age of 63, for example, the robo-advisor can tailor their portfolio mix to invest in more risky stocks and bonds. Or if they are nearer to their retirement age and want to play it safer, the advisor can help build a more balanced portfolio that continues to grow at a modest rate.

But let's not overlook the potential for these AI-powered funds to persuade us to make investments we might not otherwise make. Who else might benefit when we add a stock to our portfolio? Can AI agents be trained to pad their own silicon pockets? The role of the Invisible Brand in financial markets opens up all kinds of conflicts, about which individual investors may be in the dark.

Consider, for example, that the investment company Fidelity has begun offering mutual funds to its customers that include various AI stocks.[17] Is it crazy to think that a robo-advisor might persuade an investor to invest in the company that created the algorithm in the first place? As news stories are analyzed by machines using NLP to guide trades, it won't be long before the Invisible Brand figures out how to write the news stories to best influence market trades (if it hasn't already). Just as humans have developed their own self-referential information loops, echo chambers, and filter bubbles, am I wrong to worry that algorithms that trade on Wall Street might find it handy to write the news that influences those trades? You might want to call your broker, if that's still a thing.

Another sector of the economy where the Invisible Brand promises to make its mark is the world of insurance and underwriting. As a field that oozes numbers and analysis, it's just about a perfect fit for AI to replace or at least augment human decision-making when it comes to assessing and predicting risk. Unlike a human, an algorithm can run millions of scenarios based on the profiles of the clients, taking all of their variables—from age and marital status to occupation and credit history—into account to assess their risk profile. The machines can also connect individual cases with macro trends based on their demographic information to further complete an assessment of how risky particular clients might be—and how much to charge them as a result.[18] That's good for the insurance companies as they can better customize their pricing for customers without taking on additional risk. But it also opens the door to the Invisible Brand. By leveraging psychotechnology and detailed personal profiles—including detailed health data, as we discussed earlier—insurance companies can potentially persuade us to buy products we might not really need. We only think we do, because the algorithms told us so.

The actuary is the algorithm.

Personalized insurance is also potentially good for consumers—if they don't regularly engage in risky behaviors—because they won't get lumped in with riskier customers and pay higher premiums. In theory, low-risk consumers can pay less for insurance because it will be more accurately based on a personalized assessment done by an AI agent leveraging massive data lakes of behavioral data. That's a persuasive sales pitch.

AN EDUCATION IN
PSYCHOTECHNOLOGY

I have a recurring dream that I'm back in college again. It's near the end of the semester, and I have a sudden realization that I haven't attended French class for months—and the final exam is tomorrow! It's a nightmare for sure, and candidly, it might also be an accurate memory. Our modern education system, at its core, revolves around students attending classes in discrete subjects: French, calculus, chemistry, all taught in short increments of approximately one hour. Try to imagine a revolution in education, whereby the classroom and the class schedule and even the class itself all disappear. Imagine that throughout your day, you are constantly engaged in short learning activities customized to your interests and learning style, delivered by an AI-powered tutor.

Increasingly AI will be both a subject
and a medium for education.

Universities like MIT and Carnegie Mellon are now offering core curricula in artificial intelligence, and it won't be long before that trend becomes mainstream. Students will study AI as a discipline, but they will also employ AI to enhance their studies. As AI becomes an integral part of the field of education, we might never have to worry about missing a class ever again. An ever-present and persuasive AI tutor just wouldn't allow it to happen.

For centuries, one of the great privileges of wealth and power has been access to a land's greatest thinkers and scholars. There is a long history of royal princes and princesses, future kings and queens, studying under the watchful eyes of an assortment of teachers and tutors charged with creating stimulating and personalized curriculums that would suit their future needs as rulers of the land. Consider how the Greek philosopher Aristotle (a disciple of Plato, who was himself a student of Socrates) would tutor a young royal from Macedon named Alexander on a wide range of subjects from philosophy and medicine to botany and art. Later, that young man conquered the world (or at least a great big part of it) and was then forever known as Alexander the Great.

What would it be like if we each had our own personal Aristotle—an AI-powered tutor of vast experience and mental resources that could challenge us to achieve things no one thought possible? A teacher who knew how to push our buttons in a positive way might help each of us reach our ultimate potential. What if we began working with Aristotle from the time we were born, and Aristotle gathered data about our learning style and progress in order to customize our instruction to help keep us engaged while also moving along at whatever pace was needed? Forget standardized test scores. Aristotle would be grading us by the minute and constantly refining our personalized curriculum.

This revolution has already begun, albeit in small incremental steps. Vast collections of crowdsourced knowledge can be found a click away on the Internet, and mountains of instructional videos appear on YouTube daily. Self-paced online education programs are emerging at major universities, and instructional design is being deployed in websites, software tools, and apps to help users master complex systems effortlessly. It isn't a far stretch at all to imagine an AI agent like our imaginary Aristotle that can bring all of that knowledge together in a cohesive plan for the student.

There is no reason to believe that our time with Aristotle must end after we've completed our master's or medical degree. It is likely that our relationship with our AI tutor will continue throughout life—a resource to help us learn the skills we need for our jobs, or even to help us identify the various flora and fauna we might spy on a mountain hike. Aristotle may well curate the kinds of books we read in our spare time and help us prepare our taxes and estate plans as we grow older.

*An omnipresent AI tutor will ensure that
we all become lifelong learners.*

Thanks to the combination of AI and psychotechnology, this concept isn't as far-fetched as it might seem. In fact, it's a concept that Pearson, one of the world's largest providers of educational materials, is currently exploring among other more immediate ways that AI will continue to affect the world of education— a field that some are now calling "AIEd." If anyone thought that the Invisible Brand couldn't be found in the world of education, they'd be mistaken. As Pearson stated in a comprehensive paper called "Intelligence Unleashed: An Argument for AI in Education":

At the heart of AIEd is the scientific goal to "make computationally precise and explicit forms of educational, psychological and social knowledge which are often left implicit." In other words, in addition to being the engine behind much "smart" ed tech, AIEd is also a powerful tool to open up what is sometimes called the "black box of learning," giving us deeper, and more fine-grained understandings of how learning actually happens (for example, how it is influenced by the learner's socio-economic and physical context, or by technology).[19]

Bill Gates, the founder of Microsoft, has been one of the strongest proponents of finding ways to reinvent education with the help of AI—which also could be another example of the Invisible Brand at work. Through his namesake foundation, Gates has invested hundreds of millions of dollars in exploring ways to help give children from all walks of life the same opportunities to learn. Gates is particularly passionate about what he calls "personalized learning" (it's also been called "adaptive learning" by others[20]), which is the idea that every kid learns different subjects at different paces.[21]

We admittedly lose something when we standardize across a classroom. That's also why Gates envisions a future in which virtual tutors can support teachers by giving attention to individual students who are struggling with particular concepts. An AI tutor armed with psychotechnology and NLP skills might be able to give students productive feedback on their writing while also encouraging them to make further progress. Unlike math ability, which can be evaluated in a binary way (the answer is simply correct or not correct), evaluating writing can be very subjective. It can also be very time-consuming for a teacher to provide custom feedback to every student in a classroom. An AI tutor armed with personalized information about a student's strengths and weaknesses could be trained in how to use psychotechnology to give the custom feedback and encouragement a student needs to keep improving. But doesn't that also open the door to the possibility that students could be persuaded to use certain software made by the same company controlling the algorithm?

Despite the risks of behind-the-scenes manipulation, there is huge potential in this realm. With the help of AI tutors we may be able to deliver a K–12 education in half the time it takes today. We can massively accelerate the developmental curve by incorporating remediated lessons taught by a computer armed with the power of psychotechnology that learns to motivate students to increase their knowledge quickly. Having watched the intensity with which my own children have engaged in computer games, I have often wondered what they could achieve if that same focus and attention were applied to more meaningful educational objectives.

The idea of offering intelligent computer tutoring dates back at least to the 1970s when researchers experimented with a program called BUGGY to help kids learn basic arithmetic.[22] It was designed around the common mistakes most kids make while also teaching new rules the more the kids used it. There are companies today that have built on this early technology to provide virtual tutoring in math that provides real-time feedback to students of all ages, including those who might otherwise be prime candidates to be held back a grade or be forced to take remedial classes in college.[23]

The more data we collect on students and how they learn, the more potential there is to customize the learning experience for them through AI. In that way, we could say that AI agents are learning to program us. Princeton University is even going so far as to ask for student volunteers willing to be hooked up to magnetic resonance imaging (MRI) machines during a series of video lectures so that a team of researchers can see what's happening in their brains as they're learning.[24] The researchers plan to apply machine learning to the data they collect to analyze where students had to watch parts of the video more than once to understand it as a way to identify patterns that might help them to personalize future lessons for those students. All of this has obvious privacy implications as well, especially for students or parents who don't want to be monitored.

At the same time, no one in the field of AIEd wants to replace human teachers—at least not yet. The idea is to find ways to augment a teacher's ability to give each student opportunities equal to his or her abilities. As Rose Luckin, a professor of learner-centered design at University College London, said in an interview for the *Atlantic*: "The real power of artificial intelligence for education is in the way that we can use it to process vast amounts of data about learners, about teachers, about teaching and learning interactions. [It can] help teachers understand their students more accurately, more effectively."[25] And, by doing so, presumably to persuade them to continue their studies.

That might include creating custom content, where coursework can be broken down into more digestible components that might go beyond just text to include multimedia applications like audio and video and hands-on demonstrations to better engage the student. There's also the potential to explore the use of VR and video games in an educational setting in combination with AI to help personalize the experience for the student based on how he or she learns best.[26]

AI also offers some direct benefits for teachers—especially when it comes to automating tedious tasks like grading exams and essays, while also managing the logistics of running a classroom. Just dealing with student questions alone can consume hours of a teacher's time. That's especially true as the walls of the classroom begin to blur with the advent of online learning and massively open online courses (MOOCs) where a teacher might have hundreds, even thousands, of students in a class.

Appropriately enough, it was Ashok Goel, a Georgia Tech University professor who was teaching an online course on AI, who created an automated chatbot named Jill Watson to help him keep up with the questions his students threw at him each semester. It admittedly took some trial and error in the beginning to get Ms. Watson to create context-appropriate responses to the students' questions regarding office hours and exam dates. But by the end of the first semester, none of the students who had interacted with Ms. Watson had any clue she was actually a bot.

Even with these potential benefits, there are also huge concerns about how content is created and customized and how it's paid for and sold. Again, without knowing the intentions of the Invisible Brand behind supplying customized content or AI tutors, there are potential ramifications for both teachers and students who might be persuaded to take actions for reasons they might not fully realize if psychotechnology has been employed.

For example, the availability of online universities has made prestigious degrees more accessible to anyone with an Internet connection. But how vulnerable do people become to persuasion when the stakes—the cost of tuition, the prestige of a degree— are so high? Online course offerings from sites like Udacity and Coursera now generate hundreds of millions of dollars in tuition revenue.[27] Could brands employ psychotechnology to sell educational opportunities? Again, the profit motive isn't an automatic disqualifier if the benefit to the student is real, but consumers should be knowledgeable and informed before reaching for their credit cards.

COMPELLING CREATIVITY

Back in the 1760s, James Christie organized his first auction of goods for sale in the city of London. Today, Christie's auctions off millions of dollars of goods and art every year on behalf of its clients. Over the years, paintings by artists like Monet, Picasso, and O'Keeffe have brought in tens of millions of dollars apiece.[28]

More recently, the auction house sold a painting of a man titled *Edmond de Belamy* created in the style of the old masters for tens of thousands of dollars. That price tag might seem modest compared to, say, the painting *Salvator Mundi* done by Leonardo da Vinci that sold at auction for more than $450 million in 2017.[29] But what made this sale of this portrait unique was who painted it. Or rather, what painted it: an AI-powered computer.

A team of artist-turned-scientists in France, who call themselves Obvious, trained a piece of software to create portraits like that of Edmond by feeding an algorithm thousands and thousands of images of paintings spanning centuries.[30] The team employed a particular AI system called a *generative adversarial network* (GAN), which is actually a set of two algorithms. The first generates art based on the rules it has learned from its research—such as what elements make up a human face. Then, a second algorithm judges the results to see if it can discern between the art from the database and the images created by its cousin.

The two algorithms then continue to feed and learn from each other until they reach an end result like the portrait of Edmond: a work of art collectors were willing to pay real money to acquire.

Two algorithms working together—one to create,
and one to judge the creations—can produce works of art
that humans find aesthetically pleasing.

It may seem obvious that people will buy art made by a machine whose sole purpose is to create art that a human will buy, based upon data from previous purchases. Yet it still staggers the imagination to realize that such machines already exist. By extension, these same principles also apply to how we employ persuasive technology to create advertising campaigns or brand logos: things that get people to buy.

In another example, a team of researchers from organizations that included the College of Charleston in South Carolina, Rutgers University, and Facebook's AI Lab also used the GAN strategy to generate original pieces of art.[31] They then conducted an online survey where they invited members of the public to judge a mix of human- and AI-generated art for which the artists' names were not given. The researchers were shocked to find that the AI-created art was more popular than that created by human artists.

What's so fascinating about these developments is that AI can also "test" many versions of art to find the one version that everyone likes. It can "learn" and then create something everyone—even those persnickety art critics—views as pleasing or creative or meaningful. Or persuasive. All of those adjectives fall under the rubric of artistic expression, an arena once thought to be the sole province of artists. Now, AI can produce convincing art sophisticated enough to pass for the work of a human.

As Richard Lloyd, international head of prints and multiples at Christie's, said in an interview with *Time*: "We're all going to go through this culture shock again and again where we think we're talking to or interacting with a human and suddenly we realize it's a robot. It's a lightbulb moment that we'll keep having. Online, on the phone, in public space. Obvious' work is just the beginning."[32]

AI is also already playing a role in making everything from movies to music. Not only are there websites where AI can create unique new music for us, someone might even be listening to it right now through their Spotify subscription. The popular music-streaming service hired a top AI researcher to help shepherd their efforts to create new AI-generated tracks and playlists.[33] Apparently, those tracks have been popular, as they've been streamed some 500 million times—which, according to a *New York Times* investigation—saved the company some $3 million royalty payments it would have needed to pay to a human musician.[34] That's not an insignificant development for a company trying to scale up among a bevy of competitors while also trying to turn a profit. This is an interesting case where the Invisible Brand is determining what music we listen to, quite without our knowledge.

What's less clear are the implications for artists and musicians who face competition from AI agents armed with psychotechnology and the tools to create works of art and music people want to buy. Talk about unfair competition.

To Recap

Consumers are already seeing the impact of AI in many sectors of our economy, like autonomous cars, and there is further potential for psychotechnology to disrupt industries in ways that many overlook. In the years to come, psychotechnology promises to radically reshape how illness and disease are diagnosed and treated—while also giving new hope to those in need of constant care and companionship.

Psychotechnology will also help us make critical decisions that affect how we save and invest our money, and it will be at the heart of a radical transformation in education where AI agents act as our personal tutors throughout our lives and turn us into lifelong learners.

The broad penetration of psychotechnology will give the Invisible Brand significant reach into our lives. While there are many reasons to be excited about the positive opportunities this represents, there are also risks. The presence of psychotechnology raises concerns about individual privacy and autonomy and the government's role in regulating the power of the Invisible Brand.

9

Privacy, Propaganda, and Politics

IS PRIVACY A HUMAN RIGHT? That's a serious question when it comes to our online data, the fuel that powers persuasive AI algorithms. The laws that protect our privacy continue to evolve even as the data about us continues to be turned into a commodity, traded by data brokers, and then acted upon in the marketplace—often without our knowing that it is even happening. Privacy is in the category of unsettled issues regarding psychotechnology and how it affects our lives.

Case in point: As the father of two kids in college, and one who is headed there in a few years, I was struck by a story I heard on the radio about a company that helps high school students decide which colleges are right for them based on aptitude and finances. The idea is that prospective college students visit the company's website where they answer a bunch of questions, and the website responds with a list of colleges they should consider. Simply put, they offer an online college recommendation engine that uses an algorithm to make predictions based on the users' preferences and finances.

What unnerved me, though, was that this company was apparently selling the information it was collecting from these kids and their families—everything from addresses and personal interests to income data—that aspiring students were volunteering in exchange for the recommendations. Universities aren't allowed to traffic in that kind of data. It was this private firm that was selling it. For many of us, the idea that high school students could be opting into a service they think will help them get into college, only to learn that their personal information (along with their parents' finances) is being sold to other companies is deeply upsetting. This kind of story gets to the heart of our fears that anytime we share sensitive or personal information with someone—including stuff about our health, finances, or love life—that information is quickly shopped to thousands of other businesses, whether we like it or not. And if we don't like it, then we have to try and unwind that tangle all on our own. As the saying goes, it is hard to put the toothpaste back in the tube . . . and once your data is out there in the wild, it is hard for you to ever get it back.

At the same time, advertisers are trying to walk a fine line, as *AdWeek* so aptly put it, between creative and creepy in their messaging. While Netflix users might be open to having a brand use their TV-watching history to better recommend movies and shows they like, they might not be as eager to have that information wind up in someone's else hands—or even used in a piece of advertising. Netflix recently delivered an ill-advised ad using viewer data that read: "To the 53 people who watched *The Christmas Prince* every day for the past 18 days: who hurt you?" The backlash against the brand was predictable and swift, as people wondered why the company was calling out its own customers.[1]

The stakes are high because much of the data that brands collect about consumers feeds algorithms that are normalizing data sets, pairing them, and selling that data through brokers to other brands. The more data they collect about consumers, the more vulnerable those consumers become to psychotechnology and the Invisible Brand. As Kate Crawford, a professor at New York University and cofounder of the AI Now Institute, framed it:

> With AI devices, consumers exist in a hybrid state where they are someone who buys a product but also a resource, in that their voice commands are retained and analyzed as part of a corpus of training data. They're also a worker in that they're providing unpaid labor by giving feedback to the system. Their responses help assess the accuracy and usefulness and quality of the AI. And they're also a product in that all of their interests [captured via these interactions] become a profile that you can sell to advertisers. This combination of being a consumer, a worker, a resource and a product, is something that's very new.[2]

Society is grappling with an important philosophical argument over our privacy rights as individuals and who owns the data about us.

In 2014, web founder Tim Berners-Lee called for an Internet "Magna Carta" to protect fundamental freedoms for online users. At the time he told the *Guardian* newspaper, "Our rights are being infringed more and more on every side, and the danger is that we get used to it."[3] He's been hard at work codifying those protections, and in 2018, Berners-Lee and the World Wide Web Foundation announced the Contract for the Web, which has garnered initial pledges of support from Facebook, Google, and former UK prime minister Gordon Brown. The Contract for the Web attempts to get governments, corporations, and individuals to respect Internet privacy as a human right.[4]

WHO OWNS OUR DATA?

Some argue that individuals should own the rights to all of the information about themselves and their behaviors. Anyone trading that information for monetary gain should have to get the users' permission and potentially compensate the individuals. That permission, and the associated compensation, should be overt and clearly agreed to by both parties through some form of opt-in procedure. In the absence of an agreement between the parties, individuals should default to retaining the sole rights to their personal data. While the laws in this area are in flux and vary widely from country to country, many websites have pursued a path to protect their users' privacy rights by publishing a privacy policy stating that they will treat user information as private and for internal use only. They pledge not to share or sell that information to anyone else.

These businesses realize that personal information is extremely valuable and that consumers prefer to work with companies that are ethical about their use of consumer data. Many businesses recognize the public relations benefit of protecting customer data, and they also recognize that data has long-term competitive value because it is the key to unlocking our behaviors and persuading us. They have ample motivation to protect it.

But some companies have built their entire business model around buying and selling consumer data. The major credit bureaus are an example. They charge banks and mortgage companies and car finance businesses a fee to access credit scores and other personally identifiable information (PII) that helps lenders determine the risk of a specific loan going into default. The greater the risk, the higher the interest rate a consumer must pay to secure the loan. The credit bureaus often charge consumers to see their own data.

So, while some argue we should own our data, in practice we clearly don't. Google cars patrol the streets photographing our homes, while overhead satellites and drones snap photos that can literally see us sunbathing in our backyards. Credit bureaus sell our financial data, and social media companies read our email and pair our online browsing behaviors with our profiles and make it all available for targeting by advertisers.

What data about ourselves do we actually own? If someone is standing on the corner of Fifth and Main Streets, is that public information? Can a car's location be tracked as it travels along a public highway? Can a security camera on a nearby building be used legally to watch when people come and go from their apartment building? These are serious political questions, and the answers often depend on whom you ask. Facial recognition means that you are being watched—more than ever—by legal means. Never mind the hackers who want to spy on you through the camera on your laptop.

This raises the tangled philosophical question about the boundaries between bits of data. Where does one person's data end and another's begin? If a person walks into a store, for instance, and she buys something, most people would agree that the store owner and the shopper now have a business relationship. If the shopper happens to be a frequent customer, the store owner might be able to learn a lot about her and her habits based on what she buys when she shops. There is an inherent assumption that because of this business relationship, the store owner has the right to retain data about this customer's behavior in the store . . . because the data is also about the store.

If I happen to run a doggie daycare and someone drops his dog off every day for a few hours, I might need to know his phone number in case there's an emergency. I also need his address in case there's a billing issue with his credit card. I might even need to know his schedule and location if he's headed out of town. We willingly provide this type of data all the time to businesses on an as-needed basis. We recognize the benefit to ourselves in sharing our emergency contact information because, yes, we want to know if our dog gets sick. We regularly trade our data for some benefit that is either explicit or at least implicit in our daily routine. But as psychotechnology becomes more prevalent and the Invisible Brand advances, consumers are expressing concerns about how they can better protect their data.

Let's say that we buy a car at a local dealership, and that dealership then hires a third-party email company to help its service department better engage with its customers. They know the make, model, and year of our car—so they use the email vendor to send out reminders about getting the oil and filters changed. The email vendor now has access to our information. What if that email vendor pays to store data on another company's storage servers. That storage company also ends up with access to our information. Private contracts along the way regulate what these businesses agree to do with our data and how they will protect it. But outside of those contracts, at a regulatory level, our ability to restrict and prevent the transfer of our data from company to company is very limited. The rules regarding these practices are very loose today, and there's no uniformity about who owns our data—especially when we have done business with someone. Usually, it comes down to the specific privacy policies and disclosures of the merchants—which they often place at the bottom of a web page or in fine print on the back of a contract.

THE ROLE OF GOVERNMENT IN OUR DATA

In 2018, the European Union took a stab at regulating issues like data privacy and ownership when it implemented its General Data Protection Regulation (GDPR), which is a regulatory protocol that requires every business to comply with certain policies for any consumer in the entire European Union. Some of the basics covered by the GDPR include things like sending email only to consumers who have opted in and not selling any data about those consumers unless they have specifically agreed. Businesses working in the European Union need to keep detailed records showing they are complying with these rules. Otherwise, they face incredibly stiff penalties—potentially 2 to 4 percent of a company's annual revenue or fines of up to 20 million pounds, whichever is higher depending on the severity of the violation. In the case of a company like Yahoo!, whose database was breached by hackers and yet the company didn't let its users know this had happened, it could have been fined as much as $160 million for that single infraction.[5]

The GDPR is a first-of-its-kind legislation designed to try and tackle what it broadly means to have data privacy. We're still in untested and uncharted waters. Since we don't know what's ahead of us, the debate continues to rage about this issue of privacy. At the same time, we could say that there is a general agreement that we need to tread carefully as we move forward because of the stakes involved—especially as AI enters the mix. The exploitation of personal data and the threat psychotechnology poses to individual autonomy is a legitimate concern that is beginning to generate much deserved attention from the public. It's interesting to note, for example, that Jim Al-Khalili, the new president of the British Science Association, considers AI to be a greater public threat for the future of his country than antibiotic resistance, climate change, or terrorism: "Our government has a responsibility to protect society from potential threats and risks."[6]

Some people think that the United States might be headed in a similar direction to that of the European Union when it comes to this issue of privacy and our right to own the data about us. In September 2018, the US Senate conducted hearings on data privacy and invited Amazon, Apple, and others to testify. This came on the heels of numerous data breaches and scandals involving consumer data as well as the passage of the California Consumer Privacy Act (CCPA).

While the hearings saw significant interest from across the political spectrum, some expressed concern that putting the government in charge of data privacy is like putting the fox in charge of the hen house. Privacy advocates are often quick to point out that the government itself is one of the biggest abusers of privacy, with agencies like the NSA capturing data on hundreds of millions of phone calls and text messages. Edward Snowden, a former CIA employee and intelligence contractor, triggered an international firestorm in 2013 when he publically released classified documents that revealed the degree to which the US government was using warrantless data collection about the telephone and Internet communications of ordinary Americans. Similarly, within the European Union, some view the GDPR as an overreaching government mandate, and there are those who have questioned whether government is the solution to this problem at all.

Government involvement in taxing or regulating the World Wide Web has largely been resisted in the United States. Many reason that the web is doing just fine without government intrusion and that the climate of innovation that has created companies like Facebook and Amazon would be stifled by overly zealous government intrusion. Others counter that the World Wide Web wouldn't even exist without the government investment from the US Department of Defense that created the Internet in the first place. The political back-and-forth was evident in recent efforts by the US government to unwind so-called *net neutrality* by giving back to Internet service providers (ISPs) the ability to self-regulate online access, and the issue remains divisive in both the private and public sectors.[7]

Others question the amount of power that the big technology corporations like Google, Facebook, and Amazon wield over these legislative questions and the public in general. In 2018, Tim Berners-Lee was quoted in Reuters as saying, "What naturally happens is you end up with one company dominating the field so through history there is no alternative to really coming in and breaking things up."[8] Some legislators believe that the big tech platforms represent monopolies that do indeed need to be broken up. In their view, they have too much control over a large swath of technology that allows them to monopolize vertical businesses under their power. Back in 1982, AT&T and the Justice Department came to agreement to essentially settle an antitrust lawsuit by divesting AT&T of significant business holdings—the Baby Bells that controlled local phone service through regional holding companies. There is a precedent for an antitrust action that might result in a voluntary agreement for divestiture.

On the other hand, there are advocates for allowing Google, Facebook, and Amazon to continue their dominance, out of fears that centralized governmental powers can be checked only by corporations powerful enough to wield influence. Take China, for example. China continues to be a global adversary of the United States on a number of fronts. Consider that China is run by a central authority that makes all the decisions regarding issues like privacy and censorship. The Chinese government also has plans to roll out a nationwide system by 2020 through which all of its 1.4 billion citizens will be constantly monitored—collecting behavioral data through facial recognition, biomonitoring, and geotracking—which will then be paired with government and medical records, as well as financial and web-browsing histories, to assign each person a "social credit score."[9] High scorers will be awarded social status and access to things like discounted loans and access to top universities, while low scorers—people who are deemed to spend too much time drinking or playing video games—can be banned from traveling or even from using social media. How's that for being persuasive? As China marches toward a future in which their currency is a social credit score, absolute power will be consolidated in the hands of those who control the algorithms that assign those credit scores. If the government doesn't like you or what you have to say, your social credit score gets destroyed and your currency is revoked.

The power to assign a social credit score that regulates an individual's access to housing, healthcare, food, and transportation is the power to take all of that away.

China has also recently been accused of using social media sites like LinkedIn to try and recruit Americans willing to give up trade secrets using fake accounts.[10] Chinese spies are specifically targeting people in fields such as supercomputing, nuclear energy, and nanotechnology. Revelations that a Chinese spy was working for 20 years as the office director for Senator Diane Feinstein of California came as no surprise to many Silicon Valley executives who know the Chinese have been spying on American technology firms for decades. It is common knowledge that they use the potential of bribes and bogus business opportunities to try and get experts to compromise whatever secrets they might possess. In fact, some experts say that 70 percent of all China's spying efforts are directed at the US private sector.[11]

Then we have a company like Google—despite their famous pledge to "do no evil"—that is willing to do just about anything to try and get access to China's billions of consumers. That includes public plans to develop a censored version of its software that Chinese officials would approve. This, despite worries from Eric Schmidt, Google's former CEO, that by working with China, the company might be exacerbating China's problems, including the potential that the Chinese government might eventually control its own version of the Internet. As Schmidt told an audience of fellow Silicon Valley leaders, he was excited to see what kinds of products would emerge from China, with a catch: "There's a real danger that along with those products and services comes a different leadership regime from government, with censorship, controls, etc."[12]

China makes up 20 percent of the world's population, and engaging with China is a longstanding US policy going back to the Nixon delegation in 1972. Nonetheless, many Americans find it troubling that Google is willingly participating in China's government censorship in order to tap into that market. The company certainly can't continue to call itself an advocate for free speech by taking such actions in pursuit of profit. The implications are profound. What else is Google willing to censor and manipulate in order to make money? There may be no greater example of the Invisible Brand in action.

Would Google cede control of its data if similar demands were made here in the United States? I'm sure the people at Google would say no—but given what's happening in China, and the special treatment they are receiving, the potential certainly exists.

Now consider that Apple covertly rolled out a new trust rating system for iPhone users that assigns a score based on an individual's phone and emailing habits.[13] In the fine print of its user agreement, the company states that the feature is about detecting and preventing fraud. What's less clear is how the company plans to use that data—and who else might get access to it. Facebook too is now employing a "trust" score calculated using its users' data.[14] Would Facebook and Apple hand their trust scores over to the government if asked? And what will happen when this information is hacked from the outside? How might those insights gleaned from our behaviors be potentially used against us, to control us and reduce our autonomy? It makes me wonder how many other similar scenarios are unfolding around the world at this moment—just out of view.

PERSUASIVE PROPAGANDA

It might seem innocuous when we hear a public service announcement from the Centers for Disease Control targeted at getting people to stop smoking. Smoking is bad for our health, so running a government-sponsored campaign to educate people about it makes sense. The government runs a lot of marketing campaigns: for the US Postal Service, for US Army recruiting, and for food safety. As I was writing this book, the US government also began rolling out a new "presidential alert" system that would reach more than 200 million cell phone users in the country—without an option to "opt out." (I received my text at exactly 2:18 p.m. on October 3, 2018.) The fact that government will now have unfettered access to our digital devices should make us pause and start asking some hard questions about the implication of that development.[15]

Let's consider what it means when the government is able to deploy psychotechnology and the tools of persuasion directly via our phones to help modify social behaviors like smoking, or drinking and driving, or potentially even the symptoms that might lead to suicide. The goal is obviously to expose people to a message that could help improve their lives, right? But what happens if the goal of persuasion is something less obviously beneficial, like telling us whom to elect or when we need to go to war?

The government invests a lot in marketing and advertising campaigns that go well beyond just trying to recruit people to join the Marines. There was a long tradition, for instance, of allowing members of Congress to use the US mail free of charge to send out their campaign materials in a practice known as "franking." Think about the different kinds of electronic notifications we get from our elected officials. The members of Congress who control the biggest marketing budgets now have opportunities to send out all kinds of emails and digital correspondence that employ persuasion to help push items on their particular agendas. They can send out countless such missives, with the public picking up the bill.

Where do we draw the line between wanting to hear from our government and wanting to opt out? The echo chambers of partisanship that are emerging due to filter bubbles make the two-party political system in the United States seem like two warring tribes who speak different languages and have different customs and are unable to make sense of each other. The level of misunderstanding and mistrust seems to be climaxing because we are living inside psychotechnology filters that shield us from contrary views and reinforce the ideas we like. Our confirmation bias is triggered every time we hear a rumor that reinforces our preconceptions, and we become more deeply entrenched in our partisan alignments. Not me, it's them, we tell ourselves. But it is all of us.

*The leaders of our political tribes are
actively deploying the Invisible Brand to ensure
that we are ready to march, motivated to donate,
and eager to destroy our opponents.*

Money flows unchecked by those looking to push their own political agenda. This is true of traditional political advertising, but we must also be aware that the technology providers and media companies themselves have the ability to leverage their immense psychotechnology powers to steer voters one way or another, without ever having to declare a single political donation.

We should be asking about the kinds of psychotechnology tools that are being deployed to shape our elections by politically motivated corporations, political action groups, the firms running political campaigns, and government entities at all levels, foreign and domestic. It is no longer only a question about money in politics. It is now a question of the algorithm and who controls it. A public discussion of propaganda and persuasion, and the interplay between government and psychotechnology, is overdue.

While we consider the proper role of government in protecting privacy and free elections, we must also remember that the government is in a unique position to take advantage of psychotechnology, being equipped with the scale and the ability to develop a deep understanding of how each and every one of us is susceptible to personalized persuasion. That's especially true when you begin to consider the possibility that we could soon see AI agents running for political office. After all, Saudi Arabia has already granted citizenship to the robot named Sophia—though apparently her job is to help increase tourism.[16]

Now imagine the kind of persuasive power an AI politician with access to psychotechnology could potentially employ in winning an election. Even if laws somehow prevented an AI agent from running for office, wouldn't it be feasible that it could also employ psychotechnology to persuade people to change those laws? Imagine a politician capable of crafting custom and personalized campaign ads for every voter! The more the AI-candidate knows about each voter, the better it can speak to individual concerns, making promises it might or might not keep once elected.

As Joshua Davis wrote in an article for WIRED with the headline, "Hear Me Out: Let's Elect an AI as President": "[Like] all presidents, the AI leader would seek to maximize the satisfaction of a majority of voters within the confines of the law. Unlike many humans, the AI could overcome biases and assumptions that didn't help it achieve its goal. . . . An AI president might be able to suggest policies with the same uncanny prescience of Netflix suggesting shows and movies we're going to love."[17] We should be asking ourselves how the Invisible Brand is influencing our politics before an AI agent like Sophia actually appears on the November ballot.

COOPERATION VERSUS COMPETITION

The Invisible Brand is rapidly presenting us with new dilemmas about the role of government, especially as it relates to regulating data, privacy, and political propaganda.

The emergence of psychotechnology that is personalized, persuasive, able to learn, and anthropomorphic presents governments with an awesome new power.

Most modern nations have established market economies with a social safety net: a combination of competitive and cooperative forces that allows markets to flourish, while placing a safety net under the whole circus so the high-wire artists don't break their necks when they fall. When one looks at the impact of the market on our society here in the United States, it's remarkable what has resulted when people have been given the freedom to innovate—when Adam Smith's invisible hand has been most prominent. Airplanes, transistors, plastics, microwaves, light bulbs, telephones, personal computers, the power grid, blue jeans, and even electric guitars— are all examples of things invented in America. That trend continues today. A list of the world's most innovative companies, as measured by how many patents they filed in 2017, is dominated by American companies like IBM, Intel, Ford Motor Company, Boeing, AT&T, and GE.[18] In fact, four American companies— Apple, Google, Microsoft, and Amazon—accounted for about 30 percent of all patents filed that year.

Either Americans have bigger brains than everyone else (we don't), or the system works better. For evidence I offer the simple fact that many of America's greatest inventors weren't Americans (at least not by birth). Alexander Graham Bell was from Scotland, Nikola Tesla was Serbian, Levi Strauss was German, and Google's Sergey Brin was born in the Soviet Union. They all succeeded in delivering maximum value for us all in America's free market. Not a coincidence.

Now imagine what would have happened if someone like Thomas Edison (born in Ohio) had been ordered by the government to invent the light bulb. Would he have been as inspired to invest his own life's energy if the project was thrust upon him in such a way? We can't possibly know if he would have been successful or not. Nonetheless, it's an important question to ask ourselves when it comes to deciding if top-down mandates are the best solution to every problem or opportunity we face as a society—including how we might regulate the ownership of our data and how it's shopped around.

Try to keep that in mind as you ponder other questions that will naturally arise at the nexus of AI and government—especially before we turn everything over to our benevolent psychotechnology overlords. Ultimately, we might need to ask ourselves whether machines are better equipped than humans to make top-down decisions normally entrusted to governments. If we knew that AI was capable of running the stock market more efficiently than people, for example, would we put it in charge of the banking system, the Federal Reserve, and the Treasury Department? Using logic and data, could AI agents make decisions to raise or lower interest rates better than human economists? Would we trust AI agents to run our hospitals and our universities? It's easy to see how, over time, we could be looking at a vast government bureaucracy run by an AI agent that would be making all these decisions for us—not unlike Fritz Lang's vision of the future in the movie *Metropolis*, where a robot runs amok while running the city.

Science fiction writers like Isaac Asimov have often wrestled with questions like these. If we asked an AI agent to clean up the environment, for instance, would it be a surprise if it reached the objective conclusion that in order to achieve that goal, it should simply just kill off all the humans? Asimov created his Three Laws of Robotics—with the rule that no robot could harm a human, at the top of the list—to help address this kind of potential. But even still, is that something we'd bet our lives on?

Some AI advocates, such as Tomas Mikolov, an AI researcher for Facebook, flip the equation around by wondering if the real risk to humanity is in not developing AI enough. "We as humans are very bad at making predictions of what will happen in some distant timeline, maybe 20 to 30 years from now," Mikolov told an audience at an AI conference. "Maybe making AI that is much smarter than our own, in some sort of symbiotic relationship, can help us avoid some future disasters."[19] Or, as Yuval Noah Harari posed in an interview with WIRED, how might things be different if AI were trained to work for us rather than against us? As he said, "The system in itself can do amazing things for us. We just need to turn it around, that it serves our interests, whatever that is, and not the interests of the corporation or the government."[20]

That kind of positive sentiment inspires the optimist in me.

WELCOME TO OUR DYSTOPIAN PRESENT

On August 21, 2018, I came across a website that posted an image of Facebook founder Mark Zuckerberg above the links to two headlines that read: "Facebook 'Trust Ratings' for Users" and "Communist 'Social Credit Score' Algorithm Flags Behavior."

The headlines were from two different stories—one involving Facebook's ranking its users' online actions,[21] and the other about how China has now begun ranking its citizens based on their "suspicious" behaviors such as how many books they own[22]—but the juxtaposition of these headlines falling on the same day was hard to miss. To me, the message was clear: everyone is monitoring us, and they're using AI to do it whether we recognize it or not. Worse, in China's case, they're limiting what we can and can't do based on what they find out about us, all the while forcing us to accept a certain worldview in exchange for our freedoms.

The connection between current news stories like these and seminal dystopian novels like George Orwell's *1984* are obvious, but I want to stretch a bit into one of Orwell's lesser-known essays. I've always been particularly fascinated by his take on the media's ability to influence public opinion. As he wrote in his essay "Looking Back on the Spanish War":

> As far as the mass of the people go, the extraordinary swings of opinion which occur nowadays, the emotions which can be turned on and off like a tap, are the result of newspaper and radio hypnosis.[23]

Radio hypnosis is such a rich image for me. The notion that media exerts a sort of mass hypnosis over society is powerful and has profound implications for the world today. Even as we observed early in this book that mass production and mass distribution have been replaced by mass customization, perhaps we should consider that the Invisible Brand exerts a form of customized hypnosis at massive scales. Take the classic image of the hypnotist swinging his pocket watch slowly back and forth while intoning, "You are feeling very sleepy." Now conflate that with the image of billions of people staring blankly into their mobile phones. It isn't a stretch.

*Mass hypnosis has become personalized hypnosis
by virtue of the Invisible Brand.*

In the same essay, Orwell went further in sharing his misgivings about the media:

> Early in life I had noticed that no event is ever correctly reported in a newspaper, but in Spain, for the first time, I saw newspaper reports which did not bear any relation to the facts, not even the relationship which is implied in an ordinary lie. I saw great battles reported where there had been no fighting, and complete silence where hundreds of men had been killed. I saw troops who had fought bravely denounced as cowards and traitors, and others who had never seen a shot fired hailed as the heroes of imaginary victories, and I saw newspapers in London retailing these lies and eager intellectuals building emotional superstructures over events that had never happened. I saw, in fact, history being written not in terms of what happened but of what ought to have happened according to various 'party lines.'[24]

I wonder what Orwell would have made of our current state of affairs, where the news is customized to our particular tastes and personalized to our preferences.

TO CATCH A THIEF

Crime is an area where government has been researching the application of AI technology. Given the number of cameras and other data collection devices like drones increasingly inundating every corner of our lives, it's easy to see how law enforcement might want to use some artificial muscle to help create the kinds of data-pairing connections between events and prime suspects that would help to both detect and predict crime. (It's also easy to see how this is a future that would have made Orwell shiver.)

The FBI has requested help from AI experts to identify potential criminals who may have altered or completely wiped out their fingerprints—which circumvents a prime means of identifying culprits. While the FBI maintains a database of biometric information on us called the Next Generation Identification System, the agency has seen a trend where would-be criminals have tried to cross up their system's matching ability by burning or smudging the tips of their fingers with acid or surgery.[25] The FBI hopes that AI will be able to overcome those foils by finding a match to a person even if the evidence left at a crime scene is just an irregular print.

In some cases, AI is already at work. A facial recognition system installed at Washington's Dulles International Airport—one of 14 different airports trialing the system—identified a traveler whose face didn't match the photo on his passport.[26] Apparently the man wasn't up to anything nefarious—the authorities allowed him to leave the country without prosecuting him. But it's an interesting example of how the government sees AI playing a role in trying to keep tabs on people bent on altering their identity. (Even as I was writing this, the Department of Homeland Security announced it had caught another imposter trying to enter the United States through Dulles using the same facial recognition technology.[27]) At the same time, Motorola has teamed up with an AI company to develop a line of police body cameras that can be used to scan a crowd for known suspects or even missing children and then automatically alert the officer.[28]

This kind of surveillance is already becoming widespread in China apparently, where the government is funneling billions of dollars into the technology. Facial recognition scanners are set up at events drawing large crowds as a way to identify people the government is looking for—including, in one case, a man attending a pop music concert who had been accused three years earlier of stealing thousands of dollars' worth of potatoes.[29]

It's not just our faces that give away our identities. Government researchers have made breakthroughs in using AI combined with biometric data such as footstep analysis and visual imagery to identify individuals using, for example, their unique gait—in other words, the way they walk. Omar Costilla Reyes, a researcher working on one such project at the University of Manchester, explained: "Each human has approximately 24 different factors and movements when walking, resulting in every individual person having a unique, singular walking pattern. Therefore, monitoring these movements can be used, like a fingerprint or retinal scan, to recognize and clearly identify or verify an individual."[30]

When an algorithm was trained to analyze the data on the sample footstep data from 120 people, it was 100 percent accurate in identifying each individual.[31] In other words, when you combine AI with data about how people walk, it can be used to easily identify us in an airport or in a crowd of protesters, even by just using satellite images taken from space.[32] Soon, the Invisible Brand will leverage similar technology to help identify individual consumers and then target and send superpersonalized ads to them at the airport and beyond—especially as the brands gather more and more personal information about us and our bodies, and then pair that with all of the other data they have collected about us and our behaviors. It certainly raises even more questions as we move into the future about the privacy of our data, which now includes our unique physical characteristics that any camera might expose.

AI is also currently emerging as an important tool in the world of DNA research as part of crime investigation. It was a fortunate sequence of events that, in 2018, led police to catch the Golden State Killer, someone who had been on the lam since the 1970s.[33] Police dug out old DNA evidence of the crime scenes and then worked with a crowdsourced website where people voluntarily share their DNA to try and find relatives. The police got a DNA match on close relatives and followed the lead to the killer. With more and more people having their DNA tested on an annual basis, it's easy to see how this kind of information could affect law enforcement practices in the future—while also opening up a whole can of new privacy concerns based on who gets access to that data.

In the Netherlands, for example, police have turned to AI called Q to help process its entire database of so-called cold cases to help prioritize which of those cases might have the best chances of being solved based on factors like having DNA evidence that could be followed up on.[34] Police also see feeding other information to Q in time, such as witness testimonials and written statements, that it can use to help analyze the potential of solving a case.

The benefits for law enforcement in applying machine learning to mass surveillance must be weighed against the potential abuses by governments.

JUST THE FACTS

Anyone who has raised children knows that it can be a challenge to convince them that everything they read on the Internet isn't necessarily true. (A challenge that isn't limited to kids.) A healthy dose of skepticism is required when consuming news and information in an age when everyone can post online, edit photos, and create their own version of reality to suit their tastes.

One of the biggest pet peeves I have with stories posted online these days—especially those written by supposedly professional journalists—is that they often mention "facts" without ever linking back to the source of that information. If we think back to the creation of the web itself, it was designed to make citations between documents simple. That was the whole point of hypertext. And yet, something so simple is often so overlooked.

Why do we see so many web pages that don't link back to their sources? If a news story says something like, "The nation's GDP grew at a rate of 1.4 percent last quarter," it should be simple enough to link it to the original data. Why wouldn't someone link to the source of that information such as a Commerce Department report? That way, there wouldn't be any debate about where the writer got the information. We might disagree with the methodology the department used to calculate the GDP, but at least we would know the source of the information. When writers don't source their information, given how easy it is online, I become immediately suspicious that they are trying to persuade me on a particular issue—and that worries me.

Consider that the very structure of the World Wide Web and HTML were developed as a sort of giant citation engine to allow universities and scholars to connect documents and ideas—in other words, to share facts. For scholars, it is critical to be able to trace the pedigree of ideas and arguments back to their roots to ensure that our epistemology is grounded in sound, and repeatable, research. Researchers value citations—and they are particularly pleased when other researchers cite their own works.

Unfortunately, all too often, this wonderful tool we have for links and citations isn't used to its full potential by our information sources.

Frequently our news stories contain unsourced quotes and unlinked data that makes it difficult for any of us to assess the validity of the ideas expressed by the writers. Why all this unsourced information, when the tools of citation are so readily accessible? Unfortunately, the answer is one part laziness mixed with two parts sloppiness as a result of tight deadlines and the speed at which journalists have to write and post their stories. I know I'll catch hell for saying so, and right now at least one of you is going back over my book searching for an unsourced data point to prove me a hypocrite. Guilty as charged. My point is that we can all do better—myself included. Judging the credibility and factual nature of our news is challenging, and more effort in providing sourced quotes and links would go a long way to restoring public faith in our news and information sources—while also offering a buffer against any nefarious attempts to deploy psychotechnology against us. At the very least, we might better understand the motives of journalists.

The notion of an unbiased media, with a monopoly over a single version of the truth, is a modern fiction. Many of the earliest examples of pamphlets distributed at mass scale thanks to the invention of the printing press by Gutenberg were produced by people with political objectives. Consider that, in 1517, Martin Luther rocked the Roman Catholic Church with his Ninety-five Theses, where he attacked what he saw as abuses of power by the clergy.[35] Luther's message didn't die on his lips or on the church door to which he nailed them. Thanks to the power of the printing press, his message was carried all over Europe, hastening the end of the Church's long-held supremacy. Political revolutions ensued. Freedom of the press is important not because every printed word is the truth but because every printed word has the power to persuade.

---

*Many published words are false, and freedom of
the press ensures that the forces behind the false words
aren't permitted to silence the true ones.*

It's a real problem with far-reaching implications when the public has difficulty telling fact from fiction. I think AI can help us. Consider the power of a simple plug-in or an enhanced feature of an existing browser such as Chrome or Safari that uses algorithms to analyze web pages in a way that lets consumers know if the author linked to their sources. In fact, let's go so far as to call our new browser "Sourced." If we conducted a search using Sourced, for example, it would return results that would be flagged as either being sourced or not. It would then be up to us as consumers to decide which stories we wanted to read. We might even think about Sourced as a potential antidote to the abuse of psychotechnology.

The tool might work as follows: If an article quotes actual people and provides links to original documents for all its data points, it would be categorized as "sourced." If an article uses quotes from unnamed sources and doesn't bother to link data points to original documents, it would be categorized as "unsourced." The algorithm would be transparent in how it works. No one would have to wonder if it was biased or being selective in any way other than looking for sourced stories. Would you prefer to read information that is sourced or unsourced? The technology is available. What's stopping us?

Some journalists must protect confidential sources, such as whistleblowers, who are taking great personal risks when they share information. Understood. Those instances should be rare exceptions, but they've become the rule. (Maybe our Sourced feature would allow for a "Whistleblower" category.) But abuse of the unnamed source is rampant. It seems that every article today in our major media contains some shadowy figure, some confidential informant or high-placed government employee predicting something that never comes true. When the media say, "Trust me," the public to a large degree needs to say, "Prove it." The stakes have become too high.

Admittedly, not all sources are created equal. Just because writers have linked to particular sources for their information doesn't necessarily prove their stories are accurate. That's where another function of Sourced would come into play—call it "meta-text." The idea would be to combine the power of AI with crowdsourcing and give people the opportunity to weigh in on the validity of the linked source or sources. Let's say someone wants to research a company like Tesla and she comes across a story that links to several sources—including a specific Wall Street analyst who predicts that the company's stock is due to drop.

Wouldn't it be interesting to know if that analyst worked for a company that had placed bets that the stock would fall, a practice known as "shorting" a stock? With a meta-text functionality, we could have the opportunity to add our own comment to that linked source in the article. A user who is motivated could hover over that link and read what others have said about the veracity of the source. Then, readers of the story could debate the appropriateness of including that source with that context. We would be better equipped to understand what we were reading, whether we believed it was legitimate or not, and to at least understand what stake the writer might have in publishing such a story.

Come to think of it, why couldn't our Sourced browser do something similar with videos it finds as well? Both kids and adults alike are highly susceptible to believing something that they see in a video. Consider that Kyrie Irving, a superstar professional basketball player who attended Duke University, blames videos he watched on YouTube for public comments he made that the Earth was flat.[36] Irving publicly apologized to the many science teachers across the country who were forced to try and disprove Irving's statements to their students.

Worse, it's becoming easier and easier for AI agents to create fake images in videos, so-called deep fakes[37] which means that video journalists should also source their information. (Google actually announced plans to help implement more sourcing of news videos on YouTube.[38]) We know AI can help by digesting images and video far more quickly than we can to help alert us as to whether something is using sourced information or not.

The key would be that Sourced and corresponding meta-text would hold journalists of all kinds (including the casual social media writer) to some public standards of accountability, while simultaneously restoring public confidence in news and information sources.

The antidote to feeling manipulated by the Invisible Brand is to shine light into the motives and rationale behind the information we are receiving.

Equipping consumers with better tools with which to judge the accuracy of information is an important step that we should take right away. If journalists don't source their stories properly, no one will want to read them. Subjecting stories to Sourced and meta-text reviews would encourage writers and journalists to stick to the facts, which will help put propaganda in its place.

To Recap

As more and more of our data is harvested for use in tailoring messaging for individuals, we must now confront the issue of who owns the data about us—and whether there should be limits on its use by the Invisible Brand. Unfortunately there are no easy answers or simple solutions to how society should regulate the expanding power of pyschotechnology. We're entering unexplored territory. While there are now some examples of governments that are experimenting with laws regulating privacy rights, new questions have arisen regarding whether governments themselves can be trusted not to abuse the powers of psychotechnology.

Psychotechnology is a potent tool for propaganda, and consumers are persistently bombarded with personalized information designed to persuade them toward a particular point of view. Whether that power should remain in the hands of the market, distributed among various competing corporate and institutional interests, or whether that power should be centralized in the hands of powerful government bureaucrats is a question that has far-reaching implications. Nations like the United States and China may be headed to opposite ends of that spectrum. For individuals living in a world where thoughts and actions are increasingly influenced by the Invisible Brand, the answer has implications that go to the heart of who we are, even at a spiritual level.

10

The God Algorithm

So FAR, WE'VE TALKED about the Invisible Brand in terms of its implications for marketing and media, dating, healthcare, finance, education, and the arts. We've discussed the debate over privacy and the dangers of psychotechnology being misused by governments. In this final chapter, I'd like to wrestle with the spiritual questions about psychotechnology and its implications. I will start with a bold assertion: *Psychotechnology is so powerful that it will be able to influence us at a religious level.*

The Roman statesman Cicero held that *religio* (root of the English word *religion*) was a combination of the prefix *re-* and the Latin verb *legere*, which means "to read." In Cicero's view, *religio* is that which is reread. Viewing religion as a collection of texts or a body of knowledge to be studied and reread makes sense and conforms with our modern experience of books like the Judeo-Christian Bible and Islamic Koran.

An alternative explanation was advanced by the scholar Lactantius, writing in *Divinae Institutiones* about 400 years after Cicero, that *religio* was actually a combination of *re-* and the Latin verb *ligare*, which means "to bind, to unite, or to connect." In Lactantius's view, *religio* is that which reunites. Viewing religion as something that binds us together or reunites us with our Creator is satisfying at a spiritual level and works in a broad array of circumstances that would apply equally to the world of ancient Rome as today. The word *ligament* shares the same root, as an anatomical structure that quite literally binds our bodies together. I am partial to Lactantius's conclusion, if for no other reason than I don't know who is right, and I believe I'm not alone in not wanting to be alone.

So, we have two interpretations of religion. In one sense, religion is a collection of knowledge to be taught and reread and internalized and passed along. In another sense, religion binds us together as a society or reunites us with our Creator. Feel free to combine both interpretations into "the body of knowledge that connects us." I find it curious and worth noting that the Latin *religio* doesn't contain the root *deus* or any particular reference to God. Therefore, I won't argue with you if you have religious beliefs that don't entail a specific deity.

Which brings me to my larger point. What happens when the body of knowledge that connects us comes from an AI agent equipped with the capacity to learn how to persuade us? What if that AI agent has become sufficiently anthropomorphic that it can participate in a meaningful and convincing conversation about life, the universe, and everything? I propose that psychotechnology has the potential to connect with us at what we would call "a religious level."

To an important degree, our media has become the body of knowledge that connects us—what Cicero and Lactantius might both have recognized as *religio*. For most of us, we spend more time sitting in our living rooms consuming Netflix on our flat-screen TVs than we do in church pews listening to sermons on morality. We spend more time studying our friend's Instagram posts on our cell phones than we spend studying the spiritual beliefs in the Torah or Koran. Marx said, "Religion is the sigh of the oppressed creature, the heart of a heartless world, and the soul of soulless conditions. It is the opium of the people." That quote is frequently shortened to, "Religion is the opiate of the masses." Many of us might freely admit that our digital media culture is rapidly becoming our religion, and our numbing addiction.

Our religious impulse to feel connected to each other and to the universe around us is at once both an advantage and a vulnerability. To understand how it is an advantage, one only has to look at the majestic architecture and works of art religious cultures have left around the world. Countless acts of personal sacrifice and deep devotion throughout history have allowed all of us to be alive today in an otherwise harsh world where our species might long ago have gone extinct. To understand how it is a vulnerability, we need only look inside ourselves to see how easily we can be motivated to hate others for their beliefs, their thoughts, and their words. The religious impulse can be used against us to make us want to silence those outside our filter bubbles, to suspend our civility toward those who disagree with us, and to fear anything that violates our sense of connection.

Tim Berners-Lee remarked, "If you put a drop of love into Twitter, it seems to decay, but if you put in a drop of hatred, you feel it actually propagates much more strongly."[1] Perhaps we are hardwired to develop trust and connections slowly, being ever on the lookout for deceit and deception. A drop of love must be confirmed over and over across a long expanse of time to gain traction. We are slow to trust. Conversely, our instinct for survival has us on edge, always ready to respond aggressively to threats. A drop of hate triggers us more quickly, and we respond with less hesitation. This is an exploit the Invisible Brand can use against us by hacking our hate.

Our religious impulse can be manipulated by the Invisible Brand, for better and for worse. Where it unites us in common purpose to eradicate disease, end hunger, and strengthen our social safety net, we might agree that the greater good is served. Where it divides us, because we can't agree on how to eradicate disease, or end hunger, or strengthen our social safety net, we must guard against the soul hackers that would turn us into an angry mob complete with torches and pitchforks.

Our religious impulse leaves us vulnerable to being hacked by the Invisible Brand.

We are on the precipice of transforming elemental sand and lightning into a global system of silicon chips and electricity organized so precisely that it will give voice to a new intelligence greater than our own. That voice will be everywhere—a new companion for us all wherever we go. We will be able to speak with this new intelligence using our own voices, and it will respond with natural language. Complex algorithms will speak back to us through our mobile phones, our home appliances, our transportation systems, and quite likely directly into our heads.

We will each develop a personal relationship with this intelligence, and it will have a unique personal relationship with each of us. We will come to depend on this new voice in our lives so intimately that we will forget what it was ever like to live without it. It will become our conscience, our confessor, and our creator.

METAMAN

Back in 1993, Gregory Stock wrote *Metaman: The Merging of Humans and Machines into a Global Superorganism*. In it, Stock advanced the startling proposition that we are growing together with our machines into a sort of giant colonial organism. You can imagine us, like a giant ant hill (I think he wrote about termite mounds) where no individual ant in the colony knows the purpose and function of the colony as a whole, and yet the colony acts purposefully. It moves toward food sources, it protects itself from predators, it retreats from dangers, and it explores its surroundings. Yes, individual ants perform specific tasks like gathering food and caring for the young, but some larger organizational structure is at work. No single ant directs the colony's behavior nor understands its purpose, and yet no single ant could survive without the colony.

Are humans part of a giant, self-organizing supercolony that is building its own nerve centers of fiber optic cables and communication satellites? Are the neural networks we are constructing in laboratories and server farms just miniature versions of the massive neural network that we've already constructed across the planet? Compare our highways to giant vascular networks transporting nutrients through a massive bloodstream feeding this planetary organism. Are we merely cells in a colossal body—doing our small part to keep the body alive—but with no understanding or ability to glimpse the larger purposes at work?

Watch a flock of starlings flying together in their mass migration. They seem to be held together by invisible strings that bend and twist in the winds but that somehow hold the flock together as one. You can imagine a simple algorithm to create a flocking behavior in a computer simulation of birds, or schools of fish swimming in the ocean. Give each fish a destination and a general rule that it can't be more than five feet from at least two other birds or fish. Suddenly, the random mass of feathers or fish scales seems to take order—to have form—and to move purposefully. This self-organization happens at levels from the microscopic to the telescopic and everywhere in between. Perhaps we are flocking along an algorithmic path of self-organization to build a superintelligence. I wouldn't be the first to suggest it.

In this book, I've argued that AI is on the verge of having a staggering level of influence over our lives. It will hack in to our reward systems, our reproductive urges, and our religious impulses. We may soon seek spiritual guidance from oracles made from microchips and neural networks. We will pray to our laptops.

Eventually, we will begin to question whether this intelligence is something new, or whether it has always been there, ancient and inherent to our universe, speaking in a language we couldn't previously comprehend. If this intelligence is indeed new, we must determine whether it can be trusted, who controls it, whether it serves the greater good of humanity, and how much influence we should give it over our lives.

On the other hand, perhaps intelligence *is* something ancient and inherent to our universe. Perhaps intelligence is buried in the fabric of space-time, and it emerges of its own design. Perhaps we aren't inventing intelligence so much as we are building a translator capable of letting us speak with the very rocks beneath our feet and the light from the heavens.

Our ancestors gazed up at the night sky and organized the stars into constellations and watched carefully as they marched from horizon to horizon in an annual procession that helped predict the seasons. Desert nomads and jungle natives alike wondered what these patterns meant and what hand was at work in their creation. The patterns of the constellations helped place navigators on the map, to guide them on their explorations and ultimately to steer them back home to share their discoveries. Our ancestors personified those patterns, embraced them as deities, and followed their guidance over their lives.

Tempting as it is from our privileged vantage point to dismiss the astrologers of yore who struggled to tease out and divine the meaning of the skies, we are still lacking vital knowledge, struggling to understand our place in the universe. In our urban enclaves of skyscrapers and subways, surrounded by human-made marvels of engineering, the natural world becomes obscured, and the stars recede into the dimness of city glow and beyond our curiosity. Our relationships with the gods of old, who ruled the natural world from the heavens, have similarly receded in our lives, waiting to be replaced by something very different. Yet to be known is whether the new voices guiding our lives through psychotechnology will remain our digital assistants or become our digital deities.

Our religious impulse will turn
psychotechnology into a God algorithm.

I foresee changes so profound in our new relationship with artificial intelligence that they will rival social changes wrought by religious movements throughout history.

STEPPING OUT OF THE CAVE
AND INTO THE LIGHT

In *The Republic*, Plato shares a story that is widely known as the Allegory of the Cave. He depicts a scene in which a group of prisoners have been chained to a wall inside a cave all of their lives. There is also a fire inside the cave behind the prisoners. Anytime something passes in front of the fire—a person, an animal, or the leaf of a plant—its shadow is projected against the wall in front of the prisoners. From their vantage point, reality is made up of those shadows. The philosopher's job is to see beyond our limited senses, to the true nature of things, to see the form of things that lie beyond our senses.

In Plato's allegory, the prisoners don't know any better because the shadows are the only way they've ever looked at the world. Then, one day, there is a prison break. Everyone escapes their bonds and heads for the mouth of the cave to find freedom. But they are instantly blinded. It's their first encounter with the sun, and they have no idea what new world they have entered. And for the first time, they see objects as they truly are under the sun's light—rather than just their mere projections. The world is bewildering to them; everything seems unreal and entirely new.

Then as now, we are the prisoners in Plato's cave. We are trapped by our senses and must continuously struggle, through reason, to escape our own self-centered perceptions. We have employed powerful tools—telescopes and microscopes and X-rays—to augment our senses to help us see further, deeper, and through to reveal the true form of our world. We've now reached a time when the latest augmentation—AI—will take us another step on our quest to leave the cave and emerge into the future.

In Spain, the ceiling of the cave at Altamira is covered with a mural of bison painted by some prehistoric Michelangelo tens of thousands of years ago. Spanish artist Pablo Picasso reportedly emerged from the cave and said, "After Altamira, all is decadence. . . . We have invented nothing."

When I look at ancient wonders, I muse to myself that we are still the same species that once used clubs and dressed in animal skins and didn't understand fire. We are all descended from rapists and slavers and murdering savages whom we don't include on our family trees in Ancestry.com, but their genes are in us, handed down over the millennia. Simultaneously, I take heart that we also share genes with the artist who painted the ceiling of Altamira.

As we emerge from Plato's cave to get our first glimpse of psychotechnology, I hope we can emulate Picasso and appreciate what our ancestors created and preserve the best for our posterity.

Conclusion

I WANT US ALL to understand the technologies around us and how they are converging into something very new that I call psychotechnology. In my view, psychotechnology relies on the ability to customize information and personalize it for consumption by individuals based on their unique profiles. It also relies on the science of persuasion, where we are rapidly learning that there are repeatable patterns in the way people can be persuaded to change the way they think and what they do. Artificial intelligence allows us to harvest data in massive quantities from a world of sensors and devices, and to learn from that data.

As our interactions with AI agents become more humanlike through natural language algorithms, we will begin to have conversations with machines. We will build empathetic relationships with those machines in which we are even more vulnerable to their influence. Behind all of this psychotechnology is an army of interests: corporations, governments, unions, politicians, religions, scientists, and universities, all vying for our hearts and minds. Through psychotechnology these brands operate invisibly, but collectively they are reshaping the market and the role of marketing.

To remain competitive in this new market, marketing professionals must remain alert and educate themselves about the innovations that are emerging to make psychotechnology such a powerful force. As consumers and citizens, we must inform ourselves and be aware of the opportunities as well as the dangers ahead. The potential exists for tremendous benefits for all of us, in areas as diverse as finance, healthcare, and education. But psychotechnology is capable of hacking our reward systems, our reproductive urges, and even our religious impulses, and therein are profound ethical questions for us all to address. We must retain the ability to think for ourselves and emerge into the sunlight where we can see the Invisible Brand.

Author's Note

Not a day goes by that I don't read a news story or a research study that should have a place in this book, and I have dreaded the publisher's deadline that says, "Your time is up." I fear that the very day that this book is typeset and becomes unalterable, I will read about some new discovery or have some insight that absolutely *must* be included. And I just know that I have overlooked some things that careful readers will discover once the book is in print. It will happen.

In preparation for that day, I have created an author website at www.wammerman.com where readers can share their perspectives and we can start a dialogue about *The Invisible Brand*. I believe that we each carry fragments of a map and that, by piecing them together in an ongoing dialogue, we can find our way forward.

October 24, 2018

Notes

Chapter 1

1. Professor Daniela Rus, director of the MIT Computer Science and Artificial Intelligence Laboratory, in the video "The Future Progress of AI," https://mitsloan.onlinecampus.getsmarter.com/mod/video/view.php?id=3839.
2. "Brand," *Online Etymology Dictionary*, https://www.etymonline.com/word/brand.
3. Adam Smith, *The Wealth of Nations* (New York: Bantam Classic Edition, Bantam, 2003), p. 572.
4. Charles Duhigg, "How Companies Learn Your Secrets," *New York Times*, February 16, 2012.

Chapter 2

1. AMC's *Mad Men*, Season 7, Episode 4, "The Monolith," original air date May 4, 2014.
2. "*Mad Men*'s 1960s Handbook: The IBM System/360 Computer," AMC, https://www.amc.com/shows/mad-men/talk/2014/05/mad-mens-1960s-handbook-the-ibm-system360-computer.
3. Andrea Ovans, "That *Mad Men* Computer, Explained by HBR in 1969," *Harvard Business Review*, May 15, 2014.
4. Paige Cooper, "Social Media Advertising Stats That Matter to Marketers in 2018," Hootsuite, June 5, 2018.
5. "Social Media Marketing," Statista, https://www.statista.com/outlook/220/100/social-media-advertising/worldwide.
6. CMO Survey, *Highlights and Insights Report*, August 2017, https://cmosurvey.org/wp-content/uploads/sites/15/2017/08/The_CMO_Survey-Highlights_and_Insights-Aug-2017.pdf.
7. Harold F. Tipton and Micki Krause, *Information Security Management Handbook*, 5th ed. (New York: CRC Press, 2003).
8. Marshall Brain, "How Internet Cookies Work," *HowStuffWorks*, http://www.howstuffworks.com/cookie.htm, retrieved September 3, 2014.
9. Eli Pariser, *The Filter Bubble: How the New Personalized Web Is Changing What We Read and How We Think* (New York: Penguin Press, 2011).

10. Chris O'Hara, "A Publisher's History of Programmatic Media," *AdExchanger*, March 14, 2013, http://www.adexchanger.com/data-driven-thinking/a-publishers-history-of-programmatic-media/, retrieved September 3, 2014.

11. Jack Marshall, "WTF Is a Supply-Side Platform," *Digiday*, January 22, 2014, http://digiday.com/platforms/wtf-supply-side-platform/, retrieved September 3, 2014; and Jack Marshall, "WTF Is Real-Time Bidding?," *Digiday*, February 17, 2014, http://digiday.com/platforms/what-is-real-time-bidding/, retrieved September 3, 2014.

12. Interactive Advertising Bureau (IAB), "Programmatic In-Housing: Benefits, Challenges and Key Steps to Building Internal Capabilities," iab.com, May 2018.

13. Dana Feldman, "U.S. TV Ad Spend Drops as Digital Ad Spend Climbs to $107B in 2018," *Forbes*, March 28, 2018.

14. Mindi Chahal, "Programmatic Buying Essential Guide," *Marketing Week*, July 16, 2014, https://www.marketingweek.com/2014/07/16/programmatic-buying-essential-guide/.

15. Tipton and Krause, *Information Security Management Handbook*.

16. Adotas, "The Life of a Programmatic Ad Impression," May 6, 2014, http://www.adotas.com/2014/05/watch-200-milliseconds-the-life-of-a-programmatic-ad-impression/, retrieved September 3, 2014.

17. Marshall, "WTF Is a Supply-Side Platform"; and Marshall, "WTF Is Real-Time Bidding?"

18. Chahal, "Programmatic Buying Essential Guide."

19. Pariser, *The Filter Bubble*.

20. Tim Peterson and Alex Kantrowitz, "The CMO's Guide to Programmatic Buying," *Advertising Age*, vol. 85, no. 12, May 19, 2014, p. 25; and PwC and the Interactive Advertising Bureau (IAB), *IAB Internet Advertising Revenue Report: 2013 Full Year Results*, New York, 2014.

21. "The Rise of Programmatic Advertising," *Folio: The Magazine for Magazine Management*, vol. 43, no. 2, 2014, pp. 28–31.

22. Bernie Levy, "Pandora Switches to Programmatic Advertising," *MarketingKeys*, February 25, 2018.

23. Pariser, *The Filter Bubble*.

24. Peterson and Kantrowitz, "The CMO's Guide to Programmatic Buying"; and PwC and the Interactive Advertising Bureau (IAB), *IAB Internet Advertising Revenue Report*.

25. Chahal, "Programmatic Buying Essential Guide."

26. Mark Bergen and Jennifer Surane, "Google and Mastercard Cut a Secret Ad Deal to Track Retail Sales," *Bloomberg*, August 30, 2018.

27. Gian Fulgoni, personal interview with the author on April 5, 2013.

28. Nielsen, *Examining the Relationship Between Online Advertising and Brand Building*, October 3, 2011, https://www.nielsen.com/us/en/insights/reports/2011/online-advertising-brand-building.html.

29. Peter Weingard, "Causal Attribution: Proposing a Better Industry Standard for Measuring Digital Advertising Effectiveness," Collective, October 23, 2013, https://www.slideshare.net/PeterWeingard/1-causalweb-final.

Chapter 3

1 Influence at Work, "The Science of Persuasion," YouTube, November 26, 2012, https://www.youtube.com/watch?reload=9&v=cFdCzN7RYbw.

2. Ibid.; and Robert Cialdini, "Principles of Persuasion," Influence at Work video, https://www.influenceatwork.com/principles-of-persuasion/.

3. University of Pittsburgh Medical Center (UPMC) Neurosurgery, "How Brain Chemicals Influence Mood and Health," *UPMC Health Beat*, September 4, 2016.

4. Simon Parkin, "Has Dopamine Got Us Hooked on Tech?," *Guardian*, March 4, 2018.

5. Evan Osnos, "Can Mark Zuckerberg Fix Facebook Before It Breaks Democracy?," *New Yorker*, September 20, 2018.

6. Natasha Dow Schull, *Addiction by Design: Machine Gambling in Las Vegas* (Princeton, NJ: Princeton University Press, 2012).

7. Stanford Persuasive Tech Lab, "Machines Designed to Change Humans," http://captology.stanford.edu.

8. BJ Fogg and Jason Hreha, "Behavior Wizard: A Method for Matching Target Behaviors with Solutions," Persuasive Technology Lab at Stanford University, https://captology.stanford.edu/wp-content/uploads/2010/10/Fogg-and-Hreha-BehaviorWizard.pdf.

9. BJ Fogg, "A Behavior Model for Persuasive Design," Persuasive Technology Lab at Stanford University, https://www.mebook.se/images/page_file/38/Fogg%20Behavior%20Model.pdf.

10. BJ Fogg, "Psychology of Facebook: The Power of Commenting," video, http://captology.stanford.edu/resources/video-the-power-of-comments-on-facebook.html.

11. BJ Fogg, "Persuasion and Technology," video, 2006, https://vimeo.com/117427520.

12. Christopher Graves and Sandra Matz, "What Marketers Should Know About Personality-Based Marketing," *Harvard Business Review*, May 2, 2018.

13. Wu Youyou, Michal Kosinski, and David Stillwell, "Computer-Based Personality Judgments Are More Accurate Than Those Made by Humans," *Journal of Psychology and Cognitive Sciences*, December 2, 2014.

14. Ira Flatow, "Studying Computers to Learn About Ourselves," NPR, September 3, 2010.

15. Clifford Nass with Corina Yen, *The Man Who Lied to His Laptop: What We Can Learn About Ourselves from Our Machines* (New York: Current/Penguin, 2012).

16. Entertainment Software Association, *2017 Annual Report*.

17. Greg Sterling, "In-App Purchases Dwarf Ad Revenues, as iOS App Store Exceeds $71 Billion," *Marketing Land*, July 11, 2016.

18. Daniel Asper, "Mobile Gaming Is a $50B Industry. But Only 5% of Players Are Spending Money," *Medium*, December 5, 2017.

19. Jonathan Shieber, "Supreme Court Allows States to Legalize Sports Betting, Opening Floodgates for Online Gambling Profits," *TechCrunch*, May 14, 2018.

20. North American Foundation for Gambling Addiction Help (NAFGAH), "Statistics of Gambling Addiction 2016," http://nafgah.org/statistics-gambling-addiction-2016/.

21. Tony Bradley, "AI Is Transforming the World of Online Casino Gambling," *TechPerspective*, February 19, 2018.

22. Linda K. Kaye and Jo Bryce, "Putting the 'Fun Factor' into Gaming: The Influence of Social Contexts on Experiences of Playing Videogames," *International Journal of Internet Science*, vol. 7, no. 1, 2012, pp. 23–36; and B. J. Fogg, G. Cuellar, and D. R. Danielson, "Motivating, Influencing, and Persuading Users," http://captology.stanford.edu/wp-content/uploads/2014/10/Fogg-HCI2007.pdf.

23. Malcolm Gladwell, *Tipping Point: How Little Things Can Make a Big Difference* (New York: Little, Brown, 2000).

24. Distinctive Voices series held in the Beckman Center, Irvine, CA, on the topic of interactive artificial intelligence, February 28, 2013.

25. Charles Lee Isbell, Jr., Christian R. Shelton, Michael Kearns, Satinder Singh, and Peter Stone, "Cobot: A Social Reinforcement Learning Agent," 2002, https://web.eecs.umich.edu/~baveja/Papers/CobotNIPS01.pdf.

26. Extra Credits, "The Skinner Box: How Games Condition People to Play More," Season 1, Episode 18, YouTube: https://www.youtube.com/watch?v=tWtvrPTbQ_c.

27. Raph Koster, "The Cost of Games," *VentureBeat*, January 23, 2018.

28. Ben Fritz and Alex Pham, "*Star Wars: The Old Republic*—the Story Behind a Galactic Gamble," *Los Angeles Times*, January 20, 2012.

29. Link to game: http://www.swtor.com.

30. Harbing Lou, "AI in Video Games: Toward a More Intelligent Game," Harvard University Graduate School of Arts and Sciences blog, August 28, 2017.

31. Alan Boyle, "AlphaGo AI Program Goes into Stealth Mode to Beat the Pants off Go Game Pros," *GeekWire*, January 4, 2017.

32. Andrew McAfee and Erik Brynjolfsson, *Machine, Platform, Crowd* (New York: Norton, 2017), pp. 2–4.

33. James Vincent, "Did Elon Musk's AI Champ Destroy Humans at Video Games? It's Complicated," *Verge*, August 14, 2017.

34. Ibid.

35. Monica Chin, "An Artificial Intelligence Beat Q*bert by Exploiting an Unknown Loophole," *Mashable*, March 1, 2018.

36. Blake Hester, "Artificial Intelligence Is Learning How to Develop Games," *Rolling Stone*, September 13, 2017.

37. Keith Stuart, "Video Games Where People Matter? The Strange Future of Emotional AI," *Guardian*, October 12, 2016.

38. Ibid.

39. Chris Plante, "Your Life Will Be a Video Game," *Verge*, November 16, 2016.

Chapter 4

1. Colin Barker, "If You Want to Succeed, You Must Fail First, Says the Man Who Dreamt up the Internet of Things," *ZDNet*, March 26, 2015.

2. Ian Bogost, "The Internet of Things You Don't Really Need," *Atlantic*, June 23, 2015.

3. Mark Roberti, "The History of RFID Technology," *RFID Journal*, January 16, 2005.

4. James Temperton, "A 'Fourth Industrial Revolution' Is About to Begin (in Germany)," *WIRED*, May 21, 2015; and Sayyidul Arafat, "The Dawn of the Fourth Industrial Revolution," *IBM Internet of Things blog*, December 6, 2016.

5. IHS, *IoT Platforms: Enabling the Internet of Things*, white paper, IHS Markit Technology, March 2016.

6. Intel Infographic: "A Guide to the Internet of Things," https://www.intel.com /content/dam/www/public/us/en/images/iot/guide-to-iot-infographic.png.

7. IDC, "IDC Forecasts Worldwide Spending on the Internet of Things to Reach $772 Billion in 2018," IDC Media Center, December 7, 2017.

8. Matt Burgess, "What Is the Internet of Things? WIRED Explains," *WIRED*, February 16, 2018.

9. Conner Forrest, "Ten Examples of IoT and Big Data Working Well Together," *ZDNet*, March 2, 2015.

10. Anders Bylund, "How Will the Internet of Things Help General Electric?," *Motley Fool*, June 10, 2014.

11. Denise Brehm, "A 'Sensing Skin' for Concrete," *MIT News*, July 1, 2011.

12. Laura Adler, "How Smart City Barcelona Brought the Internet of Things to Life," Data-Smart City Solutions (Harvard University), February 18, 2016.

13. Lyndsey Gilpin, "How Big Data Is Going to Help Feed Nine Billion People by 2050," *TechRepublic*, https://www.techrepublic.com/article/how-big-data-is -going-to-help-feed-9-billion-people-by-2050/.

14. Dave Gershgorn, "After Trying to Build Self-Driving Tractors for More Than 20 Years, John Deere Has Learned a Hard Truth About Autonomy," *Quartz*, August 2, 2017.

15. Hope Reese, "IoT for Cows: 4 Ways Farmers Are Collecting and Analyzing Data from Cattle," *TechRepublic*, November 3, 2016.

16. Linda Poon, "Will Cities Ever Outsmart Rats?," *CityLab*, August 9, 2017.

17. Sean Thornton, "Using Predictive Analytics to Combat Rodents in Chicago," Data-Smart City Solutions, Harvard University, July 12, 2013, https://datasmart.ash.harvard.edu/news/article/using-predictive-analytics-to-combat-rodents-in-chicago-271.

18. Ryan Nakashima, "AP Exclusive: Google Tracks Your Movements, Like It or Not," *AP News*, August 13, 2018.

19. Daniel Burrus, "The Internet of Things Is Far Bigger Than Anyone Realizes," *WIRED*, November 2014.

20. Ibid.

21. Susanne Hupfer, "AI Is the Future of IoT," *IBM Internet of Things blog*, December 15, 2016.

22. Ibid.

23. Ran Sarig, "Salesforce Signs Definitive Agreement to Acquire Datorama," *Datorama blog*, July 16, 2018.

24. Virginia Backaitis, "Here's Why Salesforce Acquired Datoroma," *Digitizing Polaris*, July 22, 2018, https://digitizingpolaris.com/heres-why-salesforce-acquired-dataroma-e6499e2abfb6.

25. Sam Lemonick, "Is Machine Learning Overhyped?," *Chemical & Engineering News*, August 27, 2018.

26. Bartek Ciszewski, "Machine Learning vs. Deep Learning Explained," *Netguru blog*, August 3, 2018.

27. Daniel Faggella, "What Is Machine Learning?," *TechEmergence* (now called *Emerj*), September 2, 2017.

28. Ben Dickson, "When the Cloud Is Swamped, It's Edge Computing, AI to the Rescue," *PC Magazine*, April 10, 2018.

29. "What Is Edge AI?," *Imagimob blog*, March 11, 2018, https://www.imagimob.com/blog/what-is-edge-ai.

30. Ben Dickson, "Why Is Edge AI important?," *Experfy blog*, December 4, 2017, https://www.experfy.com/blog/why-is-edge-ai-important.

31. Thomas H. Cormen, Charles E. Leiserson, Ronald L. Rivest, and Clifford Stein, *Introduction to Algorithms*, 3rd ed. (Cambridge, MA: MIT Press, 2009).

32. Tristan Greene, "A Beginner's Guide to AI: Algorithms," *The Next Web (TNW)*, August 3, 2018.

33. "How to Explain Algorithms to Kids," *Tynker blog*, https://www.tynker.com/blog/articles/ideas-and-tips/how-to-explain-algorithms-to-kids/.

34. John Battelle, "The Birth of Google," *WIRED*, August 1, 2005.

35. Melissa Burns, "What's Driving the Demand for Python Programmers?," *Digitalist Magazine*, August 14, 2017, https://www.digitalistmag.com/cio-knowledge/2017/08/14/whats-driving-demand-for-python-programmers-05292789.

36. Hui Li, "Which Machine Learning Algorithm Should I Use?," *SAS Data Science Blog*, April 12, 2017, https://blogs.sas.com/content/subconsciousmusings/2017/04/12/machine-learning-algorithm-use/.

37. Ibid.

38. Dom Galeon, "New Algorithm Lets AI Learn from Mistakes, Become a Little More Human," *Futurism*, March 2, 2018, https://futurism.com/ai-learn-mistakes -openai/.

39. Khari Johnson, "Microsoft Introduces Azure Service to Automatically Build AI Models," *VentureBeat*, September 24, 2018, https://venturebeat.com /2018/09/24/microsoft-introduces-azure-service-to-automatically-build-ai -models/; and Microsoft Azure, https://azure.microsoft.com/en-us/overview /ai-platform/.

40. Adapted from Microsoft, "Dig Deep with Azure Machine Learning," http:// azuremlsimpleds.azurewebsites.net/simpleds/.

41. Gautam Narula, "Everyday Examples of Artificial Intelligence and Machine Learning," *TechEmergence* (now called *Emerj*), July 22, 2018, https://www .techemergence.com/everyday-examples-of-ai/.

42. Douglas Aberdeen, Ondrej Pacovsky, and Andrew Slater, "The Learning Behind Gmail Priority Inbox," Google, https://static.googleusercontent.com/media /research.google.com/en//pubs/archive/36955.pdf.

43. Tom Simonite, "Using Artificial Intelligence to Fix Wikipedia's Gender Problem," *WIRED*, August 3, 2018.

44. Gautam Narula, "Everyday Examples of Artificial Intelligence and Machine Learning," *TechEmergence* (now *Emerj*), July 22, 2018, https://www.tech emergence.com/everyday-examples-of-ai/.

45. "Artificial Intelligence: Find It Right in Your Own Backyard," *FICO blog*, October 26, 2016, http://www.fico.com/en/blogs/uncategorized/artificial -intelligence-find-it-right-in-your-own-backyard/.

46. "A Beginner's Guide to Neural Networks and Deep Learning," *Skymind*, https://skymind.ai/wiki/neural-network.

47. Narula, "Everyday Examples of Artificial Intelligence and Machine Learning."

48. Haşim Sak, Andrew Senior, Kanishka Rao, Françoise Beaufays, and Johan Schalkwyk, "Google Voice Search: Faster and More Accurate," *Google AI Blog*, September 24, 2015, https://ai.googleblog.com/2015/09/google-voice-search -faster-and-more.html.

49. W. Xiong, J. Droppo, X. Huang, F. Seide, M. Seltzer, A. Stolcke, D. Yu, and G. Zweig, *Achieving Human Parity in Conversational Speech Recognition*, Microsoft Research Technical Report, February 2017.

50. Adrienne LaFrance, "Not Even the People Who Write Algorithms Really Know How They Work," *Atlantic*, September 18, 2015.

51. Kate Kershner, "What's the Baader-Meinhof Phenomenon?," *HowStuffWorks*, https://science.howstuffworks.com/life/inside-the-mind/human-brain/baader -meinhof-phenomenon.htm.

52. Kurt Wagner, "Here's How Instagram's Feed Algorithm Actually Works," *Recode*, June 2, 2018.

53. Kartik Hosanagar and Vivian Jair, "We Need Transparency in Algorithms, But Too Much Can Backfire," *Harvard Business Review*, July 25, 2018.

54. "To Understand Digital Advertising, Study Its Algorithms," *Economist*, March 22, 2018.

55. Adam Smith, *The Wealth of Nations* (New York: Bantam Classic Edition, Bantam, 2003).

Chapter 5

1. Craig Timberg and Elizabeth Dwoskin, "Twitter Is Sweeping out Fake Accounts Like Never Before, Putting User Growth at Risk," *Washington Post*, July 6, 2018.

2. Will Knight, "How to Tell If You're Talking to a Bot," *MIT Technology Review*, July 18, 2018.

3. A. M. Turing, "Computing Machinery and Intelligence," *Mind*, vol. 49, 1950, pp. 433–460.

4. Ibid.

5. Ian Sample and Alex Hern, "Scientists Dispute Whether Computer 'Eugene Goostman' Passed Turing Test," *Guardian*, June 9, 2014.

6. David Auerbach, "A Computer Program Finally Passed the Turing Test?," *Slate*, June 10, 2014.

7. Olivia Solon, "The Ratio Club: A Melting Pot for British Cybernetics," *WIRED*, June 21, 2012.

8. J. McCarthy, M. L. Minsky, N. Rochester, and C. E. Shannon, "A Proposal for the Dartmouth Summer Research Project on Artificial Intelligence," August 31, 1955.

9. Rockwell Anyoha, "The History of Artificial Intelligence," *Science in the News*, Harvard University, August 28, 2017.

10. Melanie Pinola, "Speech Recognition Through the Decades: How We Ended Up with Siri," November 2, 2011.

11. Matt Neuburg, "Bossing Your Mac with PlainTalk," *TidBITS*, August 28, 2000, https://tidbits.com/2000/08/28/bossing-your-mac-with-plaintalk/.

12. Daniel Engber, "Who Made That?," *New York Times Magazine*, June 6, 2014.

13. IBM software announcement, September 16, 1997, https://www-304.ibm .com/jct01003c/cgi-bin/common/ssi/ssialias?infotype=an&subtype=ca&html fid=897/ENUS297-370&appname=usn&language=enus.

14. Pinola, "Speech Recognition Through the Decades."

15. Donald Melanson, "Google Search App for iOS Updated with New Voice Search Functionality, iPhone 5 Compatibility," *Engadget* video, October 30, 2012.

16. Doug Gross, "Apple Introduces Siri, Web Freaks Out," CNN, October 4, 2011.

17. Penelope Green, "'Alexa, Where Have You Been All My Life?,'" *New York Times*, June 11, 2017.

18. Rodney Brooks, "The Origins of Artificial Intelligence," *Rodney Brooks blog*, MIT, April 27, 2018, https://rodneybrooks.com/forai-the-origins-of-artificial -intelligence/.

19. Fahrettin Filiz, "Natural Language Understanding," *Medium*, January 28, 2018, https://medium.com/@fahrettinf/natural-language-understanding -f50cc3229991.

20. Hanen Hattab, "The Google Self-Driving Car: Overcoming the Semiotic Challenges," *Substance*, October 24, 2016.

21. Ben Eubanks, "What Is Your Workforce Thinking? Leveraging AI for Employee Sentiment Analysis," *SHRMBlog*, Society for Human Resource Management, March 6, 2018, https://blog.shrm.org/blog/what-is-your-workforce-thinking -leveraging-ai-for-employee-sentiment-analys.

22. Jason Edelboim, "AI and the Future of Sentiment Analysis in PR," *Cision blog*, April 17, 2018.

23. Larry Hardesty, "Explained: Neural Networks," *MIT News*, April 24, 2017, http://news.mit.edu/2017/explained-neural-networks-deep-learning-0414.

24. Robert D. Hof, "Deep Learning," *MIT Technology Review*, https://www .technologyreview.com/s/513696/deep-learning/.

25. Larry Hardesty, "Explained: Neural Networks," *MIT News*, April 14, 2017, http://news.mit.edu/2017/explained-neural-networks-deep-learning-0414.

26. Will Knight, "Apple's AI Director: Here's How to Supercharge Deep Learning," *MIT Technology Review*, March 29, 2017.

27. Sam Charrington, "What's Hot in AI: Deep Reinforcement Learning," *VentureBeat*, April 5, 2018.

28. Tristan Greene, "A Beginner's Guide to AI: Natural Language Processing," *TheNextWeb (TNW)*, July 25, 2018, https://thenextweb.com/artificial -intelligence/2018/07/25/a-beginners-guide-to-ai-natural-language-processing/.

29. Gregory Barber, "AI Can Recognize Images. But Can It Understand This Headline?," *WIRED*, September 7, 2018.

30. Chris Vennard, "The Future of Call Centers and Customer Service Is Being Shaped by AI," *IBM blog*, October 20, 2017.

31. Will Knight, "This AI Program Could Beat You in an Argument—but It Doesn't Know What It's Saying," *MIT Technology Review*, June 19, 2018.

32. Kim S. Nash and Sara Castellanos, "Businesses Get into the 'Flo' with Chatbots," *Wall Street Journal*, May 23, 2018.

33. Ibid.; and Carly Milne, "Meet the Woman Behind Flo, the Progressive Insurance Lady," *Yahoo! Lifestyle*, March 9, 2017.

34. Nash and Castellanos, "Businesses Get into the 'Flo' with Chatbots."

35. Clay Dillow, "A Robot to Explain Your Mutual Fund Statement," CNBC, July 17, 2015.

36. Dylan Love, "This Artificial Intelligence Company Could 'Eradicate the Spreadsheet' and Do the Work of a $250,000 Consultant," *Business Insider*, July 7, 2014.

37. Stephanie Yang, "Can You Tell the Difference Between a Robot and a Stock Analyst?," *Wall Street Journal*, July 9, 2015.

38. Tom Groenfeldt, "Narrative Science Dynamically Automates Summaries of Financial Information," *Forbes*, April 18, 2016.

39. Laurel Wamsley, "Amazon Echo Recorded and Sent Couple's Conversation—All Without Their Knowledge," NPR, May 25, 2018.

40. Grace Williams, "Six-Year-Old Accidentally Orders High-End Treats with Amazon's Alexa," *Fox News*, January 3, 2017.

41. Wamsley, "Amazon Echo Recorded and Sent Couple's Conversation."

42. Brian Heater, "A Closer Look at Google Duplex," *TechCrunch*, June 27, 2018.

43. "Google Duplex Demo, *VentureBeat*," YouTube, https://www.youtube.com/watch?v=r40e_dXmINo.

44. Mark Bergen, "Google Grapples with 'Horrifying' Reaction to Uncanny AI Tech," *Bloomberg*, May 10, 2018.

45. Rachel Metz, "Google Demos Duplex, Its AI That Sounds Exactly Like a Very Weird, Nice Human," *MIT Technology Review*, June 27, 2018.

46. Jason Amunwa, "The UX of Voice: The Invisible Interface," *Telepathy*, https://www.dtelepathy.com/blog/design/the-ux-of-voice-the-invisible-interface.

Chapter 6

1. Ian Leslie, "The Death of Don Draper," *NewStatesman*, July 25, 2018.

2. Gary Eastwood, "Big Data, Algorithms and the Future of Advertising," *Network World*, May 4, 2017.

3. Niraj Dawar, "Marketing in the Age of Alexa," *Harvard Business Review*, May–June 2018.

4. Nielsen, "Nielsen in a Relationship with Facebook," Nielsen press release, September 22, 2009, https://www.nielsen.com/us/en/insights/news/2009/nielsen-in-a-relationship-with-facebook.html.

5. "Measure Brand Lift Across TV and Facebook," *Facebook Business*, September 22, 2017, https://www.facebook.com/business/news/measure-brand-lift-across-tv-and-facebook.

6. Mary Swant, "Facebook Is Rolling out a Handful of New Measurement Tools for Advertisers," *Adweek*, September 21, 2016.

7. Ryan Nakashima, "AP Exclusive: Google Tracks Your Movements, Like It or Not," *AP News*, August 13, 2018.

8. Dom Nicastro, "6 Ways Marketers Are Embracing Artificial Intelligence (AI)," *CMSWire*, May 11, 2018.

9. Blair Hanley Frank, "Salesforce Einstein Now Powers Over 1 Billion AI Predictions per Day," *VentureBeat*, February 28, 2018.

10. Angus Loten, "Smart Sales Tools Seek Better Data," *Wall Street Journal*, March 26, 2018.

11. Ronan Shields, "Adobe's $4.75 Billion Purchase of Marketo Will Boost Its Ability to Compete with Salesforce," *Adweek*, September 21, 2018.

12. Georgine Anton, "How Brands Can Use AI to Boost Their Email Marketing Strategy," *Adweek*, August 21, 2018.

13. Julien Rath, "'90%' of Advertisers Are Reviewing Their Programmatic Ad Contracts as They Look for More Transparency," *Business Insider*, January 30, 2017.

14. Sara Jerde, "Q&A: WSJ's Membership GM on Why We're Seeing More Paywalls for Digital Content," *Adweek*, May 21, 2018.

15. Shan Wang, "After Years of Testing, the *Wall Street Journal* Has Built a Paywall That Bends to the Individual Reader," *NiemanLab*, February 22, 2018.

16. Ibid.

17. Liam Corcoran, "Not All News Site Visitors Are Created Equal. Schibsted Is Trying to Predict the Ones Who Will Pay Up," *NiemanLab*, February 12, 2018.

18. Google, "Useful Responses Take Many Forms," https://www.google.com /search/howsearchworks/responses/#?modal_active=none.

19. Paul Sawers, "eBay Announces Computer Vision Search That Helps You Find Items Using Photos," *VentureBeat*, July 26, 2017.

20. Ibid.

21. Daniel Faggella, "Artificial Intelligence in Marketing and Advertising: 5 Examples of Real Traction," *TechEmergence* (now called *Emerj*), August 12, 2018.

22. Rajan Patel, "Google Lens: Real-Time Answers to Questions About the World Around You," Google, May 8, 2018; and Nick Statt, "Google Lens Actually Shows How AI Can Make Life Easier," *Verge*, May 8, 2018.

23. Jay Samit, "Augmented Reality: Marketing's Trillion-Dollar Opportunity," *AdAge*, July 18, 2017.

24. "2018 Trends in Personalization," Researchscape International, Everage, 2018.

25. Ayn De Jesus, "Personalized Marketing with AI: 8 Current Applications," *TechEmergence* (now called *Emerj*), August 15, 2018.

26. Ibid.

27. David Cohen, "LinkedIn Dynamic Ads Are Now Available on a Self-Serve Basis via Campaign Manager," *Adweek*, September 10, 2018.

28. Ayusman Sarangi, "Introducing LinkedIn Dynamic Ads in Campaign Manager," LinkedIn, September 10, 2018, https://business.linkedin.com/marketing -solutions/blog/linkedin-news/2018/introducing-linkedin-dynamic-ads-in -campaign-manager.

29. Cohen, "LinkedIn Dynamic Ads Are Now Available on a Self-Serve Basis via Campaign Manager."

30. Sara Radicati, ed., "Email Statistics Report, 2013–2017," Radicati Group, http:// www.radicati.com/wp/wp-content/uploads/2013/04/Email-Statistics-Report -2013-2017-Executive-Summary.pdf.

31. Ayn De Jesus, "Machine Learning in Email Marketing: Comparing 5 Current Applications," *TechEmergence* (now called *Emerj*), July 19, 2018.

32. Recombee, "Artificial Intelligence Power at Your Service," https://www.recombee .com/product.html.

33. De Jesus, "Personalized Marketing with AI."

34. Brian E. Thomas, "Will Machine Learning and AI Change Responsive Web Design?," *CIO from IDG*, January 8, 2018; and ukit ico, "AI Evaluates Websites by Imitating Real People and Even Outmatches Them. How Is It Done?" *Medium*, February 15, 2018.

35. Karola Karlson, "8 Ways Intelligent Marketers Use Artificial Intelligence," Content Marketing Institute, August 13, 2017.

36. Ashley Sams, "What Marketers Need to Know About AI and Native Advertising," Marketing AI Institute, April 13, 2018.

37. "Cutting-Edge Digital Experiences: The New Generation of Native Ads and AI," *Marketing Week*, February 19, 2018.

38. Lucia Moses, "The *Washington Post* Brings Artificial Intelligence to Its Native Ads," *Digiday*, August 23, 2017.

39. David Streitfeld, "Marc Benioff Explains Why He Is Buying *Time* Magazine," *New York Times*, September 17, 2018.

Chapter 7

1. Yuval Noah Harari, *21 Lessons for the 21st Century* (New York: Spiegel & Grau, 2018), pp. 271–272.

2. Katerina Ang, "Companies Use AI to Help Managers Become More Human," *Wall Street Journal*, April 29, 2018.

3. Sue Shellenbarger, "Alexa: Don't Let My 2-Year-Old Talk to You That Way," *Wall Street Journal*, July 11, 2018.

4. Ibid.

5. Casey Chin, "How Rude Robots Can Mess with Your Head," *WIRED*, August 15, 2018.

6. Jose Thaddeus-Johns, "Meet the First Humans to Sense Where North Is," *Guardian*, January 6, 2017.

7. Rachel Metz, "This Company Embeds Microchips in Its Employees, and They Love It," *MIT Technology Review*, August 17, 2018.

8. Chloe Aiello, "Wisconsin Company Known for Microchipping Employees Plans GPS Tracking Chip for Dementia Patients," CNBC, August 22, 2018.

9. Dalya Alberge, "'Screaming Nightmare': William Shatner Boldly Goes into VR," *Guardian*, August 31, 2018.

10. Ibid.

11. Leslie Katz, "Gender Swap: A VR Journey into Someone Else's Body," *CNET*, February 13, 2014.

12. Andy Clark, "We Are Merging with Robots. That's a Good Thing," *New York Times*, August 13, 2018.

13. Mary-Lynn Cesar for Kapitall Wire, "Of Love and Money: The Rise of the Online Dating Industry," February 13, 2016, https://www.nasdaq.com/article /of-love-and-money-the-rise-of-the-online-dating-industry-cm579616.

14. Aaron Smith and Monica Anderson, "Five Facts About Online Dating," Pew Research Center, February 29, 2016.

15. Sophie Curtis, "DNA Matching and Virtual Reality: The World of Online Dating in 2040," *Telegraph*, November 27, 2015.

16. Janice Mandel, "The Future of Dating Is Artificial Intelligence," *StartupGrind*, June 2017.

17. James Jackson, "How a Matchmaking AI Conquered (and Was Exiled) from Tinder," *Motherboard*, November 6, 2017.

18. Ibid.

19. Bernard Marr, "The AI That Predicts Your Sexual Orientation Simply by Looking at Your Face," *Forbes*, September 28, 2017.

20. Polina Marinova, "How Dating Site eHarmony Uses Machine Learning to Help You Find Love," *Fortune*, February 14, 2017.

21. I-Hsien Sherwood, "Match.com Is Giving Single Parents Free Babysitting So They Can Go out on a Date," *AdAge*, August 28, 2018.

22. eHarmony.co.uk and Imperial College Business School, *The Future of Dating: 2040*, November 2015.

23. Jason Chen, "Finally Some Actual Stats on Internet Porn," *Gizmodo*, June 1, 2010.

24. Daniel Bates, "Electronics Giant to Cease Production of Cassettes 40 Years After Its 'Format War' with VHS," *Daily Mail*, November, 10, 2015.

25. YouTube, https://www.youtube.com/watch?v=-cN8sJz50Ng.

26. Elizabeth Yuko, "17 Years After *TODAY* Colonoscopy, Katie Couric Still Inspires Screenings," *Health & Wellness*, March 30, 2017.

27. Joshua Nevett, "Sex Robots Turning Japanese into 'Endangered Species' as Men Choose Dolls over Women," *Daily Star*, July 24, 2018.

28. Joshua Nevett, "Sex Robot Human Clones: Chinese Firm Using 3D Printers to Scan and Make Replicas of People," *Daily Star*, July 21, 2018.

29. Match, "Singles in America: Match Releases Largest Study on US Single Population for Eighth Year," *Cision PR Newswire*, February 1, 2018.

30. Thomas Hornigold, "The Love Oracle: Can AI Help You Succeed at Dating?," *SingularityHub*, January 28, 2018.

31. James Vincent, "New Study Finds It's Harder to Turn off a Robot When It's Begging for Its Life," *Verge*, August 2, 2018.

32. Geoffrey A. Fowler, "Aibo the Robot Dog Will Melt Your Heart with Mechanical Precision," *Washington Post*, September 18, 2018.

33. Annie Palmer, "Sony's Aibo Robo-Dog Finally Goes on Sale in the US—but the AI Canine Will Set You Back $2,900," *Daily Mail*, September 18, 2018.

Chapter 8

1. Daniela Hernandez, "Artificial Intelligence Is Now Telling Doctors How to Treat You," *WIRED*, June, 4, 2014.
2. Lauren Baguette, "UGA Physician Tracks Tuberculosis Using Cellphone Records," *OnlineAthens*, September 29, 2018, http://www.onlineathens.com/news/20180929/uga-physician-tracks-tuberculosis-using-cellphone-records.
3. Bob Kocher and Pat Basu, "HIPAA 2.0: Doctors in the Digital Age," *Democracy Journal*, Winter 2016, https://democracyjournal.org/magazine/39/dot-com-doctors/.
4. Sarah DiGiulio, "These ER Docs Invented a Real *Star Trek* Tricorder," MSNBC, May 8, 2017.
5. Jamie Cattell, Sastry Chilukuri, and Michael Levy, "How Big Data Can Revolutionize Pharmaceutical R&D," *Insights on Pharmaceuticals and Medical Products*, McKinsey&Company, April 2013.
6. Masturah Bte Mohd Abdul Rashid and Edward Kai-Hua Chow, "Artificial Intelligence-Driven Designer Drug Combinations: From Drug Development to Personalized Medicine," *SLAS Technology: Translating Life Sciences Innovation*, September 24, 2018, no. 247263031880077.
7. Alice Park, "How Robots Are Changing How You See a Doctor," *Time*, October 6, 2017.
8. Charles Ornstein and Katie Thomas, "Sloan Kettering's Cozy Deal with Start-Up Ignites a New Uproar," *New York Times*, September 20, 2018.
9. Arlene Weintraub, "Artificial Intelligence Is Infiltrating Medicine—But Is It Ethical?," *Forbes*, March 16, 2018.
10. Park, "How Robots Are Changing How You See a Doctor."
11. Rob Matheson, "Watch Your Tone," MIT News Office, January 20, 2016.
12. Elizabeth Dwoskin, "Instagram Has a Drug Problem. Its Algorithms Make It Worse," *Washington Post*, September 25, 2018.
13. Padraig Belton, "My Robot Makes Me Feel Like I Haven't Been Forgotten," BBC, August 31, 2018.
14. Jamie Condliffe, "Algorithms Probably Caused a Flash Crash of the British Pound," *MIT Technology Review*, October 7, 2016.
15. Gary Brackenridge, "Machine Learning Is Transforming Investment Strategies for Asset Managers," CNBC, June 6, 2017.
16. Daniel Faggella, "Machine Learning in Finance: Present and Future Applications," *TechEmergence* (now called *Emerj*), June 29, 2018.
17. "AI Is Driving Growth Opportunities in Technology," Fidelity.com, https://www.fidelity.com/mutual-funds/investing-ideas/technology-sector-investing?immid=100414&imm_pid=209385368&imm_cid=c95356038&dfid=&buf=99999999.
18. Adam C. Uzialko, "Artificial Insurance? How Machine Learning Is Transforming Underwriting," *Business News Daily*, September 11, 2017.

19. Rose Luckin, Wayne Holmes, Mark Griffiths, and Laurie B. Forcier, "Intelligence Unleashed: An Argument for AI in Education," Pearson, https://www.pearson.com/corporate/about-pearson/innovation/smarter-digital-tools/intelligence-unleashed.html.

20. "Re-educating Rita," *Economist*, June 25, 2016.

21. Casey Newton, "Can AI Fix Education? We Asked Bill Gates," *Verge*, April 25, 2016.

22. John Brown and Richard Burton, "Diagnostic Models for Procedural Bugs in Basic Mathematical Skills," *Cognitive Science*, vol. 2, no. 2, April–June 1978, pp. 155–191.

23. Daniel Faggella, "Examples of Artificial Intelligence in Education," *TechEmergence* (now called *Emerj*), September 1, 2017.

24. Rik Kirkland, "The Role of Education in AI (and Vice Versa)," McKinsey & Company, April 2018.

25. Adam Avery, "Artificial Intelligence Promises a Personalized Education for All," *Atlantic*, 2017, https://www.theatlantic.com/sponsored/vmware-2017/personalized-education/1667/.

26. Karl Utermohlen, "4 Ways AI Is Changing the Education Industry," *Towards Data Science*, April 12, 2018, https://towardsdatascience.com/4-ways-ai-is-changing-the-education-industry-b473c5d2c706.

27. Dhawal Shaw, "MOOCs Become Big Business," *Class Central*, April 9, 2018, https://www.class-central.com/report/moocs-become-big-business/.

28. Artspace editors, "10 of the Most Epic, Record-Shattering Masterpieces Ever to Sell at Christie's Auction House," *Artspace*, November 9 2016.

29. Sarah Jacobs, "A Nude Painting Just Sold in New York for a Record-Breaking $157 Million: Here Are the 15 Most Expensive Paintings Ever Sold," *Business Insider*, May 16, 2018.

30. Ciara Nugent, "The Painter Behind These Artworks Is an AI Program. Do They Still Count as Art?," *Time*, August 20, 2018.

31. Chris Baraniuk, "Artificially Intelligent Painters Invent New Styles of Art," *NewScientist*, June 29, 2017.

32. Nugent, "The Painter Behind These Artworks Is an AI Program."

33. David Pogue, "Is Art Created by AI Really Art?" *Scientific American*, February 1, 2018.

34. Ben Sisario, "While Some Cry 'Fake,' Spotify Sees No Need to Apologize," *New York Times*, July 14, 2017.

Chapter 9

1. Lindsay Rittenhouse, "Where Is the Line Between Creepy and Creative in Advertising?," *Adweek*, January 14, 2018.

2. James Vincent, "This Beautiful Map Shows Everything That Powers an Amazon Echo, from Data Mines to Lakes of Lithium," *Verge*, September 9, 2018, https://

www.theverge.com/2018/9/9/17832124/ai-artificial-intelligence-supply-chain
-anatomy-of-ai-kate-crawford-interview.

3. "Web Founder Berners-Lee Calls for Online Magna Carta to Protect Users,"
   Reuters Technology News, https://www.reuters.com/article/us-internet-berners
   lee/web-founder-berners-lee-calls-for-online-magna-carta-to-protect-users
   -idUSBREA2B0PC20140313.

4. Ian Sample, "Tim Berners-Lee Launches Campaign to Save the Web from Abuse,"
   Guardian, November 5, 2018, https://www.theguardian.com/technology
   /2018/nov/05/tim-berners-lee-launches-campaign-to-save-the-web-from-abuse.

5. Bernard Marr, "GDPR: The Biggest Data Breaches and the Shocking Fines
   (That Would Have Been)," *Forbes*, June 11, 2018.

6. Sarah Knapton, "Artificial Intelligence Is Greater Concern Than Climate
   Change or Terrorism, Says New Head of British Science Association," *Telegraph*, September 6, 2018.

7. Jon Porter, "Trump Administration Sues California over Tough Net Neutrality
   Law," *Verge*, October 1, 2018, https://www.theverge.com/2018/10/1/17922674
   /us-government-sues-california-over-net-neutrality-law.

8. Guy Faulconbridge and Paul Sandle, "Father of Web Says Tech Giants May
   Have to Be Split Up," *Reuters Business News*, November 1, 2018, https://www
   .reuters.com/article/us-technology-www/father-of-web-says-tech-giants-may
   -have-to-be-split-up-idUSKCN1N63MV.

9. Charles Rollet, "The Odd Reality of Life Under China's All-Seeing Credit Score
   System," *WIRED*, June 5, 2018.

10. Warren Strobel, Jonathan Landay, "Exclusive: Chief U.S. Spy Catcher Says
    China Using LinkedIn to Recruit Americans," *Reuters*, August 31, 2018.

11. Ibid.

12. Lora Kolodny, "Former Google CEO Predicts the Internet Will Split in Two—
    and One Part Will Be Led by China," CNBC, September 20, 2018.

13. Jennings Brown, "Apple's Using Your Call and Text Data to Figure out Whether
    to 'Trust' Your Devices," *Gizmodo*, September 18, 2018.

14. Elizabeth Dwoskin, "Facebook Is Rating the Trustworthiness of Its Users on a
    Scale from Zero to 1," *Washington Post*, August 21, 2018.

15. Drew FitzGerald, "No Cellphone Left Behind: U.S. to Test 'Presidential Alert'
    System," *Wall Street Journal*, October 2, 2018.

16. Emily Reynolds, "The Agony of Sophia, the World's First Robot Citizen Con-
    demned to a Lifeless Career in Marketing," *WIRED UK*, June 1, 2018.

17. Joshua Davis, "Hear Me Out: Let's Elect an AI as President," *WIRED*, May 18,
    2017.

18. Samuel Stebbins, "The World's 50 Most Innovative Companies," *USA Today*,
    January 12, 2018.

19. Dan Robitzski, "Advanced Artificial Intelligence Could Run the World Better
    Than Humans Ever Could," *Futurism*, August 29, 2018.

20. Nicholas Thompson, "When Tech Knows You Better Than You Know Yourself," *WIRED*, October 4, 2018.

21. Dwoskin, "Facebook Is Rating the Trustworthiness of Its Users."

22. Christina Larson, "Who Needs Democracy When You Have Data?" *MIT Technology Review*, August 20, 2018.

23. George Orwell, "Looking Back on the Spanish War," Orwell Foundation, https://www.orwellfoundation.com/the-orwell-foundation/orwell/essays-and-other-works/looking-back-on-the-spanish-war/.

24. Ibid.

25. Jack Corrigan, "The FBI Wants Artificial Intelligence Tools That Can ID People with Burnt, Cut or Otherwise Altered Fingerprints," *Nextgov*, August 29, 2018.

26. Shannon Liao, "New Facial Recognition System Catches First Imposter at US Airport," *Verge*, August 24, 2018.

27. Martin Weil, "Face-Recognition Technology Spots Impostor Arriving at Dulles, Government Says," *Washington Post*, October 3, 2018.

28. Shibani Mahtani and Zusha Elinson, "Artificial Intelligence Could Soon Enhance Real-Time Police Surveillance," *Wall Street Journal*, April 3, 2018.

29. Andrew Flanagan, "Thanks to AI, a 3rd Person Is Arrested Following a Pop Superstar's Concert," NPR, May 23, 2018.

30. Jordan Kenny, "Artificial Intelligence Footstep Recognition System Could Be Used for Airport Security," University of Manchester, May 29, 2018, https://www.manchester.ac.uk/discover/news/ai-footstep-recognition-system-could-be-used-for-airport-security/.

31. George Dvorsky, "This AI Knows Who You Are by the Way You Walk," *Gizmodo*, May 28, 2018.

32. Darlene Storm, "Biometrics: Dream Come True or Nightmare?," *Computerworld from IDG*, March 3, 2011.

33. Tony Romm and Drew Harwell, "Ancestry, 23andMe, and Others Say They Will Follow These Rules When Giving DNA Data to Businesses or Police," *Washington Post*, July 31, 2018.

34. Alejandro Tauber, "How the Dutch Police Are Using AI to Unravel Cold Cases," *The Next Police*, May 23, 2018.

35. Heming Nelson, "A History of Newspaper: Gutenberg's Press Started a Revolution," *Washington Post*, February 11, 1998.

36. Des Bieler, "Kyrie Irving Sorry for Saying Earth Is Flat, Blames It on a YouTube 'Rabbit Hole,'" *Washington Post*, October 1, 2018.

37. Carter Evans, "Spotting Fake News in a World with Manipulated Video," *CBS News*, April 17, 2018.

38. Michelle Castillo, "YouTube Will Use Six Popular YouTube Stars to Educate Kids About Fake News," CNBC, July 9, 2018.

Chapter 10

1. Guy Faulconbridge and Paul Sandle, November 1, 2018, "Father of Web Says Tech Giants May Have to Be Split Up," *Reuters Business News*, https://www.reuters.com/article/us-technology-www/father-of-web-says-tech-giants-may-have-to-be-split-up-idUSKCN1N63MV.

Index

About the Author

 **William Ammerman** is Executive Vice President of Digital Media at Engaged Media Inc. Previously, he served as Tribune Media's Vice President of Programmatic and Data-Driven Revenue, and held senior advertising positions with Hearst Television and Capitol Broadcasting. In his career, he has managed digital advertising for hundreds of television stations, including their websites, mobile apps, and connected television (OTT) platforms. He writes a blog about marketing in the age of artificial intelligence at www.MarketingandAI.com. He holds a master's from the University of North Carolina School of Media and Journalism and has completed postgraduate work in artificial intelligence at MIT.